John Murray

The knapsack guide to Norway

John Murray

The knapsack guide to Norway

ISBN/EAN: 9783741177705

Manufactured in Europe, USA, Canada, Australia, Japa

Cover: Foto ©Thomas Meinert / pixelio.de

Manufactured and distributed by brebook publishing software
(www.brebook.com)

John Murray

The knapsack guide to Norway

KNAPSACK GUIDE TO NORWAY.

THE

KNAPSACK GUIDE

TO

NORWAY.

WITH A MAP

LONDON:
JOHN MURRAY, ALBEMARLE STREET.
PARIS: A. & W. GALIGNANI & Co.; XAVIER.
CHRISTIANIA: DENNETT.
1864.

LONDON:
PRINTED BY WOODFALL AND KINDER,
MILFORD LANE, STRAND, W.C.

PREFACE.

The object of this Edition is to present the Norway Guide to Travellers in a more portable form than the older Editions.

Detailed information regarding the ways of reaching Norway must be sought in the Handbooks describing the countries passed through.

As far as Norway is concerned, it is hoped that this volume will be found a tolerably complete Guide. Information gathered on the spot, and by personal experience, regarding Inns, Posting, &c., has been added to this Edition, which is also furnished with special hints regarding Sporting and River Fishing in Norway.

NORWAY.

SKELETON ROUTES.

ROUTE 21.

CHRISTIANIA TO BERGEN, OVER RINGERIGET AND THE FILLE-FJELD.

Distance, 49⅝ N. miles.

Stations.	Norsk Miles.	Remarks.
From † Christiania		
To † Sandvigen i Bærum	1½	
† Humledal i Hole...........	1⅜	Pay for 2 miles; but not returning.
* † Vik i Hole................	1⅞	To see Krogkleven, hire horses and guides at Sundvolden, a little short of Vik.
* Klækken i Hougs	1½	Excellent quarters.
† Hadelands Glassworks....	⅝	Southern end of Rands Fjord, whence a steamer goes to Odnæs, ½ mile short of † Sköien.
† Kittelsrud i Jævnager....	1¼	In winter use the road to Thingelstad by Grinaker Church.
† Thingelstad i Gran.........	1	Hilly road; 3 hrs.' stage.
† Smedshammer i Gran.....	1½	Good road.
† Nordre Sand i Land.......	1⅛	Ditto.
† Björnerud i Land	1⅛	
* † Sköien i Land............	1½	First-rate station.
* † Tomlevold i Land........	1⅝	Ditto.
* † Gravdalen i S. Aurdal..	1⅝	Pay for 2 miles.
* † Frydenlund i N. Aurdal	1⅝	Pay for 1⅞.
† Fagernæs i N. Aurdal.....	1¼	Good road, and fair station.

Stations.	Norsk Miles.	Remarks.
† Reien i Slidre	1¾	
† Stee i Slidre..................	1¼	
† Öilös i Vang	1	
† Thune i Vang	¾	An excellent road.
† Skogstad i Öie...............	1¾	
* † Nystuen i Öie.............	1	Pay for 1½. Summit of Fille-Fjeld.
* † Maristuen i Lærdal......	1½	
† Hæg i Lærdal................	1	Pay for 1¼.
† Husum i Lærdal	¾	Pay for 1⅛. Borgund Church on the left.
† Blaaflaten i Lærdal	1⅜	Good road.
T. * Leirdalsören i Lærdal..	1	Boats may be had without delay to Gudvangen. Steamer weekly to Bergen; passage ca. 33 hrs.
* Gudvangen	4¾	By boat on Sögne Fjord; 8 to 10 hrs. row.
† Stalheim i Vos	1½	Road lies through Nærödal, up Stalheim's Cleft, a wonderful corkscrew road; see the Foses at base of hill.
† Vinje i Vos.....................	1	See Vinje Church.
† Tvinden i Vos.................	⅝	See Tvinden Fos.
† Vossevangen i Vos..........	1	Excellent Hotel at Jersin's.
* Evanger i Vos	1¼	
* Bolstadören i Vos...........	1	Half this stage by boat. Good fishing.
Dalseidet i Haus..............	¾	By water.
Dale i Haus	⅝	By land; wretched station.
Garnæs i Haus..................	2¼	By water.
Lone.....................................	¾	Fair road.
T. † Bergen............................	1½	
	50½	

ROUTE 22.

BERGEN TO CHRISTIANIA BY LEIRDALSÖREN, THROUGH HALLINGDAL AND HEMSEDAL.

Stations.	Norsk Miles.	Remarks.
From T. † Bergen		
To † Hæg i Borgund...	2[illegible]	Vide Route 21.

STATIONS.	Norsk Miles.	REMARKS.
† Bjöberg i Hemsedal........	2¼	Pay for 2¾ going west. Rest ½ br. at Breistölen; heavy road.
† Tuff i Hemsedal	1⅝	Pay for 2⅜.
† Ekre i Hemsedal...........	1⅓	Heavy stage.
† Löstegaard i Gols...........	1	
† Haftun i Gols	⅞	Going west pay for 1¼.
† Næs.....	1⅛	Good inn at Landhandler Meidells; can go by water to Sorteberg, and in winter on the ice to Hamremoen.
† Islandsrud i Næs	1	
† Aavestrud i Flaa...........	1¼	
Gulsvig i Flaa Annex.........	1¾	
Sorteberg i Krydsherred.....	1⅞	Pay for 2 m.
* Hamremoen i Krydsherred	1¼	Here one can take steamer on the Kröderen.
* † Hövland i Lunder	1⅝	
† Veeme i Hole...............	1	Good road.
Hönefos	1	Hotel, Mad. Glatvedt's. Good road.
† Vik	1	
T. † Christiania..............	4¼	Vide Route 21.
	45⅛	

ROUTE 23.

CHRISTIANIA TO BERGEN, THROUGH DRAMMEN, KONGSBERG, TELLEMARKEN, AND HARDANGER.

STATIONS.	Norsk Miles.	REMARKS.
From T. † Christiania		
To † Sandvigen	1¼	
† Ravnsborg i Asker	⅞	Good road.
† Gjellebæk i Traneby.......	1⅜	Pay for 1¼; but for 1⅛ returning.
T. † Drammen	1⅛	
† Haugsund....................	1⅞	A steamer runs several times daily to and from Drammen. Town stage.
T. † Kongsberg................	2	Must stop at Rustuen ¾ br.

Stations.	Norsk Miles.	Remarks.
† Tinnœs..	2⅛	Pay for 3¼. Stop 1 hr. at Jerngruben, half-way.
† Lysthuus or † Søm	½	See Tin Fos; and Hitterdal Church, 1 Eng. mile from station.
† Mossebo	1¾	
† Mœlandsmo i Hjertdal ...	1½	
† Nordgaarden i Sillejord...	2⅛	
Berge i Brunkeberg	1¾	
Mogen i Hoidalsmo	1¼	Roads lead hence to Laurdal on Bandags Vand, to Moland and Mo.
Sundeli i Vinje...............	1¼	
Jamsgaard	1⅛	
Tofsland	1⅜	
Midtvedt i Haukelid.........	1⅛	Post-road ends here.
Hörre i Röldal	6	On horseback.
Seljestad...................... ...	2	
Skare........	1	
Hildal...............	1	Good road; ¾ mile by sea, ¼ road.
* Bustethun i Odde...........	1	Steamer to Bergen weekly during June and July. Passage 21 hrs. From Odde to Vik a day's journey by boat: and thence a 10 hrs.' walk to Vöring Fos.
Helleland........................	2	By water; on E. bank of Sör Fjord.
Utne...........	1	,, on W. ditto.
Vikör.............	2⅛	,, on N. do. of Hardanger Fjord.
Jondalsören	1	,, on S. ditto.
Gjermundshavn	2	
Huse...............................	1¼	On high road to Bergen. (Vide Route 24.)

ROUTES FROM KONGSBERG TO RIUKAN-FOSS. (Vide p. 99.)

(1) From Kongsberg		
To † Tinnœs	2⅛	See above.
† Lysthuus or † Søm	⅓	Ditto.
Tinösset	3	Stage 4 hrs.; rest ½ hr. half-way. Can take Skyts hence to Sanden i Mœl.
Aasiöen i Hofvin..	1⅙	By boat.

STATIONS.	Norsk Miles.	REMARKS.
Sanden i Mœl..................	2	By boat. Send "forbud" for horses to meet at Mœl Church.
* Dal..............................	1	Half-way between Mœl and Riukan-fos. Hence on horseback, a 2 hrs.' ride, and 40 min. on foot to
Riukan-fos	1	
(2) From Kongsberg		
To Moen............................	1	
* Bolkesjö	2	Hence one can drive to Graver i Hoviml, 8 m., and row over Tinsöen to Sand. See above.
Kopsland..........................	1⅝	
Tinöset	1	See above.

ROUTE 24.

CHRISTIANIA TO HAMMERFEST AND NORTH CAPE, ROUND THE COAST BY LAND TO NAMSOS, THENCE BY STEAMER.

STATIONS.	Norsk Miles.	REMARKS.
From Christiania		
To T. † Drammen................	4	Vide Route 23.
† Östre i Sande	1	New, good road.
† Revaa i Sande................	⅛	
† Holmestrand	1¼	
† Solleröd i Undrumsdal....	1⅞	First part hilly.
† Fyldpaa i Sæm	¾	Good road.
† Sörby i Stokke	⅞	
† Haukeröd i Sandherred ..	1	
T. * † Laurvig	1½	Fair road.
† Vasbotten i Brunlangsnæs	⅛	Good road.
† Launer i Eidanger	1¼	Ditto.
† Brevig or † Stathelle......	1⅛	Hilly stage.
† Rönholt i Bamble..........	1⅛	Heavy stage.
† Tyvand and Hœgland i Sanikedal	3	Ditto.
† Holte or Österöd i Gjerustad	1¾	Half the stage up, half down hill.

Stations.	Norsk Miles.	Remarks.
† Röd i Gjerstad	1¼	Pay for 1⅜. Bridge over Holtsund. Hence to Österriisöer, 1⅛ m., pay for 2 m.; or by water direct, 1 m.
† Angelstad i Holt	1⅝	Pay for 1⅜. First part very hilly. To Tvedestrand, ⅝ m., and to Næs Iron Works, ⅛ m.
† Brække i Östre Möland...	1⅛	Hilly.
† Blödekjær or T. * † Arendal	1⅛	Fair hotel near the quay.
Lærrodstveit i Öiest	¾	Fair road.
Bringsværd i Fjære	⅛	Ditto. To Grimstad, ⅛ m.
Landvig........................	¾	Good road.
T. † Lillesand	1⅜	Hilly.
Trede i Birkenæs	1⅛	Excellent road.
Aabel i Birkenæs	⅛	Pay for ¾; good road.
† Kostøl i Tved	1⅜	Mostly a new road; bridge now over Topdals Elv.
T. Christianssand	1⅛	Hilly.
† Lunde i Sögne	1¾	
† Vatne i Holme	1¾	Very hilly. Cross Trys Fjord ferry.
T. * † Mandal	1¼	Order the horses to meet at the bridge over Mandals Elv, unless passing the night here. First part very hilly.
† Vigeland i Valle	1¼	
† Fahret i Lyngdal	2⅛	
Tjomsland i Lyngdal.........	1	
Rörvig i Fedde	1⅛	Hilly road. Going west, order horses to meet at Fedde; eastwards, at Rörvig.
Fedde	¼	Ferry over Fedde Fjord, often difficult to cross with southerly wind.
T. * Flekkefjord	1⅛	Very hilly road. May be reached by water from Fedde, 1⅛ m.
Birnæs i Bakke.....	1¾	Hilly.
Nysted or Moi i Lunde	1¼	Or by water, ⅞ m.
Eye i Hankestad	1 [illegible]	Good road.
Refsland i Hækkestad.,.......	[illegible]	Ditto.
Svalestad i Helleland.........	[illegible]	
Slettebö i Egersund	1	Ditto.
Hegrestad i Egersund	1	A few hills near Tegnsbridge.
Hölleland i Ogne	⅜	Hilly.

Stations.	Norsk Miles.	Remarks.	
* Haar i Varhoug	1	Good road; excellent quarters.	
Hobberstad I Varhoug	⅞	Ditto.	
Ree i Time	1⅛	Ditto.	
† Skeiene I Höylands	1⅜	Ditto.	
T. Stavanger	1¼		
Gangenæs i Rennesö	1	By water.	
Judebergel I Findö	1	Ditto.	
Ramsvig i Sternerö	1	Ditto.	
Nerstrand	1	Ditto.	
Vigedalsöaen i Vigedal	1¾	Ditto.	
Tuset	¼	Ditto.	
Ölen i Fjeldberg	1	By land; heavy stage.	
Etnesöen	1	Ditto; or by water.	
Lechnæs i Skonœvig	⅞	By land, pay for 1⅞; or 2 m. by water.	
Ölfernæs	⅝	By water.	
Vahlen	¾	By land.	
Helvigen	1	Ditto.	
Huse	1¼	By water.	
Sundfjord	½	By land.	
Sœrvold	1½	By water.	
Öftestu	½	By land; pay for 1.	
Hatvigen	½	By water.	
Ousören or Indre Moberg	⅞	By land.	
† Nedre Sandven	1¼	Ditto.	For land route from Bergen to Systad, see page 114.
T. † Bergen	1½	Ditto.	
Bukken i Sund	2⅛		
† Alværströmmen	2	By water.	
Kiilströmmen	2¼	Ditto.	
Skejerjehavn	1¼	Ditto.	
Sognefœst	1⅛	Ditto.	
T. * Leervig	1¾	Ditto.	
Systad	1		
Skaar	1	By land.	
Flœkke	1⅛	Ditto.	
Dale	⅞	Ditto.	
Eidevig or Sveen	1⅛	By water.	
Langeland	1	By land.	
Förde I Förde	1	Ditto; pay for 1¼ returning.	
* Nedrevasenden	1⅜	Ditto.	
Skei or Övrevasenden	1½	By water, on Jölster Vand.	
Förde i Bredheim	⅝	By land.	
Reed	1⅛	By water, over Bredheim Vand.	

Stations.	Norsk Miles.	Remarks.
Moldestadt	⅛	By land.
Udvigen	1	Ditto.
Faleidet	1	By water.
Kjosebunden	1⅛	By land.
Grodaas	⅛	By land, or ⅛ by water over Horningdals Vand.
Haugen	¾	By land.
Thronstad	⅞	Ditto.
* Hellesylt	¾	Ditto. Steamer hence direct to Aalesund.
Slyngstad	2⅛	By water or by land.
Andamn	1⅛	
* Söholt	⅞	By land: hence to Aalesund. (Vide Route 30.)
† Hellingsgaard	1¼	By land, over Örskoug Fjeld.
* Vestnæs	1	Ditto.
T. Molde	1⅛	Across Romsdal Fjord.
* Lönset	1	By land.
Eide	1	Ditto.
Istad	¾	
Hœgeim	1	
Angvik	1	By road.
Bækken	⅛	By water.
Bolseth	⅜	By road.
Stangvik	⅝	By water.
Aasen	1⅜	By road.
Honstad	⅞	Ditto.
Qvammen	1⅝	Ditto.
Holte	1⅛	Ditto.
Garberg	1	
Langseth	1	A shorter route than by Kalstad. (Vide p. xviii.)
Moe	1	
† Fandrem	1	The Örkla Elv is crossed.
† Örkedalsören	⅛	Heavy stage, but better than by By, going north.
† Eli	1⅜	Heavy stage.
† Saltnæsanden	1	Ditto. Excellent road hence to Trondhjem.
Esp	⅜	
T. † Trondhjem	1¼	
Haugan	1⅜	Easy stage.

STATIONS.	Norsk Miles.	REMARKS.
Sandfarhuus	1⅜	Excellent road; bridge over Stordals Elv. Going north, order horses to meet at Sandfarhuus; going south, at Helle.
Forbord	1	
Vordal	1	Pay for 1¼.
Hammer	¾	Very hilly.
† Nordre Skjerve	⅝	Good road.
* Levanger	1	Beautiful scenery. Steamer to Trondhjem twice a week all the year.
Holme	1⅛	Good road. See St. Olaf's Church.
Röske	1	
* † Steenkjær	1⅜	Generally a steamer to and from Trondhjem.
Östvig	1¼	
Elden	1⅛	Heavy road.
* Overgaard	1	Pay for 1⅛.
* Bangsund	1½	Pay for 2 m. Heavy road over Auskaret.
Spillum	1	Bangsund ferry is crossed; takes ¼ hr.
Namsös	1	Drive ¾, and by water ¼.

TO FISKUM FOS.

From Spillum		
To Hund	1¼	Good road. Ferry over Namsen.
Haugan	1	Easy stage.
Vie	1⅛	Cross Namsen by ferry.
Fosland	1	New road.
Fiskum Fos	1⅛	

FROM NAMSÖS TO HAMMERFEST BY STEAMER.

	Hours.	
From Namsös		
To Foslandsosen	3	For route in open boat, vide p. 126.
Rörvig	4	
Gutvig	3	
Bronösund	3	

Stations.	Hours.	Remarks.
Vivelstad	3	
Tjötö	1	
Sövig	1	
Sannesöen	1	
Kobbedal	1	
Hemnæsberget	4	
Vigholmen	2	
Indre Kvarö	2	
Selsövig	1	
Rödö	1	
Melöværet	2	
Gilleskaal	3	
Bodö	2	
Kjerringö	2	
Grötö	3	
Balstad	4	
Stamsund	2	
Henningsvær	1	
Svolvær	2	
Steilo	4	
Lidland	9	
Lödingen	2	
Sandtorv	3	
Harstadhavn	2	
Haonvig	3	
Kastnæshavn	2	
Klöven	2	
Gibostad	2	
Maalsnæs	3	
Tromsö	3	
Carlsö	4	
Havnæs	3	
Skjervö	2	
Lippen	3	
Hasvig	3	
Talvig	5	
Strömmen	2	
Bosekop	1	
Komagfjord	3	
Hammerfest	3	Here a steamer goes to Vardö and Vadsö, fortnightly.

ROUTE 25.

CHRISTIANIA BY STEAMBOAT ROUND THE COAST TO TRONDHJEM, HAMMERFEST, AND VADSO.

(Vide p. 137, and Route 24.)

ROUTE 26.

THE MOST DIRECT ROUTE FROM CHRISTIANIA TO TRONDHJEM BY EIDSVOLD, THE MIÖSEN, GUDBRANDSDAL, AND THE DOVRE FJELD.

Stations.	North Miles.	Remarks.
From T. † Christiania		
To T. † Eidsvold Bakken......	6	Rail, 3 hrs. Three trains up and down from June 15 to Aug. 15; at other times, two. Good hotel at railway station. Road route given p. 142.
T. * † Lillehammer	11	By steamer on the Miösen, leaving Eidsvold on arrival of morning train.
† Aronsveen i Öier	1⅜	Good road. Daily diligence between Lillehammer and Elstad.
† Holmen i Thrötten	1⅝	
† Nedre Losnæs i Fodvang...	1¼	
* † Elstad i Ringebo	¾	Good road from Lillehammer.
* † Listad i S. Fron..........	1⅜	
* Öien i N. Fron...............	⅝	Excellent quarters.
* † Storklevstad i Qvams.	1¼	Col. Sinclair's monument is passed.
* † Breden and Bredevangen i Sels.	1½	For winter, Breden is the station; in summer, Bredevangen.
* † Moen i Sels	⅞	Road passes Kringelen, where Sinclair was killed.
* † Rommundgaard i Sels ...	⅞	The pass of Rusten is traversed.
* † Brendhaugen i Dovre...	1	Good road; good quarters.
* † Toftemoen i Dovre..	1	
T. * † Dombaas i Lesje......	1	Heavy, sandy road; station on left of road. Route to Molde branches off.
† Fokstuen on Dovre.........	⅞	Pay for 1 mile. Going north, 2 hrs. required; going south, 1 hr.

STATIONS.	Norsk Miles.	REMARKS.
* † Jerkin on Dovre	$1\frac{3}{4}$	Good road. Arrange to sleep here.
† Kongsvold on Dovre	$\frac{7}{8}$	Pay for 1 mile.
* † Drivstuen i Opdal	$1\frac{5}{8}$	Good new road.
* † Rise i Opdal	$1\frac{1}{8}$	Pay for $1\frac{1}{4}$; heavy stage.
* † Ny-Övne i Opdal..	$\frac{7}{8}$	Good station; trout-fishing.
* † Nystuen i Opdal...........	$1\frac{1}{8}$	
† Aunsbjerg i Remnebo......	1	New road made in 1862. Good shooting.
† Bierkager i Remnebo	1	

Bjerkager to Trondhjem through Meldal.

Haarstad i Rennebo	$1\frac{1}{4}$	This route through Meldal and Örkedal is preferable, because there are several fast stations, and the scenery is very beautiful.
Grut i Meldalen	$1\frac{1}{4}$	
† Kalstad i Meldalen.........	1	The road to Christiansund branches off here. R. 24.
* † Gumdal i Svorkmo	$1\frac{3}{8}$	Pay for $1\frac{1}{2}$.
† Fandrem i Örkedal .... &c. &c. &c.	$1\frac{1}{4}$	Poor station, vide R. 24. From Fandrem one can drive to † Örkedalsören, whence a steamer goes to Trondhjem twice a week all the year.
T. † Trondhjem...............	$2\frac{7}{8}$	

Direct route continued from Ny Bjerkager.

† Garlid i Sogndal............	$1\frac{1}{8}$	Horses ordered to meet on the high road.
* † Præsthuus i Remnebo...	$\frac{5}{8}$	Easy stage; but heavy returning.
Soknæs i Stören..............	1	Easy stage northwards; heavy returning; wretched quarters.
Vollan i Horrig	$\frac{7}{8}$	Good road.
Leer i Flaa......................	$1\frac{1}{8}$	Ditto.
Meelhuus	$\frac{7}{8}$	Ditto; fine scenery.
* Esp i Leinstrand............	$\frac{3}{4}$	Ditto.
T. † Trondhjem...............	$1\frac{1}{4}$	Route 24.
	$40\frac{7}{8}$	

ROUTE 27.

CHRISTIANIA TO TRONDHJEM OVER RINGERIGET TO LILLEHAMMER.

Stations.	Norsk Miles.	Remarks.
From + Christiania		
To + Thingelstad	8¾	As in Route 21.
+ Teterud i Vestre Thoten .	1⅝	Pay for 2⅜.
+ Börsvolden i Vestre Thoten	1⅞	Good road.
+ Kræmmerbakken i Östre Thoten.	1⅛	Joins route through Hurdalen, R. 28.
T. + Gjövig	1⅜	Hence one can go by steamer to Lillehammer.
+ Stokke i Vardal	1	The road lies along the Miösen.
+ Grytestuen i Vardal	1⅞	Level road.
T. + Lillehammer	1⅜	Vid. Route 26.
Trondhjem.....................	32⅞	
	51⅛	

ROUTE 28.

CHRISTIANIA TO TRONDHJEM OVER HURDALEN ON W. SIDE OF MIÖSEN.

Stations.	Norsk Miles.	Remarks.
From Christiania		
To + Dahl	4¾	By rail.
Svendsen i Eidsvold	⅜	
+ Eidsætter i Hurdalen	1⅛	Pay for 1⅛, and 1¾ returning. The road turns off after passing Eidsvold bridge.
+ Garsjo i Hurdalen.........	1⅛	Good road by Hurdals Glass-works. Pay for 1¾.
+ Grönnen i Östre Thoten...	1⅞	Pay for 2 m., and for 1¾ returning; first part heavy stage.
+ Kræmmerbakken i Thoten &c. &c. &c.	1	Vid. Route 27.
T. + Trondhjem...............	38¼	
	48½	

ROUTE 29.

CHRISTIANIA TO TRONDHJEM OVER HEDEMARKEN ON THE E. SIDE OF MIÖSEN.

Stations.	Norsk Miles.	Remarks.
From † Christiania		
To * † Minde i Eidsvold ...	6⅛	Rail to Eidsvold, and steamer to Minde; or by carriole from Eidsvold, 1½ m.; in winter, sledge on the Vormen.
† Morstu i Stange	1⅜	Pay for 1½; cross Vormen at Minde; hilly stage.
* † Korsödegaarden i Stange	1⅜	Pay for 1½. Heavy road through Morskov. Sleep here.
† Sörholte i Stange	⅞	In winter on the ice over Agersvigen to Hamar, 1⅜.
† Louisenberg i Vang	1⅝	Easy stage northwards; heavy returning. To Hamar, ⅜ m.
† Bjerke i Furnæs	⅞	Very heavy stage northwards.
† Fangberget i Ringsaker ...	1	
† Smestad i Ringsaker	1¼	
† Frengstuen i Ringsaker..	1	Level road along Miösen.
T. † Lillehammer	1¼	Vid. R. 26.
Trondhjem	32⅜	
	49⅛	

ROUTE 30.

CHRISTIANIA TO MOLDE, AALESUND, CHRISTIANSUND *vià* MIÖSEN, GUDBRUNDSDAL, AND ROMDAL.

CHRISTIANIA TO MOLDE DIRECT.

Stations.	Norsk Miles.	Remarks.
From Christiania		
To † Dombaas	31¾	Vid. R. 26.
* † Holager i Lesje	1	

Stations.	Norsk Miles.	Remarks.
* † Holseth i Lesje	1⅜	
* † Lesje Jernværk i Lesje .	⅞	
† Mölmen i Lesje	1⅛	Fine waterfall here.
† Nystuen i Lesje	1	Poor quarters.
* † Ormen i Gryten	1	Pay for 1¼ ; returning 1⅛. See the Foss, Söndre Slettefossen.
† Fladmark i Gryten.........	1	
† Horjem i Gryten	1	
T. * † Veblungsnæset i Gryten	1¼	Steamer 3 times weekly to Molde.
Torvig i Vold..................	⅜	By water on Foss Fjord.
† Alfarnæs i Veö	1¼	By land.
Söllesnæs i Veö	⅜	By water on Langfiord.
Dværnæs i Bolsö	⅞	By land.
Strande i Bolsö	¼	Across Fanne Fjord.
T. Molde	⅜	By land ; from Molde to Vestnæs, 1⅛, and so to Aalesund, see below.
	45¼	

CHRISTIANIA TO AALESUND DIRECT.

From Christiania		
To T. * † Veblungsnæs.........	41⅜	See above.
* Vestnæs	2¾	By steamer or boat skyts.
† Ellingsgaard................	1	By road, see R. 24 ; bad station.
* Söholdt	1¼	Ditto.
Sorte	1¼	Partly by water ; bad station.
Röseth	1⅛	By road.
T. Aalesund	1⅛	Partly by water.
	49⅜	

CHRISTIANIA TO CHRISTIANSUND DIRECT.

From Christiania		
To Dværnæs i Bolsö	44¼	See above.
* Lonset i Bolsö	¼	By water across Fanne Fjord.
Eide i Bolsö	1	By land.
Furseth i Öre..................	⅜	Ditto.
Gimnæs i Öre	1⅜	Ditto.

Stations.	Norsk Miles.	Remarks.
Fladseth i Fredö	¾	By water.
Bolgen i Bremsnæs	¾	By land.
T. † Christiansund	¼	By water.
	45⅝	

ROUTE 31.

CHRISTIANIA TO TRONDHJEM *viâ* VALLEY OF THE GLOMMEN AND RÖRAAS.

Stations.	Norsk Miles.	Remarks.
From Christiania		
To T. † Eidsvold-bakken	6	By rail.
† Hamar	6	By steamer.
† Grundsæt i Elverum	3⅝	By rail from Hamar; 2 hours' journey; one train leaves daily. For route from Minde vid. p. 161.
† Nygaard i Aamot	1¾	
† Arnestad i Aamot	1	Station lies 1 Eng. mile from road; but horses may generally be had at Lapstuen on the road, between which and next station pay only for 2 m. Or *vid* Storsöen; viz. † Arnestad to † Diseth, 2 m., pay for 3 m.; † Lösæt, 1 m.; take same horse to Skjörbund, ¼ m., pay for ½ m., whence a steamer runs daily, except Sundays, to Akre.
† Ophuustuen i Stor Elvedalen	2¼	
* † Söndre Messelt i Stor Elvedalen.	1¾	Excellent quarters.
† Vestgaard i Stor Elvedalen	1	
Akre i Ytre Rendalen	2⅞	Pay for 4 m.; 2 or 3 branches up the Glommen have to be crossed; heavy stage going south, requires 5 hours.
Bergsæt i Övre Rendalen ...	1⅞	Pay for 2½.
* Engen i Tyldalen	3	Pay for 4½ m.; rest half-way at Midtskoven.

Stations.	Norsk Miles.	Remarks.
* Neby i Tönset..............	$1\frac{1}{3}$	Pay for 2; heavy road going south. Travellers not caring to go to Röraas will do well to turn off by the new post route to Trondhjem. Vid. p. 167.
Tolgen	$1\frac{3}{4}$	
Ös i Tolgen	$1\frac{1}{4}$	In winter change horses at Lillesien.
T. † Röraas	$1\frac{3}{8}$	For road hence into Sweden, vid. p. 168.
† Bergan i Röraas.............	$1\frac{1}{8}$	
† Næsvold i Aalen	$\frac{7}{8}$	
† Hov i Aalen...................	$\frac{7}{8}$	Returning, pay for $1\frac{1}{8}$.
Grödt i Holtaalen	$1\frac{1}{8}$	
Langledet i Holtaalen	1	
Kirkvold i Singsaas..........	$1\frac{3}{8}$	
Bogen i Singsaas	1	Level road along Gaul Elv.
* Rogstad i Stören	1	Good road.
Vollan i Horrig................	$1\frac{1}{4}$	Ditto. Vid. R. 20.
T. † Trondhjem	4	
	$50\frac{1}{2}$	

ROUTE 32.

CHRISTIANIA TO TRONDHJEM THROUGH KONGSVINGER AND UP THE VALLEY OF THE GLOMMEN.

Stations.	Norsk Miles.	Remarks.
From Christiania		
To † Kongsvinger	$8\frac{9}{10}$	By rail; takes $4\frac{1}{2}$ hrs.

Road Route. Christiania

To † Grorud	$\frac{7}{8}$	
† Skrimstad	$\frac{7}{8}$	pay for 1.
† Klöften	$1\frac{1}{8}$	
† Lund	$\frac{7}{8}$	
† Opaker	$1\frac{1}{3}$	
† Korsmo	$1\frac{3}{8}$	
† Sundby	$\frac{3}{4}$	
T. † Kongsvinger	$1\frac{1}{8}$	
	$8\frac{1}{2}$	

Stations.	Norsk Miles.	Remarks.
† Brandvold	1⅜	On E. side of Glommen, or on W. side 1⅛ m. over Gjölstad Sound.
† Kirkenær	1⅛	
† Austad i Hof..............	1¼	Cross Flissund.
† Mœlby i Aasnæs	⅞	
† Elsæt i Aasnæs...........	1⅛	
† Bækkevold i Elverum ...	2⅛	Rest half-hour at Houmb.
† Grundsæt	⅛	Vide Route 31.
&c. &c. &c.		
Trondhjem	35⅛	
	53⅛	

ROUTE 33.

TRONDHJEM TO STOCKHOLM *viâ* VARDAL AND SUNDSVALL.

Stations.	Norsk Miles.	Remarks.
From Trondhjem		
To * Levanger	7⅜	Vide Route 24.
Næs	1⅛	Good road.
Garnæs........................	1	Heavy road. Guddingsbakker are passed.
Suulstuen...........	1⅛	Pay for 3 m. Heavy road.
† Sandvigen.........	1¼	
Mœlen in Sweden	1⅛	Vide Route 64, "Handbook for Sweden."
	14	

ROUTE 34.

ALTEN TO TORNEA BY KAUTOKEINO.

Stations.	Norsk Miles.	Remarks.
From Alten		
To Kautokeino	16	Across the Fjelds, or 19 m. by Ladnejaure and Masi. No horses to be had here. Forbud should be sent from Bosekop to Karesuando, in Sweden, to meet here.

STATIONS.	Norsk Miles.	REMARKS.
Karesuando	10	
Muonioniska............	10	By water; or 16 from Kautokeino by the winter road.
Kolare	10	
Kexisvara................	3	Kengis Bruk, about 1 hour's drive S. of Kexisvara, is a better place to put up at.
Kardis	3½	
Pello..............................	2½	
Tortola	2	
Juskengis	1	
Mariosaara.........	1¼	
*Maratengi	1	
Niemio	1¼	
Pækkila	1¼	
Korpikula........................	1⅜	A good new inn here.
Kukkola	1⅜	
Vojakola	1⅛	
* Haparanda and Tornea...	1	The whole journey may be done in from 10 to 12 days.
	67⅜	

ROUTE 35.

CHRISTIANIA TO STOCKHOLM *vid* KONGSVINGER TO CARLSTAD, ETC.

STATIONS.	Norsk Miles.	REMARKS.
From Christiania		
To T. † Kongsvinger	8¼	Vide Route 32.
† Brenna........................	1⅜	
† Magnord	1¼	
Mornst, in Sweden	1	On this stage the frontier is crossed. Vide Route 67.
&c. &c. &c.		
Stockholm	57⅜	

ROUTE 36.

CHRISTIANIA TO STOCKHOLM *vid* FREDERIKSHALD, ETC.

STATIONS.	Norsk Miles.	REMARKS.
From Christiania		
To † Lian	1	On the new road.
† Riis	1[illegible]	
† Sundbye	1[illegible]	
† Smorbæk	1[illegible]	
† Dillingen	1[illegible]	Hence to Moss, [illegible] m.
† Carlshuus	1	Good road. Hence to Krabberöd, 1[illegible]; † Frederikstadt, [illegible]. Good road; cross by ferry to the town.
† Haraldstad	1¼	Pay for 1[illegible].
† Sarpsborg	[illegible]	Hilly road.
† Öiestad	1¼	The Glommen is crossed by the suspension bridge over Sarp-foss.
† Westgaard	⅞	Hence to Frederikshald, [illegible] m.
† Högdal, in Sweden &c. &c.	1[illegible]	Pay for 1¼. Swinesund is crossed; good quarters on the Norwegian side. Vide Routes 69 and 77, "Handbook for Sweden."
Stockholm	71	

ROUTE 37.

CHRISTIANIA TO HELSINGBORG *vid* GOTTENBORG.

STATIONS	Norsk Miles.	REMARKS.
From Christiania		
To † Högdal	11[illegible]	Vide Route 36.
Rist	1	The stations on the following route, though properly belonging to the Guide Book to Sweden, are given for the convenience of travellers.
Vik	1	
Skölleröd	[illegible]	

Stations.	Norsk Miles.	Remarks.
Hede	$1\frac{1}{6}$	
Rabalshede	$1\frac{1}{4}$	
Svarteborg	1	
Qvistrum	$1\frac{5}{8}$	
Harrastad....................	$1\frac{1}{8}$	On this stage Uddevalla is passed.
Grohed	$1\frac{1}{4}$	
Åsen	$1\frac{1}{8}$	
Holmen	$1\frac{3}{8}$	
Bak	$1\frac{1}{8}$	
Hede	$\frac{1}{8}$	
Kongelf By	$1\frac{1}{8}$	
Agnesberg...................	$\frac{5}{8}$	
Götteborg	1	Railway hence to Stockholm.
Kärra	$\frac{3}{4}$	
Kongsbakka By	$1\frac{1}{16}$	
Åsa	$1\frac{5}{8}$	
Backa	$1\frac{1}{4}$	
Varberg By	2	
Morup	$1\frac{3}{8}$	
Falkenberg By..............	$1\frac{1}{16}$	
Slöinge	$1\frac{3}{8}$	
Qvibille	$1\frac{1}{8}$	
Halmstad	$1\frac{1}{2}$	
Tjerby	1	
Laholm By	1	
Karup	$1\frac{5}{8}$	
Margrethorp.................	$1\frac{1}{12}$	
Engleholm By	$1\frac{1}{8}$	
Fileininge....................	$1\frac{1}{6}$	
Helsingborg	1	
	52	

STEAMBOAT TABLES FOR 1864.

BETWEEN CHRISTIANIA, GOTTENBORG, AND COPENHAGEN.

The KRONPRINDSESSE LOUISE leaves Christiania every Saturday at 6 A.M.; reaches Dröbak, 7½ A.M.; Horten, 9; Moss, 10; Vallo, 11; Frederiksværn, 1½ P.M.; Gottenborg, Sunday night. Leaves Gottenborg, Monday, 2 A.M., and reaches Elsinore about 12, and Copenhagen at 4 P.M. Leaves Copenhagen, Wednesday, at noon; reaches Elsinore at 2 P.M.; Gottenborg, Thursday, 2 A.M.; Frederiksværn, 12½ (where it meets the steamer to Christiansund): Vallö, 3 P.M.; Moss, 4 P.M.; Horten, 5; Dröbak, 6½ P.M.; Christiania, 8½ P.M.

The EXCELLENCEN TOLL leaves Christiania every Tuesday, at 6 A.M.; reaches Gottenborg at 10 P.M.; leaves Gottenborg, Wednesday, 1 A.M.; and reaches Copenhagen, 1 P.M. Leaves Copenhagen, Saturday, 11½ A.M.; Gottenborg, Sunday, 3 A.M.; Christiania, 6½ P.M.; touching at Dröbak, Horten, &c., as above.

BETWEEN CHRISTIANIA, FREDERIKSVÆRN, NYBORG, AND LUBECK.

The CHRISTIANIA leaves Christiania every Tuesday, at noon (touching at Dröbak, &c., as above); Vallö, 5½ P.M. (Meets the steamer from Christiansand.) Leaves Frederikshavn, Wednesday, 6 A.M.; Nyborg, 8 P.M.; reaches Lubeck on Thursday, 7 A.M. Leaves Lubeck, Friday, 10 P.M.; Nyborg, Saturday, 9 A.M.; Frederikshavn, 11 P.M.; Frederiksværn, Sunday, 10 A.M. (meets the packet to the West Coast); Laurvig, 11 A.M.; Vallö, 2 P.M.; Moss, 3½ P.M.; reaches Christiania, 8 P.M.

CHRISTIANIA AND HAMBURG.

The ST. OLAF leaves Christiania every other Saturday, from May 14, at 5 P.M.; Christiansand, Sunday, 5 P.M.; and reaches Hamburg, Tuesday morning. Leaves Hamburg the following Saturday, and reaches Christiania on Wednesday morning.

CHRISTIANIA AND HULL.

The GANGER ROLF or SCANDINAVIAN leaves Hull every Friday at 6 P.M.; and reaches Christiania Tuesday morning. Leaves Christiania every Friday at 5 P.M., and arrives in Hull Monday forenoon.

TRONDHJEM AND HAMBURG.

The HAKON JARL, JUPITER, or NID ELVEN leaves Trondhjem every Friday morning, and reaches Hamburg the Sunday week. Leaves Hamburg Saturdays. (Vide p. 141.)

N.B.—For steamers between Christiania and Vadsö, vid. R. 25.

NORWAY.

INTRODUCTORY INFORMATION.

1. *Routes from England to Norway.*—2. *Money, Measures, Weights.*—3. *Passports.*—4. *Modes of Travelling, Inns, Steamers, Boats, Carrioles, Four-wheeled Carriages.*—5. *Requisites for Travelling, Carrioles, &c.*—6. *Posting Regulations, Skydts Law, Sending Forbud, Table of Payments for Horses.*—7. *Danish and Norwegian Alphabet, Vocabulary, &c.*—8. *Scenery and Sketching.*—9. *Angling.*—10. *Shooting.*—11. *Succinct Account of Norway.*—12. *Historical Notice.*—13. *Government.*—14. *The People.*—15. *Productive Industry.*—16. *Commerce.*—17. *Literature, &c.*

ROUTES.

1. ROUTES FROM ENGLAND TO NORWAY.

The access to Norway is now as easy as to any other part of the Continent. Those who dislike the sea, by going to Hamburg and Kiel *vid* Calais or Ostend, Cologne, and Hanover, can limit the actual sea-voyage to a very few hours; but the quickest and cheapest route is by steamer from Hull to Christiania. A steamer leaves Hull every Friday, and arrives at Christiania on the following Tuesday, after touching at Christiansand on the Sunday. There is likewise a weekly steamer to Christiania from Copenhagen as well as from Kiel (*vide* Remarks, p. 61), the former touching at Gottenburg, the second at Korsör in the Great Belt, and at Frederikshavn.

All these steamers touch at the intermediate ports in the Christiania Fjord, with the exception of one of the Hull boats, the "Scandinavian," belonging to Messrs. Wilson and Son, which only touches at Christiansand. The Hamburg and Amsterdam boats also touch there, and, weather permitting, meet steamers going westwards round the coast to Bergen, Trondhjem, and Hammerfest, &c.

There is also weekly communication by steamer between Hamburg, Christiansand, Bergen, and Trondhjem.

A steamer runs from Hull to Bergen every three weeks during the summer. Fares, 3*l* 3*s*. Agents, Messrs. Dunkerly, Hull.

2. MONEY.—MEASURES.—WEIGHTS.

Accounts are kept in specie Dollars, Marks or Orts, and Skillings.

24 Skillings make .... 1 Mark, or Ort.
5 Marks .... 1 Specie Dollar.

There are no gold coins in Norway. The current money is of paper, silver, and copper. The paper is issued by the National Bank, and may be taken with perfect security. It passes current for its full value throughout the country. The notes are as follow:—For 1 specie dollar, on white paper; 5, blue; 10, yellow; 50, green; and red, 100.

The silver comprises pieces of 1 specie dollar, ½ do.; 1 mark, ½ do., or 12 skillings; and ¼ do., or 6 sk. Most of these are new and handsome coins; in addition to these there is abundance of small debased Danish coin still in circulation, which was issued during the war from 1808 to 1814, and which now passes current at a discount, viz.: 4 skilling pieces at 3 skillings, and the 8 skillings at 6. The copper money comprises pieces of 2, 1, and ½ sk. All these Danish coins are to be called in, and Norwegian of the same value to be issued. In the South of Norway the piece of 24 sks. is called a Mark, but in the W. and N. an Ort.

The *exchange* is regulated by the Hamburg quotations. Of late years it has ranged from 4 da. 40 sks. to 4 da. 60 sks. for the British pound sterling. The specie dollar, therefore, for common purposes, may be taken at 4*s* 6*d.*; including bankers' commission on bills, the latter must always be the price calculated upon. The English value of the Norwegian money, therefore, will stand thus:—

	s.	*d.*
1 Skilling, about	0	0½
1 Mark, or Ort, about..................	0	10¾
1 Specie dollar............................	4	6

In speaking of dollars, they are called "species," the dollars being dropped. One of the most important requisites to attend to in Norway, when not in a town, is to be amply provided with *small* money; for change even for a piece of a few skillings is most difficult to obtain, and if travellers are not prepared with the exact amount they have to pay for horses, &c., they must usually either give more than is due, or be involved in much delay and annoyance. Change may generally be obtained at the post-offices in the large towns—the banks, however, are the best places, but they are only open for about an hour every morning. The best money to take is the 5 and 1 dollar notes, and coin, from pieces of 1 mark down to those of 2 sks.

The Danish paper and silver dollars pass current in Christiania (but not in the interior) for their full value; the same description of Norwegian money will not be taken in Sweden or Denmark, except at a loss of 3 or 4 sks. each sp. dollar. Swedish paper will not be taken in Norway.

As to the best mode of obtaining money from England, see General Introduction, under head 5, Money.

Measures.—12 inches make 1 foot, and 2 feet 1 ell. The Norsk foot is equal to 1.029 English. The *Norsk mile* is 12,352 Eng. yards, or 7 Eng. miles, and 32 yards. In superficial measure, by the term "a tönde of hard corn," is meant as much land as can be sown with one barrel or tönde of rye, 1 of barley, and 2 of oats. The land measure is the "Töndeland," which is 100 square Norwegian ells; this comes near to an English acre. The fourth part of a Töndeland, or 50 square ells, is called a "Maal Jord." 16 Norwegian square feet will make as nearly as possible 17 English square feet.

Weights.—2 Lods make	1 Unze.
8 Unzen	1 Mark.
2 Marks	1 Skaalpund.*
100 Skaalpunds	1 Centner.
12 Skaalpunds	1 Bismerpund.
3 Bismerpunds	1 Vog.
16 Skaalpunds	1 Lispund.
20 Lispunds	1 Skippund.

In the S. of Norway the Skippund, Lispund, Bismerpund, and Skaalpund are used. In the W. and N. the Vog, Bismerpund, and Skaalpund.

3. PASSPORTS.

Passports are not required, but any one visiting Norway, and intending to return through any part of the Continent to England, should be provided with a Foreign Office passport, *visé* by the Norwegian and Swedish Minister, or Consul.

4. MODES OF TRAVELLING.—INNS, STEAMERS, BOATS, CARRIOLES, FOUR-WHEELED CARRIAGES.

All travellers in Norway must be prepared for some inconvenience and discomfort, even on the main roads, and for a great amount of dirt, and sometimes even of hunger, unless provided with their own provisions, on the by-roads, in the remote parts of Norway.

Modes of Travelling.—The modes of travelling in Norway have greatly improved of late years, and on some of the principal inland lakes steamers regularly ply, viz., on the Miösen Lake, on the Öiern Lake, on the Rands Fjord, on Storsöen, on the Nord-söe, and on the Bandagsvand.

On the Miösen at the northern terminus of the railway from Christiania to Eidsvold, two steamers run every week-day to Lillehammer, at the northern extremity of the lake, touching at some of the principal places *en route*, so that it is possible to reach Gudbrandsdal, a distance of 133 English miles from Christiania, within the day, at an expense, including the railway and steamer fares (1st class), of rather less than 2½ sp. d., about 11*s*. English.

Norway is capital ground for a pedestrian tour. The usual mode of traversing the land routes is, however, by posting, which is admirably arranged to suit the wants and convenience of the people. Calculating the dollar at 4*s*. 6*d*. Eng., the average cost of posting per English mile for each horse will be about 3*d*. from "Fast stations," and 2*d*. when not from a

* N.B.—100 Skaalpunds Norsk are equal to about 110 lbs. Eng. avoirdupois, or 10 per cent. more.

"Fast station." Throughout the country there are station-houses erected at certain distances upon the roads, and the distance between each forms a stage.

It is only at the FAST stations that regular post horses are kept, and this arrangement, which is recent, is now very generally introduced on the main roads. Where it is not the case the farmers (Bönder) in the district are obliged by law to provide horses in turn; and as these have frequently to be brought from a distance, it is usual, in order to avoid detention, to send a "Forbud" (avant courier) beforehand, who carries with him any luggage the traveller may not have room for. The "forbud-seddel" or note may be sent by post.

The *manner* of sending Forbud will be fully explained hereafter. It consists in forwarding a notice to each station where horses will be wanted, stating the day and hour of the traveller's intended arrival. In a few places where bridges have been erected a toll is payable until the expense has been repaid. Turnpikes there are none. The roads are all kept in repair by the adjoining landowners.

Inns.—In Christiania there are now several hotels. The Victoria, the Hôtel du Nord and "Scandinavie," are considered the best: the first is well conducted, and can be very highly recommended. In Trondhjem there is also tolerable accommodation at the Hôtel d'Angleterre, and the Hôtel Bellevue. The *Station-houses* are the inns of the country. The proprietors are small farmers, or small country traders (Landhandlers): they are bound to find travellers with beds and food at prices fixed by a tariff in each district, and which is upon the most moderate scale. On the main roads, if a proper selection be made, it is generally possible to get into good quarters, with clean beds, every night; and a tolerably good and warm meal may be obtained, if ordered beforehand by the Forbud: but when travellers deviate from the main roads, this is anything but the case, and it is prudent to take some portable provisions, such as biscuits, portable soup, and perhaps an uncooked ham, for such emergencies. Good coffee, milk, cream, and black rye bread, and in the season strawberries (Jordbær) and molteberries (Moltebær), "*rubus chamæmorus*, may be generally obtained everywhere.

For the convenience of tourists, it has been deemed expedient to give *skeleton routes* after the manner of the "Reise-Route." Thus the distances between the various stations can be seen at a glance; and it is confidently hoped that "The Guide Book to Norway" will become of more practical value than ever. The tourist is particularly requested to compare each "skeleton route" with the more detailed account in the body of the work before starting on his journey. The stations in the several routes are taken from the latest tables published at Christiania, 1864. But as they are frequently changed, and are often lone farmhouses, which do not appear on ordinary maps, the names of the parish or district in which they are situated are generally added. So that if the traveller should ever be at a loss from subsequent changes, he will at least know whereabouts on his line of road the new stations must lie.

Steamers.—As a general rule berths should be secured as soon as possible. The sea-going steamers are described above, and the period of their departure and arrival will be explained hereafter. Besides these, there are now numerous steamers plying on the inland lakes, as well as a weekly steamer along the coast from Christiania to Christianssand, Bergen, Trondhjem, Tromsöe, and Hammerfest, touching at all the intermediate stations. Another steamer runs from Hammerfest to Vardöe and Vadsöe at the entrance of the White Sea every fortnight, thus completely encircling Norway by steam communication.

From Christiania to Christianssand there are steamers three times a week, and from Christiania to the different towns and ports in the Christiania Fjord two, and sometimes three steamers daily.

The fares on board all these vessels are low; the cuisine and wine good, and very reasonable. The coasting steamers are generally much crowded during the summer. They are small, as the shallowness of the water in the passages they have to navigate between the islands will not allow of vessels of a larger draught; but they all take carriages, the freight of which is, for 4 wheels equal to one and a half ch. cabin fare; for 2 wheels, half that sum. The fares are charged, Chief Cabin, 15 sk. (about 7d. English) per Norsk sea mile, 4 English, with a deduction of 12 sk. for every 20 sea m.; and also of 25 per cent. upon the total amount of the fare where two or more persons are travelling together; but the latter deduction is confined to husbands and wives, parents and children. Fore cabin, 10 sk. per Norsk sea m., and no deduction allowed.

As the days become shorter towards the end of the season, alterations are obliged to be made in the times of arrival and departure of some of the steamers. As a general rule, therefore, before starting to join a steamboat in Norway, and particularly on the West Coast, care should be taken to inquire up to what time the printed lists issued by the Government may be relied upon. They cease running in the winter.

Boats.—Formerly the only means of travelling along the West and Northern Coast was in open boats, and though steamers have in a great measure superseded this mode of travelling, regular stations, under the management of regular station-masters (Skydskaffer) still exist, where boats may be hired at fixed rates, in which carrioles and other light vehicles may be easily transported. The charges are regulated by a tariff (see page 11). The whole of the West of Norway is so deeply indented by fjords of vast extent, that the water stages requisite to connect the road along it, Route 24, are very numerous; and it is the same with respect to the roads from Christiania to

Bergen, Aalesund, Molde, &c. The boatmen are very careful, obliging, and trustworthy.

Carrioles are the most convenient carriages for travelling in Norway, and gentlemen will do well not to encumber themselves with any other. It is the carriage of the country, and admirably adapted to it from its lightness and simplicity of construction. The carriole somewhat resembles the Italian carricola. It is usually built without springs. The shafts are long and elastic, the ends are fixed to the axletree, and the seat (which will only hold one person) is placed well forward, and, by cross pieces, rests upon the shafts, the elasticity of which prevents the occupant being jolted, except when the roads are very bad. The legs are brought nearly to a horizontal position, so that in descending the steepest hill there is no inconvenience, nor the possibility of being thrown out, in the event of the horse falling. A board is fixed upon the axletree to carry a trunk, &c., and there the man to whom the horse belongs seats himself. The trunk should be fitted with long straps running through eyes to attach it to the board. The harness is of the most simple construction, and so contrived as to fit any of the small horses which are met with. These horses are almost invariably so docile that a child may drive them with perfect safety, if they be not overladen. They are matchless for their sureness of foot, in proof of which a broken knee is very rarely seen. In summer their only food is grass, but their powers of endurance are very great. The cost of a new carriole, without springs, is about 8*l.*; and with them, 9*l.* A set of new harness costs about 15*s.* more. At times carrioles and harness may be met with second-hand, and of course cheaper, but great caution should be used to see that they are not patched up for sale. The best will always be found the cheapest in the end. A long journey made rapidly in a carriole without springs will be found very fatiguing. Suggestions will be given under the head of "Requisites for Travelling," as to fitting up a carriole. Ladies *accustomed to driving* would do well to adopt the carriole, and avoid the delay and incumbrance attendant on travelling in any other vehicle, but they should take a spring carriole, though in case of breaking one it is difficult to get it mended in the country. A spring carriole is no doubt a great saving of fatigue, but they are not constructed for heavy people, or for rough roads.

Four-wheeled Carriages.—Very light four-wheeled carriages may now be used safely on all *the main roads* of Norway, but on these only, and it is only within the last few years that it has become prudent to use these. No one can fail to observe the good engineering and striking proofs of the progress that has been made lately in improving the roads. Hollows have been filled up, hills cut down, and roads scarped out of the face of the rock, where formerly nothing much better than horse-tracks existed. The road along the valley of the Driva from Kongsvold to Rise (Route 26) is a magnificent specimen of

Norwegian engineering; and other improvements are still in progress all through the country, the Government having proposed the application of no less than 225,000 dollars annually to that purpose.

The finest scenery is in the West, which is the most mountainous. There, also, the horses, which in other parts are small, degenerate into mere ponies, which are unaccustomed to draw any very heavy carriage, and have neither the power nor habit of holding it back in descending steep hills. For these reasons it may be said that the only danger of travelling in Norway, is that of using or loading a carriage beyond the strength of the horses, than which nothing can be more dangerous or more cruel. It is also a most hazardous and inconvenient affair to get a heavy carriage across any of the water stations. See Christiania, as to the cost or hire of such a phaeton as that we have described. Particular attention should be paid as to the mode of fitting up these carriages.

5. REQUISITES FOR TRAVELLING.—CARRIOLES.

Small Money—provide an ample supply as before recommended. *Maps.*—By far the best is "Professor P. A. Munch's," which can be obtained at Christiania or Trondhjem. It is very minute and accurate, and for pedestrians crossing mountains, &c., is the only one to be trusted; price for the South of Norway, 5 sp. d. Waligorski's and Wergeland's, published at Christiania in 1846, is cheaper, but is little better than a postal chart, giving none of the varied features of the country. Single houses, glaciers, churches, and mountains especially are strongly marked in Professor Munch's Map. Roosen's Map, published in Christiania, in 1848, in two sheets, is also a good one. Price about 5 sp. d. *Forbud papers.*—Printed forms in blank may be purchased in all the towns, and a supply should be taken. *Writing materials* should not be forgotten, and a *pocket compass.*

Carrioles are so constructed that in the body there is only room beneath the seat for a winch, hammer, coil of rope, some string, a gimblet, and a few straps; all of which should have their place there, and be secured by a lock. The apron should be long enough to button over the seat, so as to keep it dry during the night, when it is mostly left without shelter, "lock-up coach-houses" being rare in Norway. The Norwegian carries his provision box between his legs in the carriole: and if not too large, there is just room for the feet to rest beyond it. The Norwegian provision boxes are called "tine," or "löbe," and are very useful. With a little arrangement the carriole may be made comfortable, and capable of carrying all that is requisite for a journey. Behind, the portmanteau, or box, can be strapped, and for that purpose leather eyes should be fastened on beneath to the board and the straps passed through them, which prevents shifting. The Norwegians generally use a box of the dimensions described under head 9 of the General Introduction, and covered with skin, or painted, to keep out wet. Upon this the peasant to whom the horse belongs fastens his sack of hay, and seats himself as best he can. A gun-case had better be slung under the body of the carriole. Fishing-rods should be carried in a solid leather case, and lashed fore and aft to the shafts; or be slung in loops from the body and the dashing-board. Saddle-bags, made upon the plan suggested under head 9, or two large, stout, leather pockets, one to be fastened on either side of the body, will be found a great comfort. They should be secured upon their upper sides by two very stout straps well *screwed* (not nailed) to the frame of the seat inside, and extending over the sides; the buckles to be on the bags or pockets. The lower sides should be buckled to straps screwed to the bottom of the carriole, which keep the bags firmly in their place. The pocket on the right may be set apart for maps, forbud papers, guide-book, list of stations at which you have ordered horses, &c. &c.; and that on the left to provisions, which can be easily and effectually protected from sun and rain by anything thrown over the bag. To the outside of the dashing-board a case for 4 bottles of wine may be strapped, and to the inside a large leathern pocket to hold the pea-jacket and mackintosh.

The pleasure of a tour in Norway so much depends on having as little baggage as possible, and that little comfortably arranged before starting, that the time occupied in having a carriole fitted up accordingly will be amply repaid. Great care must be taken to pack everything as tightly as possible which is to be strapped at the back of your carriole, as the best preventive against the constant friction to which it will be exposed from not being on springs, which in every description of carriole are used for the body alone. If travelling with your own horse, by all means take a spare set of shoes and a supply of nails. A knife, fork, and spoon, a tin box for salt, and some mustard should be taken. Meat, white bread, and biscuits, are rarely met with in Norway, save in the towns and at a few of the best stations; a brisk look-out should therefore be kept for provender, and no opportunity lost of replenishing the provision box. Preserved soup, and an uncooked ham or piece of bacon to be fried in slices, are the most portable forms of meat. Tea, if it will be wanted, should be taken from England; none good can be obtained in Norway. It can be carried very conveniently in a bottle in the bottle case. A few wax candles had better be taken, if travelling after August. Nothing but tallow dips are to be had at the stations. Capital coffee, milk, sugar, and eggs, and generally rye-bread or oatmeal-cake (flad-bröd), fish, or bacon, are met with at most of the stations. Sour milk, eaten with a little sugar and oat-cake, is delicious, and a favourite Scandinavian dish. But the staple and most nutritious food of the peasants, and which may be obtained in every hovel in Norway and Sweden, is porridge (gröd). They prepare it very carefully and admirably, and it is a capital dish to fall back upon when nothing better can be obtained.

A *dog* may be carried in a net or bag slung under the carriole, upon the Italian plan. It is always the safest way to carry a dog in that manner, in case of his being attacked by a wolf, for with that animal a dog is an irresistible temptation. Pigs and cattle will also frequently attack a strange dog very fiercely, perhaps mistaking him for a wolf.

Mr. Bennett, an Englishman, residing at No. 17, Store Strandgade, has for many years fitted out most of the English travellers with carrioles, &c. Any one, by writing to him from England, or by telegraphing from Christiansand, on the arrival of the steamer there, may get everything provided for them ready for their departure on the morning after their arrival in Christiania.

Phaetons of the lightest description, as before observed, are the only four-wheeled carriages which can with either comfort or safety be used in Norway. If a servant be taken, he drives, and the second seat in front is occupied by the person who owns the horses. The only space for luggage is, therefore, under the front and back seats. Nothing above 12 inches high will go under them. If intending to return to Christiania, the best plan is to leave everything there except what may be requisite for the time you intend to be absent. Expanding portmanteaus, not exceeding 22 inches long by 14 wide and 12 deep, or cases of sheepskin or fustian mackintosh of that size, will be found the most convenient to stow away. Bags or pockets fixed on each side of the back seat (similar to those recommended for carrioles) are a great convenience. Or provisions can be taken in a basket, which should be covered with oilskin to keep out dust and rain. A case for 4 bottles of wine may be fastened to the dashing-board. Slings should be fixed at the back of the front seat for an umbrella. A strong fork must be fixed at the back of the carriage to stay it while the horses take breath on going up hill; and two stout drags for the wheels must not be omitted. The harness should have breeching; and the whole should be carefully looked over and examined, to see that it is in good repair, particularly the reins. A hammer, winch, rope, &c., should be taken, as in a carriole. The natives do not travel much in summer, and, when they do, it is almost entirely by carriole, and thence the ignorance which prevails even in Christiania as to what is essential for safety in travelling with a 4-wheeled carriage. We cannot too strongly caution those who value their lives not to venture into the interior with any carriage of a heavier description than a phaeton, or unprovided with shafts, fork, drags, and strong harness.

Luggage Cart.—Those who have too much baggage to take with them had better purchase a little spring cart for it to be used by the Forbud (see weight allowed at p. 12). If this be not done, the common carts without springs, kept at the stations, must be used, and luggage becomes much injured by the repeated changes on the road and jolting. It is well to take a piece of tarpaulin, which can be procured from Mr. Bennett.

It may be mentioned that there is an English Church establishment sup ported by *voluntary* contributions. Service on Sundays at 11 A.M.

6. POSTING REGULATIONS, SKYDTS LAW, SENDING FORBUD, TABLE OF PAYMENTS FOR HORSES.

TABLE

OF RATES FOR HORSES, BOATS, &c., PER NORSK MILE, EQUAL TO 7 ENG. MILES

	LAND.				WATER.	
	From Fast Stations in Towns.	From ordinary Stations in Towns.	From Fast Stations in the Country.	From ordinary Stations in the Country.	From Fast Stations.	From ordinary Stations.
	Skillings.	Skillings.	Skillings.	Skillings.	Skillings.	Skillings.
For one horse . . .	48	36	30	24		
Carriole with harness	6	6	4	4		
Two-horse cart with double harness . .	6	6	6	6		
One-horse cart with single harness . .	3	3	3	3		
Saddle with bridle, or long sleigh with harness	2	2	2	2		
Harness for leaders up and down hill, or pack saddle . . .	1	1	1	1		
Each man	...	...	...	...	24	20
Each 4-oared boat . .	...	...	...	...	8	8
„ 6 ditto .	...	...	...	...	12	12
„ 8 ditto .	...	...	...	...	24	24
„ 10 ditto .	...	...	...	...	32	32

If two persons post with the same vehicle with one horse, 1½ fare is charged The above fares for boats are for such as are constructed for sailing and rowing for row-boats only the charge is one-half less.

Independent of the above rates, the post-master is entitled to 4 skillings fo each horse, or 2 skillings for each boatman ; this is termed "tilsigelse," an is allowed him as his remuneration for the trouble of ordering them for th traveller, and he is entitled to the same fee of 2 skillings for each 8 or 10 oare boat, but at fast stations no tilsigelse is paid.

Three people and the post-boy can travel with two horses, if the carriage be not too cumbersome.

On a cart with two horses in the summer, or on a sleigh in the winter, luggage to the extent of 640 skaalpunds may be carried.*

On a cart with one horse, 320 lbs.

On a carriole, chaise, cart, or sleigh with one person, 64 lbs.

But if two persons travel with one horse, they are only allowed to carry 16 lbs.

The load of a horse with a pack-saddle is 192 lbs.

Persons hiring boats may load them with as many people or goods as they can safely carry without any extra charge.

Although the law fixes the weight of luggage as above stated, yet, unless the traveller has imprudently encumbered himself with a very undue quantity, and attempts to overload the horse or vehicle, no question as to the exact weight is ever mooted.

Skydts Law.—The following is an abstract of the act passed by the Storthing of 1845.

At stations which are not fast, if the Forbud arrives three hours before the time at which the horses or boatmen are required to be at the station, and if they are not there when the traveller arrives, the owner of the horses or the post-master is fined one specie dollar for each horse or boatman; and when the traveller does not arrive at the time he has stipulated, but detains the horses or boatmen beyond one hour, he has to pay one quarter of the rate for a mile, for each horse or boatman, as waiting money, and the post-master can refuse to supply him until this be paid. If the traveller does not arrive within three hours of the time he has appointed, the owner of the horses is not bound to wait any longer, and has a right to claim, as detention money, one-half of the rate for a mile for each horse, and each boatman may claim a similar payment.

If the traveller's late arrival has been caused by his having been detained at one of the previous stations, and he brings a certificate to that effect, which the post-master, under a penalty of 3 dollars, cannot refuse to give him, he is not bound to pay any detention money, but the party who caused the delay has to pay it. If detained in consequence of the weather, or of any accident which prevented his proceeding, and which is proved by the certificate of the post-master, he is not bound to pay this charge.

At stations which are not fast, and to which no Forbud has been sent, if the horses are a ¼ of a mile, ½ a mile, or a mile distant from the station, the traveller must wait respectively one, two, and three hours; but should he be detained beyond that time, unless through some unforeseen hindrance, the post-

* See Norsk weights, p. 4.

master, or owner of the horses, is subject to a fine of ¼ a dollar for every additional hour that the traveller is detained.

When the traveller does not drive himself, but leaves the reins to the post-boy, no responsibility with regard to the horse rests on him, but *if he drives himself, and the horse is ill-used or driven beyond its strength, and the post-boy complains, the post-master at the next station, two other men being called in to confirm his opinion, is to ascertain the extent of the injury done to the horse, and this the traveller is bound to pay; and until he does so, the post-master is authorized to refuse to provide him with horses.* This money is to be deposited with the post-master for four weeks, so that the traveller can appeal against his decision and have the case more fully investigated.

Travellers have to pay all tolls.

Where there are no post stations, a special agreement must be made with the owners of the horses.

In towns, the horses are to meet the traveller at any spot which he shall fix upon, and in the country at any place not above ¼ of a mile from the station; beyond that distance he must pay the usual mileage rate.

Drivers are always required to keep on the right side of the road, and not to occupy more than half of it; any offence against this regulation subjects the offending party to a penalty of 1 specie dollar.

The Day-book (Dagbog).—At every station a book is kept, in which the traveller enters his name, destination, the number of horses he uses, and states any complaints he may have to make against the post-master, post-boy, or others; these books are periodically inspected by the authorities, the complaints stated in them are inquired into, and the accused parties, if they are found to have acted improperly, are punished. Should the post-master refuse to produce this book, he is liable to a fine of half a specie dollar. To this book are always attached the posting regulations, and the distances to the adjoining stations. At every post station the giæstgiver or landlord is bound to have, and produce for inspection if required, a *table of rates and charges* of the different articles of food and liquors, which rates are fixed by the authorities; but the charges are generally so moderate that few travellers appeal to this document, unless they have reason to suppose that they have been imposed upon, and are desirous of punishing the offender. At the country stations a bill is rarely, if ever, given even if asked for; the total amount claimed being merely stated.

POSTING TABLE FOR BOATS.

Distance.	IN THE COUNTRY. From Stations not Fast. 2 Men with 4-oared Boat and Sail.	IN THE COUNTRY. From Stations not Fast. 3 Men with 6-oared Boat and Sail.	IN THE COUNTRY. From Stations not Fast. 4 Men with 8-oared Boat and Sail.	IN THE COUNTRY. From Fast Stations. 2 Men with 4-oared Boat and Sail.	IN THE COUNTRY. From Fast Stations. 3 Men with 6-oared Boat and Sail.	IN THE COUNTRY. From Fast Stations. 4 Men with 8-oared Boat and Sail.	IN TOWN. From Stations not Fast. 2 Men with 4-oared Boat and Sail.	IN TOWN. From Stations not Fast. 3 Men with 6-oared Boat and Sail.	IN TOWN. From Stations not Fast. 4 Men with 8-oared Boat and Sail.	IN TOWN. From Fast Stations. 2 Men with 4-oared Boat and Sail.	IN TOWN. From Fast Stations. 3 Men with 6-oared Boat and Sail.	IN TOWN. From Fast Stations. 4 men with 8-oared Boat and Sail.
	Sp. m. sk.	Sp. m. sk.	Sp. m. sk.	Sp. m. sk.	Sp. m. sk.	Sp. m. sk.	Sp. m. sk.	Sp. m. sk.	Sp. m. sk.	Sp. m. sk.	Sp. m. sk.	Sp. m. sk.
1/8 Mile...	0 0 6	0 0 9	0 0 12	0 0 7	0 0 10½	0 0 14	0 0 8	0 0 12	0 0 16	0 0 8½	0 0 12¾	0 0 17
1/4 " ...	0 0 12	0 0 18	0 1 0	0 0 14	0 0 21	0 1 4	0 0 16	0 1 0	0 1 8	0 0 17	0 1 1½	0 1 10
3/8 " ...	0 0 18	0 1 3	0 1 12	0 0 21	0 1 7½	0 1 18	0 1 0	0 1 12	0 2 0	0 1 1½	0 1 14¼	0 2 3
1/2 " ...	0 1 0	0 1 12	0 2 0	0 1 4	0 1 18	0 2 8	0 1 8	0 2 0	0 2 16	0 1 10	0 2 3	0 2 20
5/8 " ...	0 1 6	0 1 21	0 2 12	0 1 11	0 2 4½	0 2 22	0 1 16	0 2 12	0 3 8	0 1 18½	0 2 15¾	0 3 13
3/4 " ...	0 1 12	0 2 6	0 3 0	0 1 18	0 2 15	0 3 12	0 2 0	0 3 0	0 4 0	0 2 3	0 3 4½	0 4 6
7/8 " ...	0 1 18	0 2 15	0 3 12	0 2 1	0 3 1½	0 4 2	0 2 8	0 3 12	0 4 16	0 2 11½	0 3 17¼	0 4 23
1 " ...	0 2 0	0 3 0	0 4 0	0 2 8	0 3 12	0 4 16	0 2 16	0 4 0	1 0 8	0 2 20	0 4 6	1 0 16

N.B.—At stations in the country that are not fast, two skillings per boatman must be paid extra ; and if an eight or ten oared boat be ordered, two skillings more for the boat.

Sending Forbud.—The following is the usual form of the printed Forbud papers, which may be purchased in all the towns, in blank. The words in Roman letters show how they are to be filled up.

Paa Skydsskiftet Grorud bestilles 1 siger een Hest med Sele og 2 siger to löse Heste at staae færdige.—Thorsdagen den 4de Juni, 1848. Formiddagen, Klokken.

Med Forbudet (som betales ved Undertegnedes ankomst) fölger 1 Vadsæk, og 1 Hatæske.

Christiania den 3 die Juni, 1848.

A. B.

Jeg anmoder Gjæstgiveren om at bære Omsorg for, at Forbudet strax gaaer videre, og at notere i Dagbogen naar ankommet og igjen afgaaet.

Literal Translation.

At the Skyds station *Grorud*,* there is ordered 1, to say *one* Horse † with harness,‡ and 2, to say *two*, loose Horses § to stand ready *Thursday* the 4th *June*, 1848. *Forenoon* at 11 o'clock.

With the Forbud (which is to be paid at the undersigned's arrival) there comes ‖ a *Portmanteau, and Hat-box.*

Christiania,¶ the *3rd June*, 1848.

A. B.**

I beg the Landlord to take care that the Forbud immediately goes on, and to notice in the Day-book when it arrives and again starts forward.

N.B.—Great care is requisite when filling up these papers for fixing the proper hour at which the horses will be wanted, and a *List* should be accurately made and kept of the different stations at which the Forbud papers are to be left, and the time horses are ordered at each station. This will prevent confusion or mistakes. The usual rate of travelling in a *carriole* is *one* Norsk mile (or 7 Eng.) an hour, where the roads are not very hilly; but it is always better to allow 1½ hour for each mile on account of the penalties which travellers are liable to when they arrive much after the time at which they have ordered the horses (see p. 12). With the lightest 4-wheeled carriage it takes about 20 minutes per Norsk mile longer than by carriole, and even more than that when the hills are very steep.

Forbud papers may be sent by post at a cost of *four* skillings for each paper, which is a considerable saving of expense in a long journey. But to prevent mistakes travellers should *personally* ascertain at the post-office when

* The name of the station at which the horses are to be ordered.

† Hest is the singular, Heste plural.

‡ If no horse wanted with harness, strike this out.

§ "Loose" horse means without harness.

‖ Any luggage sent by the Forbud cart should be stated here.

¶ The place from whence the Forbud paper is sent.

** Signature of the person who sends it.

the post will go the road they wish to travel. But, however they may be transmitted, in the event of several Forbud papers being sent at the same time, it is usual to number them, and write very distinctly the name of the station at which each is to be left. This is done in the margin, or at the back, together with the following

Notice to Station-Masters,

where travellers desire that dinners, &c., or beds, should be ready for them on their arrival.

Gjestgiveren paa Grorud anmodes herved om at have Aftensmad, og Senge for tre Personer færdig ved min Ankomst.

A. B.

Translation.

The Master of the *Grorud* Station is hereby requested to have *Supper* and *Beds** ready for 3 persons on my arrival.

A. B.

Should the traveller be kept waiting for horses beyond the time he has ordered them, the following is the proper form of entry to be made in the Day-book kept at the station. If not written in Norsk it will not be attended to; and it should not be made except in an extreme case, as it subjects the party complained of to a penalty, and in many places the peasants have to come from long distances to the stations.

Form of Entry in Day-book.

Undertegnede er bleven opholdt paa dette Skydsskifte ventende paa Heste, som ei ankom førend to Timer efter den, paa Forbudssedlen angivne Tid.

A. B.

Translation.

The undersigned has been detained at this Station, waiting for horses, which did not arrive until *two* hours† after the time specified on the Forbud paper.

A. B.

It sometimes happens that persons change their plans, and take another road after having sent off their Forbud papers, and horses are ordered as requested. Whenever this occurs, the forfeit money due to the owners of the horses, and also to the station-masters for ordering them, should be carefully paid, which may be done without any difficulty at the next post-office arrived at in any of the towns. Persons are not only legally liable, and will be made to pay these sums if they can be traced, but it is grossly unjust and dishonourable to evade the payment. Except at fast stations, the horses have often to be sent for several English miles from the station; besides which, when required

* Breakfast, *frokost.* Dinner, *middagsmad.*

† Or whatever the time may have been.

POSTING TABLE FOR HORSES.*

Fast Stations in the Country, and Stations not Fast in Towns.					Stations not Fast in the Country.					Fast Stations in Towns.				
Distance.	Horse without Carriole or Harness.		Horse with Carriole and Harness.		Distance.	Horse without Carriole or Harness.		Horse with Carriole and Harness.		Distance.	Horse without Carriole or Harness.		Horse with Carriole and Harness.	
	mk.	sk.	mk.	sk.		mk.	sk.	mk.	sk.		mk.	sk.	mk.	sk.
⅛ Mile ..	0	4½	0	5½	⅛ Mile	0	3	0	4	⅛ Mile ..	0	6	0	7
¼ ,, ...	0	9	0	11	¼ ,,	0	6	0	8	¼ ,, ...	0	12	0	14
⅜ ,, ...	0	13½	0	16½	⅜ ,,	0	9	0	12	⅜ ,, ...	0	18	0	21
½ ,, ...	0	18	0	21½	½ ,,	0	12	0	15½	½ ,, ...	1	0	1	3½
⅝ ,, ...	0	22½	1	3	⅝ ,,	0	15	0	19½	⅝ ,, ...	1	6	1	10½
¾ ,, ...	1	3	1	8½	¾ ,,	0	18	0	23½	¾ ,, ...	1	12	1	17½
⅞ ,, ...	1	7½	1	14	⅞ ,,	0	21	1	3½	⅞ ,, ...	1	18	2	0½
1 ,, ...	1	12	1	19	1 ,,	1	0	1	7	1 ,, ...	2	0	2	7

during the hay season, the service of both men and horses is of so much more value at home, that it is usually a loss to the farmer even when paid the full charge allowed by law. In such a country as Norway, the wrongful act of a traveller is not only prejudicial to his own reputation, but also to those who may follow him, and particularly to his own countrymen.

With the assistance of the above tables and previous information, the charges for horses, and also for boatmen and boats, may be readily calculated. The peasants are slow in calculating, but generally honest in their demands. Where any difference arises as to payment, the station-master should be applied to, and whatever he states to be the proper sum to be paid may be relied upon as correct.

The peasants who accompany the horses are not entitled to anything, but it is customary to pay them a gratuity (drikke-penge) at the rate of 3 or 4 shillings per horse per mile. The Norwegians are fond of their horses, and it both pains and irritates them extremely to see their favourites ill-used or driven faster than the usual carriole rate of one Norsk mile an hour, even when the roads are good.

* At all stations that are not "fast," 4 sk. per horse must be paid to the station master.

7. DANISH AND NORWEGIAN ALPHABET, VOCABULARY, ETC.*

The *Alphabet*.

Although the Roman character is daily gaining ground, the Gothic form is still in very general use.

The Danish Alphabet consists of 27 letters, viz. :—

Roman.	Gothic.	Pronounced.	Power.
A, a,	𝔄, 𝔞,	Ah,	*a* in *Father*.†
B, b,	𝔅, 𝔟,	Bey,	*b*.
C, c,	ℭ, 𝔠,	Cey,	*s* and *k*, as in English.
D, d,	𝔇, 𝔡,	Dey,	*d* hard, and *th* flat, as in *thus*.
E, e,	𝔈, 𝔢,	Ey,	French *é fermé*, and *è ouvert*.
F, f,	𝔉, 𝔣,	Eff,	*f*.
G, g,	𝔊, 𝔤,	Ghey,	*g* in *go*, *give*.
H, h,	ℌ, 𝔥,	Haw,	*h* aspirated.
I, i,	ℑ, 𝔦,	Ee,	*ee* in *bee*, *i* in *bill*.
J, j,	𝔍, 𝔧,	Yoth,	*y* consonant.
K, k,	𝔎, 𝔨,	Kaw,	*k*, and sometimes like *ch*.
L, l,	𝔏, 𝔩,	El,	*l*.
M, m,	𝔐, 𝔪,	Em,	*m*.
N, n,	𝔑, 𝔫,	En,	*n*.
O, o,	𝔒, 𝔬,	O,	*o* in *more*, *for*.
P, p,	𝔓, 𝔭,	Pey,	*p*.
Q, q,	𝔔, 𝔮,	Koo,	*q*.
R, r,	ℜ, 𝔯,	Er,	*r*.
S, s,	𝔖, ſ, 𝔰,	Es,	*s* hard.
T, t,	𝔗, 𝔱,	Tey,	*t*.
U, u,	𝔘, 𝔲,	Oo,	*oo* in *fool*, *u* in *full*.
V, v,	𝔙, 𝔳,	Vey,	*v* in *vein*, *w* in *howl*.
X, x,	𝔛, 𝔵,	Ex,	*x* hard.
Y, y,	𝔜, 𝔶,	U,	*u* in *pur*.
Z, z,	ℨ, 𝔷,	Set,	*z*.
Æ, æ,	𝔄𝔈, æ,	Ai,	*a* in *sale*, *ai* in *said*.
Ö, ö,	𝔒̈, 𝔬̈,	Eu,	(French) *ouvert* in *veuve*, *œu* in *cœur*, *œuf*.

* A small Danish and English Dictionary has been published at Leipsig, and may be obtained at the Foreign booksellers' in London. Rask's Danish Grammar, for the use of Englishmen, can be procured of Mr. Quaritch, 16, Castle Street, Leicester Square. Mr. Bennett's English and Norwegian Parleur may be found useful.

† Where aa occurs it is sounded nearly like the English *a* in *warm*, or the *oa* in *broad*.

Pronunciation.

In Danish every word is pronounced as it is written. One of the greatest difficulties is to distinguish between the vowels *u*, *y*, and *ö*; and very long practice is necessary to give the right sound of these.

The *Articles.*

The greatest peculiarity of the Danish language is the use of the articles.

The *indefinite* article has two forms, viz., *et* before a noun of the neuter, and *en* before one of the common gender (which includes masculine and feminine nouns); it has no plural.

	Ex. Neuter.	*Common.*
Sing.	et Land, *a country.*	en Stol, *a chair.*
Plur.	Lande, *countries.*	Stole, *chairs.*

The *definite* article of nouns substantive is *et* in the neuter, *en* in the common gender, and *-ne*, *-ene* for the plural of both genders, and always added as an affix to the nouns, as

	Ex. Neuter.	*Common.*
Sing.	Landet, *the country.*	Stolen, *the chair.*
Plur.	Landene, *the countries.*	Stolene, *the chairs.*

The *definite* article of adjectives is *det* for the neuter, *den* for the common, and *de* for the plural of both genders, as

Sing.	det skönne* Land,	*the fine country.*
Plur.	de skönne Lande,	*the fine countries.*
Sing.	den gamle Stol,	*the old chair.*
Plur.	de gamle Stole,	*the old chairs.*

The *Personal Pronouns* are—

Sing.		*Plur.*	
jeg (pronounced *yei*) ...	*I*	vi..............................	*we*
du..............................	*thou*	I..............................	*you*
han	*he*	de	*they*
hun	*she*		

De, they, is used instead of *I* in addressing a person (like the German *Sie*), in which case it is written with a capital letter.

The *Numerals.*

Cardinal.	Ordinal.
1, een, *one.*	det, den, förste, *the first.*
2, to, *two.*	—— anden, *the second.*
3, tre, *three.*	—— tredie, *the third.*

* The k is pronounced soft, as ch, like *schön* in German.

4, fire, *four.*	det, den, fjerde, *the fourth.*
5, fem, *five.*	—— femte, *the fifth.*
6, sex, *six.*	—— sjette, *the sixth.*
7, syv, *seven.*	—— syvende, *the seventh.*
8, otte, *eight.*	—— ottende, *the eighth.*
9, ni, *nine.*	—— niende, *the ninth.*
10, ti, *ten.*	—— tiende, *the tenth.*
11, elleve, *eleven.*	—— ellefte, *the eleventh.*
12, tolv, *twelve.*	—— tolvte, *the twelfth.*
13, tretten, *thirteen.*	—— trettende, *the thirteenth.*
14, fjorten, *fourteen.*	—— fjortende, *the fourteenth.*
15, femten, *fifteen.*	—— femtende, *the fifteenth.*
16, sexten, *sixteen.*	—— sextende, *the sixteenth.*
17, sytten, *seventeen.*	—— syttende, *the seventeenth.*
18, atten, *eighteen.*	—— attende, *the eighteenth.*
19, nitten, *nineteen.*	—— nittende, *the nineteenth.*
20, tyve, *twenty.*	—— tyvende, *the twentieth.*
21, een og tyve, *twenty-one, &c.*	—— een og tyvende, *twenty-first, &c.*
30, tredive, *thirty.*	—— tredivte, *the thirtieth.*
40, fyrretyve, *forty.*	—— fyrretyvende, *the fortieth.*
50, halvtresindstyve, or halvtres, or femti, *fifty.*	—— halvtresindstyvende, or femtiende, *the fiftieth.*
60, tresindstyve, or sexti, *sixty.*	—— tresindstyvende, or sextiende, *the sixtieth.*
70, halvfjersindstyve, or halvfjers, or sytti, *seventy.*	—— halvfjersindstyvende, or syttiende, *the seventieth.*
80, fjersindstyve, or otti, *eighty.*	—— fjersindstyvende, or ottiende, *the eightieth.*
90, halvfemsindstyve, or halvfems, or nitti, *ninety.*	—— halvfemsindstyvende, or nittiende, *the ninetieth.*
100, hundrede, *hundred.*	—— hundrede, *the hundredth.*
101, hundrede og een, &c., *one hundred and one.*	—— hundrede og förste, *the hundred and first.*
1000, tusende, *one thousand.*	—— tusende, *the one thousandth.*

Days of the Week.

Monday	*Mondag.*	Friday	*Fredag.*
Tuesday	*Tirsdag.*	Saturday	*Löverdag.*
Wednesday	*Onsdag.*	Sunday	*Söndag.*
Thursday	*Thorsdag.*		

Months.

January	*Januar.*	July	*Juli.*
February	*Februar.*	August	*August.*
March	*Marts.*	September	*September.*
April	*April.*	October	*October.*
May	*Mai.*	November	*November.*
June	*Juni.*	December	*December.*

VOCABULARY.

Again	*Igien.*	Biscuits	*Tvebakker.*
Aid	*Hielp.*	Black cock	*Urhane.*
Ale	*Öl.*	Boat	*Baad.* *
All	*Al* and *Alt.*	Boil, to	*Koge.*
All the same	*Slig slag*	Boots	*Stövler.*
Also	*Ogsaa.*	Bottle	*Flask.*
Altogether	*Altsammen.*	Boy	*Gut.*
Always	*Altid.*	Boy, that goes with horses	*Skydskarl.*
And	*Og.*		
Answer	*Svar.*	Brandy	*Brændeviin.*
Arm	*Arm.*	Bread and butter	*Smör og brod, Smörbröd.*
Ask, to	*Spörge.*		
As much as	*Saa meget som.*	Breakfast	*Frokost.*
As well as	*Saavelsom.*	Bridle	*Bidsel.*
At	*Til, ved.*	Brush	*Börste.*
Away	*Bort.*	Bucket	*Spand.*
Axletree	*Axel.*	Buckle	*Spænde.*
Back again	*Tilbage.*	Butter	*Smör.*
Bad	*Slem, ond.*	Buy, to	*Kjöbe.*
Bag	*Sak.*	By-way	*Afvei, sidevei.*
Barley	*Byg.*	Call, to	*Raabe, kalde.*
Basket	*Kurv.*	Can	*Kan.*
Bath	*Badekar.*	Candle	*Lys.*
Bear	*Björn.*	Cap	*Hue.*
Because	*Fordi.*	Capercailie	*Tiur* (m.), *Röy* (f.)
Bed	*Seng.*		
Before	*For.*	Carriage	*Vogn.*
Berth	*Koie.*	Carriole	*Carriole.*
Best	*Bedst.*	Cart	*Karre.*
Better	*Bedre.*	Chain	*Kjæde.*
Between	*Imellem.*	Chair	*Stol.*
Bill, the	*Regningen, nota.*	Change (small money)	*Smaa penge.*
Bird	*Fugl.*		

* Pronounced nearly like the English *boat.*

Change, to (money) *Vexle.*
Char *Rör.*
Cheese *Ost.*
Chemist's shop *Apotheke.*
Clean *Reen.*
Coat *Kiole.*
Cod *Torsk.*
Coffee *Kaffee.*
Collar, horse *Halskobbel.*
Comb *Kam.*
Come, to *Komme.*
Cook, to *Koge.*
Coverlid *Teppe.*
Cream, sweet *Flöde.*
Cup *Kop.*
Cut, to *Skære.**
Danger *Fare.*
Daughter *Datter.*
Day-book *Dagbog.*
Deep *Dyb.*
Dinner *Middags-mad.*
Do, to *Giöre.*
Dog *Hund.*
Door *Dör.*
Drink-money *Drikke-penge.*
Duck *And*, pl., *Ænder.*
Early *Tidlig.*
Eat, to *Spise.*
Eggs *Œgg.*
Eggs (boiled) *Kogte Œgg.*
,, (poached) *Blödkogte Œgg.*
Elk *Elsdyr.*
Enough *Nok.*
Evening *Qvæl, Aften.*
Every, each *Hver.*
Everywhere *Overalt.*
Exchange, to *Bytte.*
Face *Ansigt.*
Fall, to *Falde.*
Far *Langt, borte.*
Farm-house *Bönde-gaard.*
Ferry *Færge.*
Field *Mark, Ager.*
Fire *Ild.*
Firewood *Ved.*
Fish *Fisk.*
Fish, to *Fiske.*
Fishing-line *Fiske-snör.*
Fishing-rod *Fiske-stang.*
Fly *Flue.*
Fly (artificial) *Flue-angel, Flue-krog.*
Fork *Gaffel.*
Forwards *Frem.*
Fox *Ræv.*
Fry, to *Stege.*
Frying-pan *Stegepande.*
Game *Vildt.*
Get, to *Faae.*
Girl *Pige.*
Girth *Saddelgjord.*
Give, to *Give.*
Glad, I am *Det glæder mig.*
Glass *Glas.*
Go, to *Gaae.*
Grass *Græs.*
Grayling *Syk.*
Grease (for wheels) *Smörning.*
Gun *Skydegevær, Gevær.*
Gunpowder *Krudt.*
Hair *Haar.*
Half *Halv.*
Ham, or bacon *Skinke.*
Hand, right *Höjere Haand.*
Hand, left *Venstre Haand.*
Handkerchief *Lommetorklæde.*
Hare *Hare.*
Harness *Sele.*
Hasel-hen *Hjerpe.*
Hasten on *Skynde paa.*
Hat *Hat.*
Have, to *Have.*
Hay *Hö.*

* The *k* is pronounced like *h*.

Hence	*Herfra.*
Here	*Her.*
Herring	*Sild.*
Hill	*Bakke.*
Hold (of a ship)	*Rum.*
Hold of, to take	*Tage fat paa.*
Hook	*Angel, Krog.*
Horse	*Hest.*
Hour	*Time.*
Hour, half an	*En halv Time.*
Husband	*Mand.*
If	*Dersom.*
Immediately	*Strax, Øieblikkelig.*
In	*I.*
Ink	*Blæk.*
Inn	*Giæstgiver-Gaard, Værtshuus.*
Interpreter	*Tolk.*
Island	*Ö, Holm.*
Jug	*Kruus.*
Keep, to	*Holde.*
Kindle, to	*Tænde.*
Knife	*Kniv.*
Lady	*Frue.**
Lady (young unmarried)	*Fröken.*
Lake (large)	*Indsöe.*
Lake	*Vand.*
Large	*Stor.*
Late	*Sildig.*
Later	*Senere.*
Lay, to	*Lægge, sætte.*
Lead	*Bly.*
Least	*Mindst.*
Less	*Mindre.*
Letter	*Brev.*
Little	*Liden.*
Look	*See.*
Lucifer matches	*Fyrstikker.*
Luggage	*Töi*
Man, that supplies post-horses	*Skyds-skaffer.*
Many	*Mange.*
Map	*Veikart.*
Me	*Mig.*†
Meat, fresh	*Kiöd.*
Milk	*Melk.*
Mine	*Min.*
Money	*Penge.*
Money, paid for ordering post-horses	*Tilsigelse-penge.*
More	*Mere.*
Most	*Mest.*
Mountain	*Fjeld, Bjerg.*
Much	*Meget.*
Mustard	*Sennep.*
My	*Min.*
Nail	*Negl.*
Near	*Nær.*
Needle	*Synaal.*
Net (large drawing)	*Net.*
Net (smaller, and usually fixed)	*Garn.*
Never	*Aldrig.*
Newspaper	*Avis.*
Next week	*Næsten uge.*
Night, in the	*Om natten.*
Night lodging	*Nat-quartier.*
No	*Nei.*‡
Nobody	*Ingen.*
Nothing	*Intet.*
Now	*Nu.*
Oar	*Aare.*§

* *Frue*, lady, is used to wives of men of rank, namely, those who hold government appointments, such as Ministers of State, Clergy, Field Officers in the Army, and of corresponding rank in the Navy, Professors, &c., and *Fröken* to their daughters; *Madame* to the wives of Merchants and Tradesmen; *Jomfru* to their daughters.

† Pronounced nearly like the English *me*.

‡ Pronounced *nay*.

§ Pronounced nearly like the English *oar*.

Oat-cake	*Flad-Bröd.*
Oats	*Havre.*
Of	*Af.*
Often	*Ofte.*
Oil	*Olie.*
Once	*Eengang.*
One more	*Een til.*
Order, to	*Bestille.*
Our	*Vor.*
Over	*Over.*
Pancakes	*Pandekuger.*
Paper	*Papiir.*
Parsonage	*Præstegaard.*
Partridge	*Agerhöne, Raphöns.*
Pay, to	*Betale.*
Pen	*Pen.*
Pepper	*Peber.*
Physicians	*Læge.*
Piece	*Stykke.*
Pike or Jack	*Gedde.*
Pilot	*Lods.*
Pillow	*Hovedpude.*
Plate	*Tallerken.*
Pleasure	*Fornöielse.*
Portmanteau	*Vadsæk.*
Port-wine	*Portviin.*
Post-office	*Post-contoir.*
Potatoes	*Potates.*
Ptarmigan	*Rype.*
Put, to	*Sætte.*
Ready	*Færdig.*
Red deer	*Hjort.*
Reel	*Snelle.*
Rein	*Tömme.*
Reindeer	*Rensdyr.*
Return, to	*Vende tilbage.*
Ride, to	*Ride.*
River	*Elv, Flod.*
Road	*Vei.*
Roast	*Stege.*
Room or chamber	*Værelse.*
Row, to	*Roe.*
Rower	*Roerkarl.*
Rye	*Rug.*
Saddle	*Sadel.*
Safe	*Sikker.*
Salmon	*Lax.*
Salt	*Salt.*
Scissors, pair of	*Sax.*
Sell, to	*Sælge.*
Shafts, the	*Armene.*
Shall	*Skal.*
Shallow	*Grund.*
Sheets, the	*Lagene.*
Shew, to	*Vise.*
Shoe	*Sko.*
Shoe, horse	*Hest-Sko.*
Shot	*Hagel.*
Side, on this	*Paa denne side.*
Side, on the other	*Paa den andre side.*
Since,	*Siden.*
Smell, to	*Lugte.*
Snipe	*Myr-sneppe.*
Soap	*Sæbe.*
Son	*Sön.*
Speak, to	*Tale.*
Spoon	*Skee.*
Stable	*Stald.*
Stage, the	*Skiftet.*
Steamer	*Dampskib.*
Steward	*Opvarter.*
Stirrups	*Stigböile.*
Stove	*Ovn.*
String	*Snör, Hyssing.*
Strap	*Rem.*
Straw	*Halm.*
Sugar	*Sukker.*
Supper	*Aftensmad.*
Table	*Bord.*
Take, to	*Tage.*
Take care of, to	*Sörge for.*
Take care	*Passe paa.*
Tarpaulin	*Presenning.*
Tea	*Thee.*
Then	*Da.*

Thence	*Derfra.*	Water	*Vand.*
Throw, to	*Kaste.*	Waterfall	*Fos, Vandfald.*
To	*Til.*	Wheel	*Hiul.*
To-day	*Idag.*	When	*Naar.*
To-morrow	*Imorgen.*	Where	*Hvor.*
To-night	*Inat.*	Whip, driving	*Svöbe.*
Towel	*Haandklæder.*	Why	*Hvorfor.*
Town	*By.*	Why not	*Hvorfor ikke.*
Travel, to	*Reise.*	Wife	*Kone.*
Trout	*Forelle, Öret.*	Window	*Vindue.*
Trowsers	*Beenklæder.*	Wine	*Viin.*
Tub (to wash in)	*Kar.*	With	*Med.*
Twice.	*To Gange.*	Without	*Uden.*
Under	*Under.*	Woodcock	*Rugde.*
Upon	*Paa.*	Woodgrouse	*Ryper.*
Valley	*Dal.*	Wood, a forest	*Skov.*
Very	*Meget.*	Yes	*Ja, jo.*
Vinegar	*Œdikke.*	Yesterday	*Igaar.*

DIALOGUES.

Good morning!	*God Morgen!*
How do you do?	*Hvor staar det til?*
Very well, I thank you.	*Jeg takker, meget vel.*
Be so kind as to take a seat.	*Vær saa artig at tage en Stol.*
Sit down for a moment.	*Sid ned et Öjeblik.*
Where are you going?	*Hvor skal De hen?*
Show me the way.	*Viis mig Veien.*
Which is the way?	*Hvilken er Veien?*
But when shall we see each other again?	*Men naar sees vi nu igjen?*
Shall we then meet to-night?	*Sees vi saa i Aften?*
In the evening I shall be at home.	*Om Aftenen er jeg hjemme.*
At what hour?	*Ja hvad Tid?*
About six or seven o'clock.	*Omtrent Klokken sex eller syv.*
Shall I expect you then?	*Maa jeg da vente Dem?*
Good bye!	*Farvel! Adieu!*
Good evening.	*God Aften.*
I beg pardon.	*Jeg beder om forladelse.*
I don't know.	*Jeg veed ikke.*
I am very happy to see you.	*Det fornöjer mig meget at see Dem.*

I am much obliged to you.	*Jeg er Dem meget forbunden.*
Many thanks.	*Mange tak.*
Thank you (literally, thanks shall you have).	*Tak skal De have.*
Come here.	*Komme hid.*
Wait a little.	*Bie en lidt grun.*
Do you speak Danish—Norwegian?	*Taler De Dansk—Norsk.*
I cannot speak Norwegian.	*Jeg kan ikke tale Norsk.*
You must speak slowly.	*De maa tale langsomt.*
Do you understand me?	*Forstaaer De mig?*
Yes, I understand you very well.	*Ja, jeg forstaaer Dem meget vel.*
I cannot understand you.	*Jeg kan ikke forstaae Dem.*
What o'clock is it?	*Hvor mange Klokken nu?*
It is two o'clock.	*Klokken er to.*
It is half-past one.	*Den er halv to.*
It is three quarters past two.	*Den er tre quateer till tre.*
Is it possible?	*Er det muligt?*
What is that called?	*Hvad kaldes dette?*
How many miles is it from here to . . . ?	*Hvormange Mile er det herfra til . . . ?*
Is the road good?	*Er Veien god?*
Did you ever travel this way before?	*Har De reist denne Vei för?*
Are there any good inns upon the road?	*Findes gode Gjestgiversteder paa Veien?*
Is the road safe?	*Er Veien sikker?*
What conveyance can I have to . . . ?	*Hvad Slags Befordring kan jeg faae til . . . ?*
How much must I pay for each horse?	*Hvor meget maa jeg betale for hver Hest?*
How much must I give the postilion?	*Hvor meget maa jeg betale til Kudsken?*
Can I depend on having fresh horses on the road?	*Kan jeg giöre Regning paa overalt at finde friske Heste?*
I shall perform the journey on horseback.	*Jeg vil giöre Reisen tilhest.*
I have but little luggage.	*Jeg har kun ubetydeligt Töi.*
Where do we change horses?	*Hvor skifter man Heste?*
Where are the horses?	*Hvor ere Hestene?*
The horses were ordered for one o'clock.	*Hestene vare bestilte til klokken eet.*
Put grease on the wheels.	*Sætte smörning til hiulene.*
Is there a ferry?	*Er der nogen Færge?*

Put me over the river.	*Sæt mig over Elven.*
How much must we pay for the passage?	*Hvor meget maa man betale for Overfarten?*
How much does a place in the vessel cost?	*Hvor meget koster en Plads paa Skibet?*
I wish to go to . . . in the steamer.	*Jeg önsker at gaae til . . . med Dampen.*
When does the steamer go?	*Hvad tid gaaer Dampen?*
Can I have this berth?	*Kan jeg faae denne koie?*
Is there no room?	*Findes ingen Plads?*
Is there no boat here?	*Findes ingen Baad her?*
Can you procure me a boat with a couple of rowers?	*Kan man skaffe mig en Baad med et Par Roerkarle?*
Go ashore.	*Gaae til Land.*
Let the boat drop down.	*Lade Baaden slippe ned.*
Can I get a horse directly?	*Kan jeg faae en Hest strax?*
Is this the road to . . . . ?	*Er denne Veien til . . . . ?*
Can I sleep here to-night?	*Kan jeg ligge her inat?*
Can I get anything to eat?	*Kan jeg faa noget at spise?*
What kind of meat is there?	*Hvad slags Kjöd er der?*
What can you give us for supper?	*Hvad kan De give os til aftens.*
Give us whatever you have.	*Giv os hvad De har.*
I am hungry: I am thirsty.	*Jeg er sulten: jeg er törstig.*
Give me something to eat and drink.	*Giv mig noget at spise og drikke.*
What do you like to have?	*Hvad behager De?*
Fetch me some wine, bread and cheese.	*Hent mig Viin, Bröd og Ost.*
Give me a plate, please.	*Giv mig en Tallerken, vær saa god.*
Let me have a cup of coffee.	*Lade mig faae en Kop Kaffe.*
Shut the door, window.	*Luk Dören, Vinduet.*
Light a fire in the stove.	*Lægge Varme i Ovnen.*
Not too much.	*Ikke formeget.*
Bring me a tub with some cold water.	*Bring mig et Vandkar med koldt Vand.*
I wish to breakfast.	*Jeg önsker at spise Frokost.*
What do you say?	*Hvad siger De?*
Who is there?	*Hvem er der?*
Come in.	*Kom ind.*
What do you want?	*Hvad önsker De?*
Stand still.	*Staae stille.*
Go away.	*Gaae bort.*
Don't touch.	*Ikke röre.*
Let go.	*Lad gaae.*

I shall walk.	*Jeig skal spadsere.*
Are you ready?	*Er De færdig?*
Are our rooms ready?	*Ere vore Værelser istand?*
Is my bed made?	*Er min Seng redet?*
Bring me a washhand basin.	*Bring mig en Vadskevand Skaal.*
Bring me a towel.	*Bring mig et Haandklæde.*
Send the dirty clothes to the washerwoman.	*Send smudset Töi til Vaskekonen.*
Wake me to-morrow, early.	*Væk mig imorgen tidlig.*
Clean my boots.	*Börst mine Stövler.*
Bring me my shoes.	*Bring mig mine Skoe.*
How much do we owe you?	*Hvor meget ere vi Dem skyldige?*
What does this cost?	*Hvad koster den?*
It is very dear.	*Det er meget kostbar.*
Put the horse to.	*Spænde for.*
It is far too much.	*Det er alt formeget.*
Give me the bill.	*Giv mig Regningen.*
What have we to pay?	*Hvad har vi at betale?*
The bill is reasonable.	*Regningen er ganske billig.*
Here is your money.	*Her ere Pengene.*
The bill is too much.	*Regningen er for höi.*
I will not pay more than 4 marks.	*Jeg vil ikke betale mere end 4 Mark.*

N.B.—Throughout Scandinavia, where the rank of a gentleman is not accurately known, in directing a letter to him, it is usual to write in capital letters, S. T. (salvo titulo) over his name, to guard against any offence being taken in omitting or mis-stating his title.

8. SCENERY AND SKETCHING.

The grandest scenery in Norway is about that great chain of mountains which, as before mentioned, runs from N. to S. nearly throughout the whole country. The most select portions, as well as those most attainable, are comprised in the following Routes, viz., part of Route 24, from Christianssand to Molde and Christiansund; N. of Trondhjem, upon that route, the valleys of the Namsen and the Alten, and the peaked mountains in the extreme N., are also very grand, but, as a whole, will not bear comparison with the scenery S. of Christiansund, besides which the only mode of travelling N. of the Namsen is by open boats or steamers. In addition to the above, the finest scenery will be found in Routes 21, 22, and 23, between Christiania and Bergen; Route 26, Christiania to Trondhjem; Route 30, through Romsdalen to Molde; and Route 33, from Lierdalsören through the mountains to Romsdalen. To the E. of Route 26, in the interior of the country, the forests are dense and of enormous extent, and the scenery, though at times grand and very wild, is far less picturesque than upon the W. of that Route.

Sketching.—Norway is still but slightly known to artists or amateurs. Danby, senior, was there some years since, also Edward Price and Zeigler, and in 1847, West, of Bristol, made a beautiful series of more than 50 finished sketches, in his happiest manner, of the most celebrated waterfalls and districts, chiefly upon Routes 21, 23, and 30 : in addition to these, some of the beauties of Norway and Sweden have been illustrated of late years by the pencil and pen of several tourists. Everything requisite for sketching should be taken from England, as the materials to be obtained in Norway for the purpose are very inferior. Artists would do well to provide themselves with a pair of saddle bags, as horses and guides may be procured throughout the country, and the wildest parts thus be easily visited. Paper and sketches should be secured in a bag of fustian mackintosh (which is very strong), and, if securely tied at the mouth, may be immersed in water without its penetrating. Winsor and Newton's moist water-colours, and their folding seat and easel, will be found particularly convenient.

Landscape.—Except a few churches, and some of the peasants' houses in the wildest parts, there are few picturesque buildings in Norway, but the beauties of nature are of the highest order. The atmospheric effects in early morning and evening are of wondrous beauty, and peculiar to the North. The depth and gorgeousness of colour during the long twilight which follows the setting of the sun are marvellously fine, and give a poetry and charm of the most sublime character. The valleys are usually narrow, very deep, and of great extent, with a lake or river in the bottom. Waterfalls are innumerable, and the most picturesque are the smaller ones, which are found at the head and upon the sides of almost all the valleys. The *great waterfalls* are the Sarp-Fos at Sarpsborg, Route 36 ; the Larbrü Fos, near Kongsberg, and the Riukan Fos, Route 29 ; and the Foring Fos, and Östud Fos upon the Hardanger Fjord, Route 21. At the upper parts of the fjords upon the W. coast, the scenery is of Alpine character, and perfectly unique ; the fjords in many places becoming very narrow, and winding in amongst the mountains, which rise thousands of feet perpendicularly from the water. The most picturesque forms of mountains are those about Molde, Route 24 ; and between Christiansund and Stavanger, upon the same Route, there is a great variety of foliage and much grandeur in the masses of rock and forms of the mountains which there dip into the sea.

Marine.—The whole coast from the mouth of the Christiania Fjord to the N. Cape, Route 24, is rocky and mountainous, and abounds in grand subjects. Neither the towns nor craft are picturesque, but the situation of the former is eminently so in many cases. During summer there is always more fishing and bustle going on upon the S. and S.W. coast than farther N., and, upon the whole, it is perhaps the best part of Norway for marine sketching. The belt of islands which runs all up the W. coast abounds in picturesque huts inhabited by the fishermen.

Figures and Interiors.—There is a good deal of *costume* still existing in Norway, and particularly amongst the women. It is mostly to be found in the Bergen, Hardanger, and Tellemarken districts, upon Routes 21 and 23. Some of the old men are highly picturesque; their long white hair flowing down each side of the face, and surmounted by a faded red worsted cap, shirt collar open, and jacket and waistcoat ornamented with large silver buttons. In the upper parts of the Hardanger, and other fjords upon the W. coast, almost each parish has its own costume. The people are very civil, and easily persuaded to don their gala dresses for the gratification of strangers. Some of the best interiors are also in the Tellemarken and Bergen districts. These are far more picturesque than cleanly. In many cases the principal room is of a rich dark brown, from the wood smoke, and this apartment contains all the family and most of their property—this is particularly the case amongst the fishermen upon the W. coast at a distance from the towns, as well as amongst the poor in Tellemarken.

Cattle.—Norway abounds in admirable subjects of this class. Each farm having its *sæter* or mountain pasture, all the spare stock is sent up there during the summer months. A small hut is erected, where the girls in charge of the stock sleep and carry on the dairy operations. When bears are known to be in the neighbourhood, the cattle are driven in at night, and fires lighted for their protection. Nothing can be more picturesque than the subjects at times found at these chalets, when groups of every description of cattle, horses, goats, dogs, &c., and of all ages, are grouped around amidst the rocks.

Norway is particularly rich in subjects of winter scenery. At that season all the cattle have been driven in from the hills; the sledge and snow-skates (*skier*) are in request, and all is life and animation during the short period of daylight.

9. ANGLING.

The innumerable lakes and rivers in Norway, almost all of which teem with fish, render it the most attractive country in Europe for a fishing tour. Trout are abundant, and grayling, even in the lakes and streams upon the great mountain plateau, or fields, and salmon in every river where they can get up from the sea. Char, pike, and a variety of other fish are met with in most of the lakes. In the Miösen Lake, near Christiania, Route 26, it is said there are upwards of 20 different varieties of fish. But there is no doubt that salmon-fishing in Norway has deteriorated of late years, and is now very difficult to procure. The fish themselves have diminished in numbers from the more skilful modes of netting employed by the natives, and from the use of the leister, which, though contrary to law, is much practised in some rivers. English anglers, too, have become more numerous, and all the *first-rate* waters are rented by them upon regular agreements for a term of years, while the natives themselves have learned to flog the waters with bad imitations of

English flies. Still, no doubt, tolerable salmon-fishing may yet be obtained, but not by the mere casual traveller, nor unless it is made a special object. That splendid fishing was to be had there is proved by the published accounts of numerous English gentlemen. Mr. Belton, in his admirable book ("Two Summers in Norway"), first made known the salmon-fishing to be had in the Namsen and other streams; and to his experience, and also to "Sport in Norway," by Mr. Barnard, we are indebted for some of the following observations.

Salmon.—The tumultuous rapidity of the Norwegian rivers renders them admirably suited for salmon. "A knowledge of the waters which experience alone can give is needful to insure success in the northern rivers, otherwise days are lost in fishing places where there are no fish. Early in the season the deep pools below the fosses and rapids are best. Later on the fish take to the strongest streams, and in autumn lie above the largest falls and rapids." The two most celebrated streams are the Alten and the Namsen, N. of Trondhjem (see Route 24). The Guul, Route 26, towards Trondhjem; the Siva, which falls into the upper part of the Lange Fjord, Route 30; the Rauma, upon the same Route; and the Laaven, near Laurvig, Route 24, are also well spoken of. The great Tana River, to the E. of the North Cape (see Route 24), abounds in salmon, but there is no doubt that the take of salmon by nets there has decreased of late years. Many ascribe this decrease to the great number of seals which abound on the shallow banks at the mouth of this river, and which no doubt intercept many of the fish on their passage to fresh water. Still, however, it is a magnificent river, and very heavy fish are to be taken in it. The best fishing-places in it are at Seida Foss, about 40 miles from the mouth; Kjæring Foss, and at the mouths of the Valjijok and Levvojok. Any one intending to try it must be prepared for a rough life. There is no habitable house on the whole length of the river, and a tent and every necessary for camping out must be taken. Musquitoes swarm. If Tana should turn out a failure, the Pasvig and Neiden, in East Finmark, might be tried, or the Jacob's Elv on the Russian frontier, where no Englishman has probably ever fished. It is about 14 Eng. miles from Vadsö, where the steamers stop. Any one intending to try the Finmarken rivers ought to call on a hunter who lives at Piselvnas; he can give excellent information concerning the fishing and shooting in this Amt. His name is Clark. The fortnightly steamer from Hammerfest to Vadsö calls at Tana mouth, and also near the mouths of the Pasvig and Neiden. None of these three rivers would fish before the beginning of July. We have before stated that salmon are found in all the rivers upon the coast where they can get up, but as most of the streams S. of the Rauma down to the Laaven are comparatively short, and remain in a more or less turbid state till towards the end of summer, such fishing cannot be obtained in them as in the larger streams; at the same time those who have not been spoiled by the splendid sport offered by the latter, when the waters are in good order, will find ample occupation in the smaller streams, some of which, no doubt, are still unknown to anglers. This is particularly the case with those rivers which fall into the Sogne, Hardanger, and other fjords upon the W. coast, in the midst of some of the grandest scenery in the country, and where excellent general shooting may likewise be had.

The great point upon which the success of a fishing expedition to Norway depends, is to hit the proper time for it; to be neither too early nor too late. The fishing season is short, and always later towards the N. All the streams flow from the great range of mountains running from N. to S. There are always two floods every year; the first in the early part of the summer, caused by the melting of the snow in the valleys, &c., and the second arising from the breaking up of the ice in the mountain lakes, at a later period; before the latter has subsided, few if any good fish will be found in the rivers. Taking the Alten as the most northern great salmon stream on the W. coast, the mountain flood there does not subside before the beginning of July; and, upon the average, the best season for that river is from the middle of July to the end of August. Farther S. the season is usually a month or a fortnight earlier, but, throughout Norway, July and August may be considered the best months for salmon-fishing. The abundance of salmon in the great Norwegian streams may be judged of by the fact, that an English gentleman, in the season of 1847, killed 2500 lbs. weight in the Alten in 14 days, his fish averaging from 15 to 35 lbs. each. This is by no means a singular instance, many gentlemen having met with equal success, particularly in the Namsen. Evening and early morning will be found the best times for fishing during the height of the season. Though, undoubtedly, the best places on the best rivers are leased from year to year, there are still many opportunities open to the energetic fisherman, where fair sport can be obtained. In addition to the rivers already named we may mention the Ranen and Vefsen rivers in Nordlands Amt (R. 24). Sannesöen is the nearest station for the Vefsen. In N. Trondhjem Amt the Værdals Elv, a little north of Levanger, is a likely stream for salmon and trout (R. 24); and splendid fishing may be had at the famed Steenkjær (R. 24). Herr Moe, a merchant, residing at Steenkjær, can give every information. A steamer runs there weekly from Trondhjem. The Orkla Elv (R. 24) is a good river, if it is not leased. Fandrem, Gumdal (a good station), and Langsæter will be found to be the best places. The Nid Elv (R. 26) abounds with fish; and some sport may occasionally be had in Skaugdals Elv, north-west of Trondhjem, near Uddue, where the steamer stops (R. 26). The Eridsfjord Elv, midway between the Rauma and Sundals Elv (R. 24), is a good river. In 1860, 2569 lbs. of salmon were taken by one rod in 39 days. Most of the fishing on Sundals and Surendals Elv is taken up. The Lerdals Elv (R. 21), Aardals Elv (R. 21), and Aurlands Elv (R. 21) are excellent rivers. The Vosse Elv (R. 21) is a fine salmon river. Good quarters at Bolstadören, large fish have been taken here. The fishing near Stavanger is poor; but good snipe shooting may be had in the marshes in August. In the neighbourhood of Christiansand some fishing may be had in Topdals Elv (R. 24), and in Torridals Elv (R. 24). The fishing belongs to Consul Vildt, a Swiss gentleman in Christiansand, who will probably give permission. Some fair sport may also be had in Enningdals Elv, near Frederickshald (R. 36). Salmon fishing is now so much sought after by our countrymen, and such high prices given, as to render success anything but a certainty to new comers.

Trout.—The salmon-fishing in Norway has such attractions for the angler, that all the smaller fry have been comparatively neglected, few of the streams and lakes of the interior having been tried, except hastily, by those en route to or from the coast. The smaller streams and lakes will usually be found to contain a greater abundance of fish, and in better condition, than the larger waters. The best fish will invariably be found near the bottom of falls, and especially those above the larger lakes. Even upon the Dovre, and other great fjelds, the trout run to 6 lbs. In all the above-named rivers, first-class trout-fishing may be had. Indeed, there is scarcely a river in the country where trout are not plentiful. In the interior, and eastern parts of the country, the following places can be especially recommended, viz.—Dale and Strængen, at either end of Bandags Vand (R. 23); Nisser Vand (R. 23), on the road from Arendal to Tellemarken; Mjös Vand (R. 21). Good trout-fishing may be had at Hönefoss (R. 22); Vaage Vand and its tributaries (R. 26); Rena Elv (R. 31); Trysil Elv, running out of Famund Sö. Good grayling fishing may be got at Eidsvold and Minde, in August (R. 26).

The waters of the higher mountains of Central Norway should be avoided until the summer is well advanced. In the S. and lower parts of the country the season for trout-fishing may be considered as commencing about the middle of June, and ending with September.

Flies, Rods, &c.—Only inferior tackle is to be obtained in Norway; it should therefore be taken from England, and be of the very best quality. The salmon killed are so large, in some cases being 40 lbs. weight and upwards, that the strongest lines must be used. No exact directions for flies can be given: salmon take most unaccountable flies of all sorts and sizes, and of all colours. A general rule may be, to fish with large bright flies when the water is heavy, and to diminish in size as the water falls, till, late in the season, small flies on single gut are the only ones which salmon will look at. The fishing-tackle makers in London know the style of flies and patterns generally used.

A well-oiled silk line, not less than 120 yards long for the large rivers, will be found preferable to the patent mixture of horsehair and silk. The casting line should be of the strongest treble gut, and plaited, not twisted, the reel of ample dimensions and single action, and the gaff of wide curve and firm build. The rods should comprise two for salmon, a stout one not less than

16 feet long, and a second a foot shorter, and lighter, with an extra small joint and spare tops to each of them.

For trout flies, decided colours, either gay or dark, are also the best; and a great variety of colours is not so important as a good assortment of different sizes. Small Irish sea-trout flies kill well, and in the evening or at night white and brown moths. But trout vary so much in their likes and dislikes that it is useless to attempt giving any particular colour the preference. For char, the common red palmer is recommended.

Most of the rivers belong to small proprietors located along their banks. Formerly a small gratuity of ten dollars secured the exclusive right of fishing, but now, owing to the competition that has arisen, and from the avidity shown by some of our English fishermen, the prices have risen greatly; still there are probably rivers at the heads of some of the long-unfrequented fjords, which have not been explored and tried. It is customary to give to the proprietors such fish as are not required by the angler for his own use.

An experienced man has been directed by the Norwegian Government to visit all the rivers, and, where feasible, institute artificial breeding of salmon. With what success, in a country where running streams are frozen to the bottom for some months in each year, remains to be seen. Besides this, the Storthing passed a law in 1857, prohibiting the use of nets at the mouths of salmon rivers. These measures may, perhaps, have some effect in arresting the sensible decrease that has been perceived in the numbers of the fish taken of late years.

10. SHOOTING.

Norway formerly abounded in game and wild beasts; both have somewhat decreased as the population has advanced, but from the mountainous nature of the country it is always likely to remain one of the best in Europe for wild shooting. Prior to 1845 game was unprotected, and therefore destroyed at all seasons; but in the Storthing of that year a law was passed for its protection, which has proved very beneficial. It is somewhat the fashion to complain of the general scarcity of all descriptions of game in Scandinavia, but, comparing different accounts, and the supply brought into the markets, there is little doubt that game is far more abundant there than is generally imagined. The general shooting along the western coast is poor; and indeed in any part of Norway large bags must not be expected. Good shooting has been had in some of the islands off the north-western coast, but these are mostly leased by Englishmen.

Reindeer are met with in all the highest parts of the great mountain range N. of the Fille Fjeld, Route 21, up to the N. Cape. Red deer are found in the islands off the coast between Bergen and Trondhjem, and particularly in the large island of Hitteröen, near the latter city, Route 26. Elk are rare, but of late years have been met with as low down as Toten and Eidsvold, the

Northern Terminus of the Railway, but Osterdalen, Route 31, is still their favourite resort. Of wild beasts, bears and wolves are killed in all parts of Norway, and occasionally the lynx, and wolverine or glutton.

Hares are plentiful. All up the W. coast wild fowl of every description abound, and, from being so little disturbed, are easy to get at. N. of Trondhjem they are swarming. In July and August numbers of woodcocks are found about the great fjords upon the W. coast. Snipe also abound in low and swampy places. Besides these and Plover, there are of winged game the Capercailie (*Tiur*); Blackcock (*Urhane*); Hazel-hen (*Hjerpe*); Ptarmigan (*Fjeld-rype*), only found high up on the mountains; and Wood grouse (*Skov-Rype*). These last afford the best sport. They are generally to be found in dwarf willow, or alder scrub. It is useless to attempt to shoot them without dogs; no heavy bag can be made with beaters alone. A hardy setter is, perhaps, the best for ryper-shooting. An Irish water spaniel, perhaps, for duck, and other general shooting. Before the middle of August ryper are so small and lie so close as to afford no sport. By the middle of September, however, they are wild enough. Partridges are comparatively rare. The capercailie is found in all the great pine forests which abound in Norway, the buds of that tree being his favourite food. The blackcock and hazel-hen frequent the numberless valleys where the spruce fir (*Pinus abies*) abounds; and ptarmigan keep to the plateau of the great mountain range, particularly those N. of Trondhjem. Amongst the best places to select for general shooting (including *bears*) are the Fille Fjeld, and the upper parts of the Sögne Fjord, and Hardanger Fjord, Route 21; Romsdalen, Route 30; the Dovre Fjeld, Route 26; the mountains upon the Swedish frontier, Route 33; and on many of the islands along the coast. Tolerable quarters may be obtained at most of these places. The stations upon the Fille Fjeld and Dovre Fjeld are amongst the best in Norway. The general shooting in Norway has of late years deteriorated, owing partly, no doubt, to the increased facilities of communication with the large towns, where the peasants find a ready market for what they trap or shoot. Rifle shooting, too, is greatly in vogue in the country, and the Bönder may now be seen by scores, scouring the fjelds in all directions, even in the most remote corners. For elk shooting, the neighbourhood of Kongsvinger, R. 35, is the best in Norway; while for reindeer, the fjelds between Gudbrandsdal, Valders, and Bergen Stift, by the Bygdin and Gjendin lakes, and on the Lesjö and Romsdal Fjelds large herds may be found the whole year round. On the Rundene and Dovre Fjeld, between Hallingdal and Lerdal, herds of 300 to 1000 are frequently seen.

Those who make shooting a principal object of their tour, must take dogs with them, if they wish to have any sport. The gun should be a double-barrel, of large bore; one which can be depended upon for ball to the distance of 100 yards. Except the natives, those who have shot the most game and wild beasts in Norway and Sweden have rarely used a rifle. A smooth bore is quite as effective for a bear at close quarters as a rifle. Shot may be bought in the large towns; all other ammunition should be brought from England. It is dangerous work to attack a bear single-handed, for fear of only wounding him, when he will generally charge; in that case the hunter's life often depends upon his companion's shot, or his own nerve in not resisting when the bear comes in. The best chance of safety is then to lie down, with the face to the ground, and breathe as little as possible. (*Lloyd's Field Sports of the N. Europe*, vol. i. p. 198.) Numerous instances are recorded where hunters have saved themselves by adopting that plan in preference to using the butt end of the gun, or the hunting knife, against so formidable an assailant at close quarters.

The favourite haunts of the bear in summer are in the thickly wooded mountain valleys and slopes of the mountains, and particularly in the neighbourhood of the sæters, or mountain pastures, where the cattle are grazed.

Should a bear have killed a cow in the neighbourhood, and news of it be brought within a day or so afterwards, the most likely method of getting a shot is for the sportsman to watch the carcase of the cow from some place of concealment close by, till the bear returns to gorge himself upon it a second time, which he seldom fails to do, if undisturbed.

The usual native mode of killing bears is to fix three or four guns with the muzzles pointing at different angles across the carcase of a cow that has been killed, tying strings at one end to the triggers, and at the other to the cow, so that they explode when the bear returns and begins to tug at the carcase again, in which case some of the balls can scarcely fail to kill, or severely wound him. By far the greater number are killed towards the end of the winter. A good bear-skin may be bought sometimes at some of the skyds-stations for 10 or 15 dollars.

Meat being so rarely met with at the country stations, and game as seldom, although to be found near most places, a tourist's comfort in the commissariat department depends very much on the produce of his gun. Beef stewed to a jelly and poured into the windpipes of oxen becomes quite hard, and never turns mouldy; an inch of this put into a small camp-kettle with game or wild-fowl, and vegetables of any kind, makes an admirable dish. Good food is essential to health in shooting expeditions, and great care should be taken to avoid sleeping in the open air, which is most dangerous in the North.

The Ordinance of the Storthing passed for the preservation of game, &c., is dated 4th August, 1845. But material alterations were made in 1863. The following abstract may be useful to sportsmen.

Premiums for Destruction of Birds and Beasts of Prey.—Sections 1 and 2. For every bear, wolf, tiger-cat, lynx, glutton, or wolverine, of whatever age, 5 sp. ds.; for eagles, 60 sks.; mountain owls, 24 sks.; hawks, 24 sks. Skins of beasts and birds slain to be produced to Foged of district, or his deputy, who is to mark same and give a certificate for the premium.

The following tables show the number of each that have been killed from 1846 to 1855 :—

	Bears.	Wolves.	Lynxes.	Gluttons.	Eagles.
1846	219	323	104	81	1055
1847	270	259	110	88	2594
1848	264	247	144	51	2193
1849	325	197	110	96	2142
1850	246	101	118	39	2120
1851	276	281	101	50	4620
1852	202	236	118	45	3415
1853	142	191	116	51	4603
1854	198	169	94	35	3379
1855	212	235	125	72	2559

Besides about 700 or 800 mountain owls, and the same number of hawks destroyed annually.

Game Laws.—Sect. 3. Elks and stags not to be killed except between 1st August and 1st November, and then only by the proprietor of the ground. One elk and 2 stags only to be killed during that time upon each separate property. But these restrictions as to time and number, not to apply to islands which are private property, or those kept within walled parks. *Sect.* 4. Wild reindeer not to be killed between 1st April and 1st August. *Sect.* 5. No beavers to be killed for 10 years after 4th August, 1845, but it is feared that this law has come too late to prevent their total extinction. Time the same as for elks, &c. *Sect.* 6. Hares not to be killed between 1st June and 15th August. Owners of land alone entitled to kill them during rest of the year. *Sect.* 7. Female capercailie and greyhens may not be shot between 15th March and 15th August; male capercaille, blackcock, hjerper, and ryper may not be shot between 15th May and 15th August ; salmon and sea-trout not to taken between 14th September and 14th February; partridges between 1st January and 1st September.

No water-fowl used as food (birds of passage excepted) may be killed between 1st April and 15th July, or deprived of their eggs after 1st June ; but the provinces of Nordland and Finmark are excepted from this enactment as to water-fowl and their eggs.

Sect. 8. Occupiers entitled, upon their own land, to kill stags which injure crops, &c. *Sect.* 9, in addition to the owner's remedy for trespass, renders the offender liable to the following PENALTIES for game killed contrary to the above enactments. Elks, 60 sp. ds. ; stags and beavers, 30 sps. ; wild reindeer, 10 sps. ; hares, 2 sps. ; and other game, 1 sp. Unlawfully depriving nest of eggs, 60 sks. *Sect.* 10. Suits for penalties under last section to be settled in police courts. When information is lodged, the officer is to inform the accused of the amount of the penalty and inquire if he will pay it. If he agrees to do so and fails in his promise, it may be levied upon him by an execution. Should he deny the offence, then the officer will proceed to investigate the charge and decide upon it.

Fines levied to be divided between *the informer* and poor of district.

Penalties to be without prejudice, and in addition to any reparation reserved to proprietors by usual course of law, for an infringement of their rights in hunting, fishing, or preserves.

Sect. 11 repeals the game laws of 1733 and 1818 as to stags.

Lemmings (Georychus lemmus) occasionally visit Norway in great numbers. They are nearly as large as a water rat, of a tawny colour, with black stripes over the withers. They are much larger than the Siberian ones, which are about the size of a field mouse. They appear in Norway about once in every four years; impelled probably by a too great increase of numbers to leave the mountains they inhabit, and not, as many Norwegians are inclined to believe, by an instinct of the approaching winter being more than usually severe. They move from east to west in as straight a line as possible, swimming large rivers, and wide fjords, wherever they come upon them, till they reach the islands on the seaboard of the Atlantic. Occasionally, if they have been overtaken by a storm, great numbers are found floating on the surface of the water, drowned. They never appear to return eastwards. The probable explanation of this is, that most of them are devoured by the owls and hawks, which follow them. They move chiefly at night, devouring most of the herbage, or corn it may be, as they pass. Formerly the Norwegians believed them to have fallen from the clouds, and so great was the mischief caused by them, that they were solemnly exorcised by the priests.

11. SUCCINCT ACCOUNT OF NORWAY.

Sunk into a province of Denmark for so many centuries, Norway, upon recovering her independence, is left without a remnant of the conquests made by her in the days of her glory. Her possessions are confined to the W. part of the great Scandinavian peninsula, including Norwegian Lapland and the islands off the W. coast, the most important of which are the Loffodens, N. of the Arctic circle. The length of the Norwegian territory, from the most southern point at the Naze to the N. Cape, is upwards of 1100 English miles. Its breadth varies considerably, being about 40 miles at the narrowest part in the N. and 200 at the widest portion in the S. Its total area in square miles is 121,800.

The great chain of the Kiölen mountains commences in the extreme N. of Lapland, and, in conjunction with others, runs through the whole length of the peninsula. All the country is mountainous, and abounds in lakes, rivers, and forests. The leading features in Norwegian scenery are the fjelds, fjords, and valleys.

The *Fields*, or Fjelds, are the plateaux of those different ranges of mountains, such as the Dovre Fjeld, the Hardanger Fjeld, &c., which form part of the great chain from N. to S. above mentioned. These fjelds or plateaux are of vast extent, and from them the highest summits in Norway rise to about 8000 feet. On the E. side of this great chain the descent is gradual. On the W. abrupt and precipitous.

The *Fiords*, or Fjords, are arms of the sea with which the whole coast is indented, and particularly the W. The Christiania Fjord is the largest in the S. of Norway. In the W. the Hardanger and the Sögne Fjords are the most extensive; the latter runs upwards of 100 Eng. miles from the coast into the mountains. Most of these fjords upon the W. coast have several branches, and at the head of each of them there is generally a stream where salmon will be found wherever they can get up. It is upon the upper parts of the fjords on the W. coast, that the most grand as well as the most picturesque scenery in Norway exists. In many places the mountains rise perpendicularly from the water to a vast height.

The *Valleys* (Dalene). Throughout the greater portion of that chain of mountains before mentioned there are minor lateral ranges branching off, and which form deep and, for the most part, narrow valleys between them. Each has its stream and lakes. Some of these valleys are of great length, extending upwards of 100 Eng. m., and containing numerous farms. Indeed, all the best land in Norway is to be found in her valleys. It is the lower part of these valleys which, upon the W. coast, form the fjords; they are never frozen near the sea, and make some of the finest harbours in the world. The lakes and streams in Norway are innumerable, and all abound with trout. The largest lake is the Miösen, between Christiania and Trondhjem. In the N. the principal rivers are the Tana, the Alten, and the Namsen; and in the S. the Glommen, the Lauven, and the Drammen. Waterfalls are very numerous, and many of them are upon a grand scale.

Geology.—The whole Scandinavian peninsula is highly interesting to the geologist and mineralogist. Norway and Lapland are chiefly composed of primitive and transition rocks. Granite is rare, the prevailing rock being gneiss, which sometimes alternates with granite. Mica slate also abounds, and is associated with the gneiss; while in beds subordinate to both are limestone, quartz, and hornblende. The plateaux of the mountains are often covered with blocks of a conglomerate rock, in which pebbles of quartz, feldspar, &c., are imbedded, and which, being smooth and rounded, have evidently been, during a remote, but lengthened period, subject to violent friction. The southern part of Norway has frequently experienced earthquakes, and numerous instances exist, in various parts of the country, which prove that it has been upheaved by volcanic action.

Mineralogy.—The Norwegian mountains appear to be rich in minerals, of which the chief are iron, copper, silver, nickel, and cobalt.

Climate.—The climate of Norway is healthy, and the weather (except on the W. coast) is generally more steady than in England, being either good or had for a considerable period without any change. A country, however, ranging over upwards of 13 degrees of latitude, and 26 degrees of longitude, must present some varieties of climate, although it is not so much to the difference of geographical position that these modifications are to be ascribed as to other operating causes, such as vicinity to the ocean, height above the level of the sea, peculiarly sheltered situations, and a variety of other causes, which in the same latitude frequently occasion considerable difference in temperature.

In many of the fjords, the waves of the ocean literally lave the foundations of the houses; whilst the inhabitants of the interior frequently locate themselves at a height of 3000 feet above the level of the sea. Röraas parish, for instance, in which the town and copper mines of that name are situated, stands at an elevation of 3000 feet, and several inhabited valleys branching laterally from the great Akers-huus valley rise to the height of 1500 to 2000 feet.

In Norway one of the most active causes in moderating or increasing the temperature of various localities is the relation to the sea-coast; the nearer to this, the more marked are the changes which the same altitude exhibits. In several parishes in the valleys stretching laterally from the coast, this may be distinctly perceived by merely attending to the state of the crops, which are either advanced or retarded in proportion to the height at which the fields are situated. Other causes tend likewise to operate favourably or unfavourably to vegetable life; among these may be noticed the vicinity of some elevated range of rocks, which, by protecting the spot from keen northern winds, exempts it from sudden transitions of heat and cold, which other less favoured localities are greatly exposed to. Even an insignificant mountain stream, fed by the thawing of the snow as it rolls from crag to crag, until it winds its course through the level meadow-land below, will create a cold current of air, which, slight as it may appear, is sufficient to check vegetation for some space around it, while the adjoining fields are flourishing in vegetable richness. But it is principally owing to the Gulf Stream that Norway enjoys—at least, its northern and western parts—so mild a climate. "The Gulf Stream impinges on the western coast somewhere about lat. 62°. From this point of impact it takes a northerly direction, and follows the coast line to the Russian frontiers on the Arctic Ocean. It is owing to this that the mean temperature at the N. Cape, and at Christiania, during the winter months, though these places are separated from each other by 12° of latitude, is the same. But on penetrating for a few miles into the interior, out of the influence of the sea-air, the cold in winter is intense to a degree, while the heat in summer is equally oppressive. Thus at Valle in Saetersdal, lat. 59°, lying at an attitude of 1000 feet above the sea, the thermometer in summer may stand at + 42° cent., and in winter fall to—35°1" (Vide *Sport in Norway*, pp. 249, 251.)

A wooded district enjoys less of the warmth of the sun, consequently is generally more humid; in these cases a judicious clearance will tend to increase the temperature and check the severity of the frequent spring frosts which injure the corn in the eastern valleys of Norway. In other places, where the forests have served as a protection against cold and destructive winds, to which the land may from its peculiar local circumstances be exposed, much injury has been done by their indiscriminate clearance; and it is a well-known fact, that many farms, which formerly afforded remunerating crops, have been rendered unproductive solely from this cause.

Norway, on the whole, enjoys the mildest climate of any region so remote from the equator. In Iceland the limit of snow in latitude 60° is 2900 feet; on the east coast of Greenland it descends to the water's edge and forms icebergs; in the Scandinavian sea, ice is first formed in latitude 80°, whilst around the North Cape, in latitude 71° 11′, and at the head of the deepest fjords, the sea never freezes.

In Siberia, every trace of agriculture ceases at 60 degrees, whereas in Norway, oats will ripen under latitude 69°, rye under 69½°, and barley under 70°. Owing to the continuous daylight in summer, vegetable growth goes on with incredible rapidity. From observations made at Alten, lat. 65°, it has been ascertained that barley will grow 2½ inches, and peas 3 inches, in the 24 hours, for several consecutive days, and this under the same parallel of latitude as that under which the ice-bound regions of Victoria land, Disco Island, and Boothia Felix are situated!

Pinewood in the south of Norway reaches about 3000 feet above the level of the sea; farther to the north its highest limit sinks still lower. The limit of birch in the south of Norway is about 3300 feet. Above this level, and below the perpetual snow, there are capital grass runs in summer of great extent.

The *Population* taken by the census in 1845 was about 1,400,000 souls. In 1855 about 1,500,000, whilst in 1835 it was only 1,194,000. By the census of 1835 the population of Christiania was 21,757; by that of 1845 it was 30,931; in 1855 it had increased to 40,000, an increase at the rate of nearly 1000 per annum in the last 20 years. At the census taken immediately after the separation from Denmark the population did not exceed 10,000; and the total population of the country was then 514,530 less than in 1845.

The population in 1855 was divided into the following classes, viz.:—

	Heads of Families.	Families.
Proprietors of land	91,470	346,832
Farmers renting land	21,784	82,659
Feudal tenants	67,062	255,332
Squatters or Clearers	2,336	7,318
Farm Servants	36,543	27,492

	Heads of Families.		Families.
Traders	4,940	......	14,291
Proprietors of works and factories...	203	......	551
Artisans	21,694	......	43,754
Shipmasters	3,518	......	10,337
Seamen	14,034	......	20,560
Pilots	928	......	2,931
Day Labourers	41,963	......	65,247
Servants	57,644	......	106,037

Not belonging to any of the above classes, 121,574.

The number of Norwegian Laplanders in 1855 was 15,999, of whom 14,054 had fixed residences, and 1945 were Nomades.

The animal stock in the whole country in 1855 consisted of 154,447 horses, 949,935 oxen and cows, 1,596,199 sheep, 357,102 goats, 113,320 pigs, and 28,000 tame reindeer, approximately.

12. HISTORICAL NOTICE.

The early history of Norway is enveloped in darkness. Prior to the 7th century it rests solely on traditions, which, like all similar sources of information, are very imperfect, but still are probably founded on fact. The prevailing tradition is, that Odin, who came over from Asia, was the founder of the Norwegian race. The aborigines were probably a few Lapps scattered in families all over the country, till they were driven northwards, and confined to their present abodes by the influx of clans of the low German branch of the great Teutonic stock. No date of the arrival of the Northmen can be fixed, nor can it be with certainty stated whether the immigration came from the south, or whether, having come north of the Gulf of Bothnia, either by land or round the North Cape, it streamed southwards till stopped by the Gothic settlements, of which Gottenburg would perhaps have been the head-quarters. To readers of Danish, the late Professor Munch's great work, "Det norske Folks Historie," will throw much light on this branch of ethnology. He has compared the Latin accounts of the early inhabitants of the North with early Icelandic sagas and indistinct native traditions, and has extracted from them what appears to him to be the true history of the time, with rare powers of criticism. It is known that tribes of heroic barbarians inhabited the country, who divided it into several small kingdoms, and were continually at war with each other. The first monarch, of whom we have any authentic account, is Olaf Trætelia, who laid the foundation of a new power in Norway about A.D. 630. The incorporation of the petty States, of which the country then consisted, was the constant aim of his successors. (*Dunham's Hist. of Norway*, &c., v. i. p. 157.) Harald the Black subjected the southern part of Norway to his rule, and his son Harald Haarfager (the Fair-Haired) finally completed the conquest of the whole country in the latter part of the 9th century. In the commencement of his career, having been told of the charms of Gyda, daughter of the King of Hordaland, Harald sent messengers to her with the offer, not of his hand, but of his heart. Her proud reply is stated to have been, that so far from being the mistress, she would not even be the wife of a chief whose territories consisted of a few insignificant provinces, and that she would never marry any one who did not hold absolute sway over the whole country. Admiring her ambition, he vowed to the gods that he would neither cut nor comb his hair until he had subdued all Norway, and that he would do so or perish in the attempt. Upon the completion of his vow the princess became his wife, according to the custom of the period sharing that honour with eight others.

From the completion of Harald's conquest of the country in 885, down to about the middle of the 13th century, is comprised the glorious period of Norwegian history. From thence to the union of Norway and Denmark, in the latter part of the 14th century, the prosperity of the country gradually decayed, and that union during its continuance was fatal to its regeneration. Sunk into a province of Denmark, the energies of the heroic Norwegian race became palsied, and their history may be deemed a blank until their emancipation from the Danish yoke in 1814.

The conquests of Harald Haarfager induced many of the petty sovereigns whom he had subdued to emigrate, and the piratical expeditions of the sea-kings (or leaders) were made upon a much larger scale. The most celebrated of these leaders was Rolf-Ganger, or Rollo, the founder of the Duchy of Normandy, and ancestor of William the Conqueror. Rollo emigrated from the neighbourhood of Aalesund on the W. coast; see Route 24. Space will not admit of our detailing the victorious course of the Norwegian arms in Belgium, France, Spain, Italy, the British Islands, and elsewhere; but one of the most interesting facts connected with their career of conquest is their occupation of Iceland, and from thence discovering North America centuries before the time of Columbus. (See Iceland, in Route 12; also *Dunham's History of Norway*, &c., vols. I. and ii.) It was during the latter end of the 9th century that Iceland was colonized by Norwegians, and towards the end of the 10th century that America was discovered by the descendants of those settlers.

Harald Haarfager died in 933, and his successors, during several reigns, were princes of no great note, with the exception of his son Hako the Good, who, brought up in England in the court of Athelstane, was the first king who endeavoured to establish Christianity in Norway. This was in the middle of the 10th century, but Paganism was not finally eradicated until after the 12th.

There is a curious story told in "Hako the Good's Saga," with reference to the introduction of Christianity. The king was suspected of being a waverer from the old religion, and his nobles insisted on his attending a banquet held to Odin, and drinking the horse-broth in his honour, to which the king was obliged to consent, but with very bad grace. This seems to have been the test applied by the worshippers of Odin to all whom they suspected of Christianity. And certainly there was nothing which the monks and early missionaries to Scandinavia denounced more warmly than eating horse-flesh, as savouring of the ancient worship. The repugnance to eating horse-flesh, still felt by all nations of the Germanic family, perhaps has its origin from this.

In 1016 Olaf (Olave) the Second ascended the throne of Norway. He is more usually known as Olaf the Holy, or St. Olaf. After pledging himself to respect the rights of the native chiefs, in order to force Christianity upon his subjects, he not only destroyed the heathen temples, but propagated the Christian faith with fire and sword. Under the sacred banner of the Cross he perpetrated the most ruthless deeds of blood and plunder, until his atrocities raised the whole country against him.

In 1028 Canute the Great landed in Norway, and was elected King; while Olaf, deserted by his people, retreated into Sweden. He subsequently invaded the country with a view of recovering the throne, and a desperate battle was fought at Stikklestad, N. of Trondhjem (see Route 24), in which he was slain, 31st August, 1030, together with most of his followers. A few years afterwards, his body having been found incorrupt, it was considered a miracle, he was declared a saint, and the corpse taken to Trondhjem and buried there. A chapel was erected over it, which became the origin of the Cathedral. Pilgrimages were made to the shrine of St. Olaf up to the time of the Reformation. See also Trondhjem, Route 20. Several churches in London were dedicated to this precious saint.

Sweyn, the son of Canute, was deputed by him to the government of Norway, with the regal title, but upon the death of the latter, in 1035, Sweyn was driven from the throne, and Magnus I., the illegitimate son of St. Olaf, obtained possession of it. He died in 1047, and was succeeded by his uncle, Harald III., one of the greatest warriors of his age, and the founder of Osloe, now the city of Christiania. At the instigation of Tostig, brother of Harald II. of England, he invaded that country and plundered York, but was at length met by the royal forces at Stamford in Lincolnshire. A sanguinary battle took place there, 25th September, 1066, in which both Harald of Norway and the Prince Tostig were slain, with most of their army. The son of Harald (Olaf III. of Norway), with the whole of the Norwegian fleet, fell into the hands of the victorious Harald of England, who generously and immediately allowed Olaf to depart with 20 ships. Harald himself perished within 3 weeks afterwards upon the field of Hastings.

Magus III., surnamed Barford (Bare-foot), was the successor to his father, Olaf III., and became one of the most warlike and heroic monarchs of Norway. In 1098 he conquered the Isle of Man, the Shetlands, Orkneys, and Hebrides. He afterwards invaded Ireland, where he was surprised and slain in 1103, after a most gallant resistance.

His son, Sigurd I., surnamed Jorsalafare, *i.e.* Traveller to Jerusalem, is celebrated in the annals of Norway for his pilgrimage to Jerusalem, and his exploits during the voyage. He sailed in 1107, with a fleet of 60 ships, and was 4 years absent. His first winter was passed in England, where he was hospitably entertained by Henry I. Continuing his voyage, he fought several battles afterwards with the Moors in Portugal and at sea. Landing in Sicily, he was magnificently entertained there by Roger, the Norman sovereign of that island. He then proceeded to Jerusalem, where the offer of his sword was most acceptable to Baldwin. His last exploit in the Holy Land was that of joining in the siege of Sidon, and when the city was taken half the booty became his. He returned home by way of Constantinople and Germany. The fame of this expedition still lives in the memory of the peasants of the Sögne Fjord, many of whose ancestors took part in it.

Dissension and civil war followed upon the death of Sigurd, which for a time were checked, in 1152, by the good offices of the Papal Legate, Nicholas Breakspear, an Englishman, who afterwards ascended the pontifical throne as Adrian IV. He succeeded in getting a metropolitan See established at Trondhjem, with a jurisdiction not only over Norway, but also Iceland, Greenland, the Faröe Islands, Shetlands, Orkneys, Hebrides, and Man. These two last were called the "Syder-öer," or Southern Islands, in contradistinction to Orkney and Shetland. This word is no doubt the origin of the name "*Sodor*." The Legate was eminently successful, during his mission in Norway, in reforming the clergy, as well as the customs and manners of the people.

Hako IV. made war upon Scotland for the continued possession of the Hebrides, and died during the expedition in 1263. From this time commenced the decline of the national prosperity of Norway, attributed to the continued wars with Denmark, which thinned the population; and also to the monopoly of trade established by the Hanse towns, which crushed the national industry, and shackled the trade of the country so fatally as still to have left its traces upon the west coast.

Another fearful blow to the prosperity of Norway was the plague (called the Black Death), which in 1349 was brought by an English ship, which had been driven into Bergen, the crew having previously perished. In Trondhjem, the archbishop and the whole of the chapter died, with the exception of one canon. Solomon, bishop of Osloe, was the only bishop who survived. Many appalling traditions relating to this scourge are yet extant in the country. Several densely populated valleys lost all their inhabitants; the domestic animals also were smitten with this plague. The peasantry, for want of cattle and strength to labour, could not cultivate their land, and the famine which succeeded completed what the plague had begun; many districts became waste, and forests sprang up, which remain to this day, where previously cultivated fields were to be seen. Industry, trade, and navigation were stopped, and the country fell into decay, from which it did not recover for centuries.

Hako VI. married the daughter of Valdemar IV. of Denmark, and died in 1380, when the Norwegian crown descended to his infant son, then Olaf III. of Denmark, from which period, down to 1814, the two countries remained united under one sceptre. Olaf III. of Denmark and V. of Norway died young, and was succeeded by his mother, the famous Margaret, known as "the Semiramis of the North." Victorious over the King of Sweden, she subsequently united that country to her dominions, and in 1397 succeeded in obtaining the signatures of the chief nobles and prelates of the three kingdoms to the celebrated act, known as the Union of Kalmar, the chief object of which was, in future, to unite the three crowns on one head; and, with that view, it was stipulated that a perpetual peace should reign between the three countries, the subjects of each to have equal rights at the election of their sovereign, each kingdom to be governed by its own laws, and all to unite in the common defence.—(*Geyer's Histoire de Suède*, p. 84.)

From this period, and in violation of the conditions of the Union, all places of trust, in Norway, were gradually bestowed on Danish noblemen, and the most oppressive rights and privileges bestowed upon them at the expense of the Norwegian nobles, who ultimately became impoverished and extinct, or amalgamated with the peasantry. Such was the deliberate and ruthless policy of Denmark towards this noble country for upwards of 800 years, and which may account for the jealous watchfulness with which every true Norwegian regards the policy of Sweden since the Union of 1814.

The reign of Christian I. of Denmark and Norway is celebrated for his act of plunder in mortgaging part of the Norwegian dominions, the Shetland and Orkney Islands, for a portion of the dowry to be paid by him with his daughter, on her marriage with James III. of Scotland; since which time, in consequence of the non-payment of the money, those islands have been annexed to that country. See Route 12.*

In the year 1536, during the reign of Christian III., the Reformation was introduced into Norway, but it was some years before any considerable number of the Norwegians embraced the new faith. In the year 1567, during the reign of Frederick II., the Swedes made several incursions into the country, but were eventually obliged to retire; not, however, before they had laid in ashes Hammer and Sarpsborg, two considerable towns.

The most popular of all the Danish monarchs who ruled Norway was Christian IV. This king visited the country no less than 50 times during his reign, and carried on several wars with the Swedes. It was during his reign that the silver mines at Kongsberg (see Route 23) and the copper mines of Röraas were discovered, the former in 1623, the latter in 1644; both these mines are still worked, and they are the largest in Norway. This sovereign was likewise

* For Routes 1 to 10 inclusive see the "Handbook for Denmark."

founder of Christiania, in 1624, on the ruins of Oslos, and of Christiansand in 1643; he also gave his subjects a code of laws, which are still in force. In the reign of Frederick III., which extended from 1648 to 1670, the first Post was established in Norway. In the year 1770, during the reign of Christian VII., potatoes were first introduced by General Krogh, at the request of Caroline Matilda, Queen of Denmark and Norway, sister of George III. The only University was that of Copenhagen; but a few of the richest Norwegians could alone avail themselves of it for the education of their sons. Norwegians of any influence or talent were placed in offices in Denmark, and the policy of the Danish Government was to treat Norway rather as a conquered province than as an independent kingdom united to the Danish Crown. In the earlier part of the present century a brighter period began to dawn. Frederick VI. founded the University of Christiania, and there is reason to suppose that, had Norway still remained united to Denmark, she would, under the mild government of that monarch, have been more justly treated than at any former period. But Russia put an end to all these prospects. On the 27th of August, 1812, the Emperor Alexander guaranteed Norway to Sweden, in lieu of Finland, on condition that the crown prince of Sweden (Bernadotte) would join the allied sovereigns. He accepted this arrangement, which was confirmed by the great powers, and, after the battle of Leipsic, the crown prince marched into Holstein with a considerable force, and compelled Frederick VI., under the terms of the treaty of Kiel, to cede Norway to Sweden.

Many of the Norwegians were at this time prisoners of war in England, and had been offered their liberty upon giving their parole not to bear arms during the continuance of the struggle their country was making. To a man they refused these terms, and remained in prison till the war was over.

When the treaty with Bernadotte became known, the Norwegians were justly indignant at being thus transferred from Denmark to Sweden without their consent, and determined to resist it and declare their independence. The Prince Christian (afterwards the 8th king of that name in Denmark) was then resident in and Governor-General of Norway. He convoked a national diet, which was composed of 113 representatives of all classes of the people, and met at Eidsvold, near Christiania (see Route 26), on the 11th of April, 1814. The constitution, as it now exists, was then prepared. On the 17th of May following, the Prince Christian was elected King of Norway, and the diet thenceforth took the name of Storthing. The Swedes, led by Bernadotte, invaded Norway by way of Frederickshald, and the allies blockaded the coast. Longer resistance became a useless waste of life and property, and accordingly, on the 14th of August, the most favourable terms having been offered to the Norwegians, an armistice and convention were agreed to between the belligerents. Christian abdicated the throne of Norway, and Charles XIII. of Sweden was elected in his place, as king of Norway. On the 4th of November,

1814, he accepted the constitution, on which day it is therefore dated. It comprises 112 articles, the first of which declares that "Norway shall be a free State, independent, indivisible, and inalienable, united to Sweden under the same king." On the death of Charles XIII., in 1818, Bernadotte ascended the throne of Norway, as Charles John XIV. Desirous of introducing several important alterations in the institutions of the country, he is stated to have tried every means to gain a majority in his interest in the Storthing, but in vain; not a single member could be found who would abuse the confidence of his constituents. An armed demonstration was equally unavailing, and the firm, determined patriotism of the Norwegians has enabled them to resist all attempts which might have proved injurious to the interests of "Gamle Norge" (Old Norway).

On the death of Bernadotte, on the 8th of March, 1844, his son, Oscar I., was proclaimed, being then in his 45th year. Soon after his accession, King Oscar gave the Norwegians a separate national flag, which his father had denied them. He has also decreed that, in all acts and public documents relating to Norway, he shall be styled King of Norway and Sweden, instead of Sweden and Norway, as heretofore. In August, 1847, he created an order of merit for the Norwegians, "St. Olaf." These judicious arrangements, combined with his liberal and enlightened views, his scientific acquirements, and untiring industry in the duties of his high office, have endeared him to his Norwegian subjects, with whom he is most popular.

In September, 1857, King Oscar was attacked by a malady, which incapacitated him from holding the reins of government. His son, Prince Carl Louis Engène, was appointed Regent during his father's illness, and succeeded to the throne on his death in 1859, under the title of Carl XV. He was born on the 3rd of May, 1826, and married, in 1850, the Princess Wilhelmina of Holland, daughter of Prince William Frederic, a brother of the present King of Holland.

13. GOVERNMENT.

Norway is an hereditary constitutional monarchy, the mutual rights of the crown and of the people being clearly defined by the Constitution of 1814, which was subsequently guaranteed by the allied powers.

For particulars of the *Royal Family*, see "Handbook for Sweden."

The *Storthing* is elected and assembled every three years; the duration of their sittings is three months, or until the whole of the business before them be despatched; the king, however, has the power to dissolve it at the expiration of the three months. Each Storthing settles the taxes for the ensuing 3 years, enacts, repeals, or alters the laws, grants the sums which have been fixed for the different branches of expenditure, revises the pay and pension lists, and makes such alterations as it deems proper in any provisional grants made by the king during the recess. It also appoints auditors to examine all the government accounts. The minutes of the public departments, as well as copies of all treaties, are laid before it. The Storthing impeaches, and tries before a division of its own body, ministers of state, judges, and also its own members. Besides these important controlling powers, secured to it by the constitution, sworn to by the representatives of the nation at Eidsvold on the 17th of May, and accepted by the king on the 4th November, 1814, the Storthing receives the oaths of the king on coming of age or ascending the throne; and in case of a failure of the royal line, it can, in conjunction with Sweden, elect a new dynasty.

The first step taken by the Storthing, after it has been duly constituted, is to elect the Lagthing, or Upper House. This is done by choosing from among the members of the entire body one-fourth of their number; the functions of this section are deliberative, and judicial in cases of impeachment; the other three-fourths constitute the Odelsthing, or Common House; all enactments must be initiated in this section. The initiative of laws is not vested in Government alone, but any member of the Storthing can propose a law. After a bill has been passed in the Odelsthing, it is sent to the Lagthing, where it is deliberated upon, passed, rejected, or sent back with amendments to the Odelsthing; after being agreed to, it requires the sanction of the king before it can become a law. But if a bill passes through both divisions in 3 successive Storthings, on the third occasion it becomes the law of the land without the royal assent. The law for the abolition of hereditary nobility was passed by the exercise of this right in 1821.

Every native Norwegian of 25 years of age, who has been owner for 5 years, or who has a lease of at least 5 years of a farm, paying tax, or who is a burgess of any town, or possesses there a house or land to the value of 150 sp. d. (about 30*l.*), is entitled to vote in elections; but, to be elected, he must be 30 years of age, and, if a foreigner, he must have resided 10 years in Norway. The country is divided into elective districts, corresponding to our counties, and into sub-districts like our parishes. Each town having 150 voters makes a sub-district, but if the number be under 150 it is joined to the next town. When the period arrives the voters proceed to choose their electors, in such proportion that in towns 1 is chosen from every 40 voters, and in the country 1 from every 100; if the sub-district contains a smaller number than a hundred, they elect 1; from 100 to 200 voters elect 2; from 200 to 300 voters, 3, and so on. After these electors are chosen, they assemble and elect from among themselves, or from among any other qualified voters in the district, their representative in the Storthing. The greatest number of members any county or town can send to the Storthing is 4. The Storthing meets on the first week-day in February, every third year. All the meetings of the ordinary Storthings take place *suo jure*, by the terms of the constitution, and not under any writ or proclamation from the king. An extraordinary Storthing, consisting of the members of the previous Storthing, may be convened by royal authority, but it can only pass interim acts until the next ordinary Storthing. The election and meeting of the regular body cannot be postponed or controlled in any way by the executive power, and do not depend on its co-operation. The ministers of state are not allowed to sit in the Storthing; it was feared that they might exercise too much control over the members. But considerable practical inconvenience has been found to result from their exclusion, and it has been proposed more than once to rescind this clause of the constitution.

The *Religion* of Norway is Episcopal Lutheran: it remains in exactly the same state as that in which it was originally moulded after the subversion of Roman Catholicism, and there are but few individuals who hold any other creed. In fact, until very lately, no places of worship belonging to other creeds were permitted to exist. But in the Storthing of 1845 an act of general toleration was passed, which gave religious liberty to all Christians. In the Storthing of 1851 another act admitted Jews to the country on liberal conditions of equality with Christians. There is now a Roman Catholic congregation at Christiania, and another at Alten in Finmark, but, as far as is known, they have made few proselytes. Mormons are not allowed to remain in the country: most of those who belonged to this sect have emigrated to America.

The clergy, speaking generally, are a highly educated class of men, most of them being acquainted with the literature of Europe, and familiar with the standard works in the French and German languages, and with those of England; most of the clergy can converse in Latin. Taking into account the value of money in the country, their church incomes are good, the average of the livings being 200*l.* per annum. While the Roman Catholic faith prevailed in Norway, there, as elsewhere, a vast portion of the land was in the hands of the clergy, and, although despoiled of a good deal at the Reformation, the greater portion remained at the time the constitution was established, in 1814. One of the first acts of the Storthing was, therefore, to pass a law that all church lands, not glebe, should be sold, and the produce applied to educational purposes. The fund thus raised amounted to 600,000*l.* or 700,000*l.*

Norway is divided into 5 bishoprics and 336 parishes, some of which are very extensive. The performance of public worship is essentially ceremonial, as much so almost as the Roman Catholic. There are crucifixes, paintings, sculptures, and votive offerings in the churches, but no act of adoration is ever performed to any of these. There is much monotonous chanting of psalms in the service.

The patronage is in the Crown, the Minister for Ecclesiastical Affairs, and the Norwegian Council of State. They select 3 candidates, whose names are placed first on the list, which is laid before the king. He usually, but not invariably, presents one of the three thus recommended to the vacant living.

Public Instruction.—Schoolmasters are appointed to every parish, and paid partly by a rate upon the householders, in addition to a small contribution from the scholars. The instruction in these schools is usually confined to reading, writing, arithmetic, and singing. Considerable efforts are made by the clergy to promote education amongst the lower classes, and it is rare to find any young person in Norway who cannot at least read and write. Great importance is attached to the ceremony of confirmation in Norway, prior to which the applicants undergo a long and careful course of religious instruction, and are subject to rigid examination, both public and private, by the clergy of their respective parishes. In the towns there are schools of a very superior description. Sunday schools have been extensively established; and the Society of Public Good maintains a public library, in most parts of the kingdom. The only University is at Christiania, established by the Danes in 1811.

Justice.—A court of mutual agreement exists in each parish, the arbitrators being chosen by the householders every [illegible] years. For legal purposes Norway is divided into 4 *Stifts* and 64 *Sorenskriveries.* In each of the latter a law court sits once a quarter, where the Sorenskriver presides; he is assisted by 3 *Laugrettemænd*, but who, practically, are merely considered judicial witnesses. From these courts an appeal lies to the *Stifts-ret*, which sits in the chief town of each Stift, and is composed of 3 judges, with assessors. And from the Stifts-ret a final appeal lies to the *Hoieste-ret* in Christiania, which is composed of a president and 8 assessors. The judges are responsible in damages for their decisions. Capital punishment is rarely put in force. When it is, it is performed by beheading with a sword.

Great efforts are being made by the Norwegian Government to improve the criminal law, and with that object the Storthing in 1845 made a grant to enable the Government to send commissioners to England and the United States, for the purpose of inquiring into the system of trial by jury; and in 1857 they passed an act for the introduction of the system into Norway: the act, however, was negatived by the king's veto. As regards the transfer of real property in Norway, it is, perhaps, more simple, secure, and inexpensive than in any other country in Europe.

The *Press* is perfectly free in Norway, all being at liberty to print and publish what they please, but subject to responsibility for what they do publish. Newspapers are numerous and free from tax.

The *Army* comprises about 23,000 men, of which 2000 are *gevorben* (armed), and perform garrison duty; 10,000 are troops of the line, who are drawn in their several districts, and bound to serve five years; 9000 form the Landværn, which is composed of men from the line, who, after having completed their period of duty in that service, are attached to the Landværn for 10 years, making the term of service in all 15 years; and about 2000 are engineers, staff and garrison officers, and military servants. The artillery consists of 5 battalions, and the cavalry of 11 squadrons. The troops of the line are exercised in companies every summer for six weeks in their own districts, those of the Landværn for eight days. The garrison towns are Christiania, Frederikstad, Christiansand, Bergen, and Trondhjem. All officers must be educated at the Military Academy in Christiania, and they undergo rather a strict examination previous to receiving their commission. They usually reside in their several districts, and the principal part of their emolument consists in the use of a house and farm.

The *Navy.*—In future it is intended only to build steamers and gun-boats. At present the Norwegian navy consists of 3 frigates, 5 corvettes, 125 gun-boats, 5 steamers; in all 138 craft of all kinds, carrying 450 guns. 46,000 sailors are enrolled. A part of these are men in the merchant service, and a part are the fishermen on the coast; they are liable to serve whenever called upon. The three naval depôts are Horten, Fredericksværn, and Trondhjem. At Horten large sums are expended in the construction of works connected with the building and repair of vessels, and also for the manufacture of marine engines.

The *Norwegian Revenue* for the three years from 1857 to 1860 is estimated by the Government at the sum of 4,631,000 sp., about 1,000,000*l.*, viz.:—

	sp.
Customs	2,600,000
Excise on brandy	750,000
Kongsberg Mines	50,000
Stamps	85,000
Post	310,300
Interest on money belonging to the State	162,500
Money belonging to the State Obligations due to the State	219,500
Sundries, such as land-tax, police fines, legacy duties, &c.	453,700
Total	4,631,000

The principal items of *expenditure* are:—

	sp.
Royal family	111,000
Army	988,000
Navy	540,000
Civil administration, justice, and police	1,036,904
Diplomatic service	76,900
Interest on national debt	247,431
Pensions	76,700
Storthing	36,292
Carried forward	3,113,227

	sp.
Brought forward	3,113,227
Education, &c.	164,017
Improvement of roads	51,073
Post	325,300
Telegraph	97,500
Lighthouses	92,919
Improvement of agriculture	47,266
Increase to official salaries	225,000
Sundries	529,000
Total	4,645,302

The direct tax on land for the whole country is but 5700 sp.

As the peasants or farmers produce the greatest portion of the articles they consume, and scarcely purchase any luxuries, full two-thirds of the revenue being derived from the customs, the burdens fall on the higher classes, and upon those who, living in towns or along the coast, support themselves by the fisheries. It is the wish of the Government to equalize the taxation by levying a small land-tax, which would enable them to reduce some of the duties, but as the majority of members of the Storthing are peasants, this will probably be a work of some difficulty.

The Government have long been aware of the impolicy of trusting so largely to the customs, instead of availing themselves of other sources of revenue which could not be so easily disturbed by political changes.

14. THE PEOPLE.

The early and close connection which existed between the inhabitants of the United Kingdom and those of Norway and other parts of Scandinavia has left such strong traces both in the language and character of the former, that every Englishman must be sensible of it, and will probably more quickly find himself at home amongst the Norwegians than amongst any other part of the great European family. The Norwegians have the same feelings towards the English; they like them, as every Englishman who has travelled in Norway can bear witness.

Great patriotism and hospitality are two of the leading characteristics of the Norwegians; they are often cold and reserved, and combine great simplicity of manner with firmness and kindness. "Deeds, not words," is their motto. Enjoying as much practical liberty as any nation can boast of, they know and value it, and consequently are not only very independent, but particularly jealous of any encroachments from those above them.

There is not much admixture of Finnic or Lapponic (Mongolian) race with the Norwegian stock; none probably in the South, and very little in the North of Norway. The Norwegians are a tall, hardy, long-lived race. Standing in a Norwegian crowd, an Englishman of average height will find so many taller, or as tall as himself, that it is a difficult matter to see over or between their heads. The reverse of this is the case in crowds of most continental nations. Cutaneous diseases and chest affections are their worst maladies, so that those with a tendency to those disorders should by no means travel there. Otherwise, Norway is a very healthy country. Cholera raged in Christiania in 1853, and in Christiansand in 1856, but did not spread inland, or extend to Trondhjem, or the North, where it has never yet been seen. The dirt, bad drainage, and heat in Christiania are quite enough to account for cholera there; but since the great fire of 1858, when nearly one-fourth of the town was laid in ashes, a great improvement has taken place. The town is supplied with excellent water from a lake a few miles distant, and large sums of money have been expended on drainage, and other sanitary amendments.

The upper and middle classes became amalgamated after the independence of the country was established in 1814, and are comparatively few in number. The bulk of the population is engaged in agricultural pursuits, the land being mostly held in small farms. It is these small farmers, or peasants, as they are called, who now command a majority in the Storthing. Like most agriculturists they are obstinately opposed to innovations, but may easily be led by those in whom they place confidence. The besetting sin of the peasants is drunkenness, which engenders idle and dirty habits. The drudgery of the farms falls upon the women in a great measure, and they are usually less clean and well-dressed than the men, except upon Sundays and state occasions. Much *costume* still exists amongst the peasants in the wildest districts, which has been noticed under "Sketching," page 30.

15. PRODUCTIVE INDUSTRY.

Agriculture, &c.—Norway is essentially an agricultural and pastoral country, but only about 1060 sq. miles of the entire surface is supposed to be under culture, or otherwise productive. Most of the land is the property of those who cultivate it, and is called *udal*, which is equivalent to our freehold. The farms usually comprise 3 divisions: the in-field, or land inclosed for cultivation and the best hay; the mark, or out-field, also inclosed and kept for pasturing the cattle; and the *sæter* or tract of grass land in the mountains, where a shed is erected, and the cattle are pastured during the summer. A farm of average size is about 300 acres, exclusive of the sæter. All the hay and other crops, as well as the cattle, are kept under cover during the winter, which renders the homestead large in proportion to the size of the farm. Almost all the buildings are of timber, resting upon detached masses of rock, so as to allow a free current of air underneath the structure. The farmers, as was formerly the case in England, are so wedded to the system handed down to them from their ancestors, and their implements are usually of such antiquated form and rude construction, that farming is literally in its infancy amongst them, so far as regards the scientific cultivation of land, excepting in the neighbourhood of Christiania, where great improvements are in progress. Still of late years a marked improvement in this respect has taken place. Deep draining has been introduced there, and some improved implements of agriculture have been imported, the merits of which are fully appreciated.

The quantity of corn, rye, barley, oats, &c., sown in the country in the year 1855, consisted of about

2,816	quarters of	wheat,
8,850	do.	rye,
62,700	do.	barley,
38,300	do.	mixed grain,
18,600	do.	oats,
5,000	do.	peas,
277,400	do.	potatoes.

The *imports* of grain amounted to about 492,591 imperial quarters; a quantity considerably less, however, than in 1851, when 631,390 quarters were imported, or than in 1852, when the imports amounted to 602,110 quarters. But owing to the disastrous floods of 1860, by which an immense area of land was rendered unfit for agricultural purposes, the importations reached the large sum of 656,903 imp. quarters. The provinces of Hedemarken, Toten, and Smaalehnes are the great agricultural districts of Norway. Wheat is grown in a few favoured spots, but it only enters into the domestic economy of a Norwegian household as an article of luxury.

In many parts of Norway there are *corn magazines*, to which the farmers may send their surplus produce, and from whence also they may be supplied with loans of grain. The depositors receive at the rate of 12½ per cent. of increase on the corn deposited for 12 months; and the borrowers replace the quantities advanced them at the expiration of the same period, paying an increase of 25 per cent. This difference between the amount of the corn received and lent pays the expenses. These magazines are most useful, in consequence of the extreme precariousness of the crops.

The most profitable branch of rural industry appears to be that of breeding horses and cattle. The latter are small, but admirable for the dairy. The true Norwegian horse (now but rarely met with) is about 13 or 14 hands high, colour dun, with black mane, tail, and legs, and also a black stripe along the back; head small, splendid crest and mane, high shoulder, and finely proportioned. Those bred on the mountains usually run very small. In the S. of Norway horses are about 50 per cent. dearer than in the N. and W.

Forests.—Another great source of profit to the farmers in some parts of Norway is their pine and fir timber; most of it grows upon the banks of those great rivers and their tributaries which flow into the Christiania Fjord. The farmers assemble to meet the timber merchants in Christiania at midsummer, the contracts are entered into, and about 20 per cent. paid in advance. The trees are then felled, cut into lengths, and floated down the rivers in the spring to the sawmills of the merchants, where they are sawn into planks, sorted, and dried for exportation. Upwards of 8-10ths of the Norwegian timber is taken by France. Only about 1-10th, of the best quality, comes to England. The chief places from whence it is exported are Drammen, Christiania, and Sarpsborg, near Frederikstad. The total annual produce of the Norwegian forests, in timber, deals, charcoal, and firewood, is estimated at 1,000,000*l*. Oak grows only in some of the more southern provinces; there is one oak tree in a garden near Trondhjem (latitude 63½°). Beech are found in one particular district near Laurvig (latitude 59°), and a few near Christiansand. The ash (*Fraxinus excelsior*) is confined to the South of Norway. Fir, mountain ash, birch, poplar, and several kinds of willow flourish all over the country. Spruce fir is the prevailing tree of the South of Norway, but it is not found much north of the Arctic circle, where Scotch fir takes its place. Mountain ash (*Pyrus aucuparia*) grows very luxuriantly: and its clusters of berries are exceedingly beautiful in the autumn. The larch is not indigenous to Norway, but it has been planted, and thrives well near Bergen.

Currants, raspberries, and strawberries, and numerous other berries, such as the molteberry (*Rubus chamæmorus*), the whortleberry (*Vaccinium vitis Idæa*), &c., grow wild in Norway, and bear good fruit. Cherries, gooseberries, apples, pears, and all kinds of English summer vegetables ripen in the South of Norway.

Mines. — No coal has yet been discovered in Norway, which is a great drawback upon the mining operations which might otherwise be carried on; but the ores are, on the other hand, of extraordinary richness in many places. Some of the iron ores, for instance, in the S. produce 60 and even 95 per cent. of pure metal. The plan of exporting the unsmelted ores, which prevails so extensively in Cornwall, appears not yet to have been adopted in Norway.

At present the mineral productions are chiefly confined to iron, copper, silver, nickel, and cobalt.

The iron mines are numerous, but are not worked to any extent, as in all the mining districts they are restricted to a fixed quantity of fuel, which necessarily limits the produce: were this not fixed, the production might be increased for a few years, but then the forests would be altogether exhausted. The total quantity of iron obtained does not exceed 30,000 tons per annum, but it is of the finest quality.

The total produce of copper varies from 400 to 500 tons. It is shipped to Germany, Holland, and France. The Röraas copper mines are among the oldest in Europe, having been worked for upwards of 200 years. The Kongsberg silver mines belong to the State, and for a series of years have returned an annual profit of about 200,000 dollars, although the number of men employed to work them is less than 400; the metal occurs chiefly in the form of native silver, and beautiful crystallized specimens are occasionally met with; there is one in the museum at Copenhagen which weighs about 500 pounds. Since their commencement these mines have produced upwards of six millions sterling.

Fisheries.—The inhabitants of the Norwegian coast throughout its whole extent, as well as those of the great fjords in the W., are almost entirely supported by the fisheries, which are estimated at upwards of 1,000,000*l.*, and which give employment to between 20,000 and 30,000 men. The most important are the cod and sey, which are carried on during February and March about the Loffoden Islands and other parts of the N. coast. Nearly 3000 boats are employed, the largest of which are about 3 tons burden.

The herring-fishery is chiefly carried on between Bergen and Stavanger. It usually commences after the cod season is over; and the annual produce is about 1,000,000 barrels.

From Bergen to the Naze there is also an extensive take of lobsters, most of which are exported to London alive. During the season there are two lines of packets between Norway and England constantly employed in this trade. In the summer large quantities of mackerel are taken off the S. coast and are extensively salted for winter use in Norway. Great numbers of salmon are also taken upon the S. coast, and in all the rivers where they can get up throughout Norway.

Manufactures are almost entirely domestic, the division of labour being carried to a less extent in Norway than in almost any other part of Europe. The Norwegian peasant has few wants, and unites most trades in his own person and family, purchasing nothing which can be raised or made upon his own farm; yet of late years numerous manufactories have been established for working up the natural products of the country, for which the numerous waterfalls supply a great abundance of water power. Besides a great number of brandy distilleries there are breweries, tobacco manufactories, sawmills, iron foundries, and smelting works scattered all over the country. The cotton-spinning and weaving factories for the production of the coarser kinds of cloth have not been able to compete with the English wares, in spite of a high protective duty.

Almost all the towns in Norway are upon or near the coast, and import such manufactures as they require; these comprise German, French, and English.

16. COMMERCE.

Internal trade in Norway is at present upon a very small scale, arising from the habits of the peasantry, as before stated, as well as the thinness of the population, the mountainous nature of the country, and badness of the roads.

The latter, however, are being improved as fast as the national resources will permit, and in the best manner.

The *Bank of Norway* is in Trondhjem, and has branches in Christiania, Bergen, and Christiansand. For further particulars see Trondhjem, Route 26.

Foreign Trade of late years has been exceedingly prosperous. Duties on imported articles have been relaxed, as far as compatible with the exigencies of the State, and a great advance has been made towards adopting the principles of free trade. The result so far has been, not only to encourage intercourse with foreign nations, but to stimulate the energies of the Norwegians to develope the internal resources of their country.

The *Exports* from Norway are chiefly deals and timber, fish, and minerals. Of the former, upwards of 500,000 loads are annually shipped to France, England, Denmark, Holland, and Belgium.

Between 400,000 and 600,000 barrels of herrings are annually sent to Sweden, Denmark, and the Baltic ports. The produce of the cod-fishery, which comprises the fish both in a dried and salted state, cod-liver oil, and cod roes, is very great. The fish are sent to Russia, France, Spain, and Italy; the oil to Germany and Holland; and the roes to France and the N. coast of Spain, where they are used as bait in the sardine fishery. Of late years granite has been extensively exported to Hamburg, where it is used for the foundations of houses and other purposes.

The *Imports* comprise all kinds of colonial produce, wines, and the manufactures of Germany, France, and England, particularly the latter; salt, coals, iron wares, and a great variety of articles of luxury, for which prosperity invariably creates a demand.

The *Commercial Marine* shows great activity. In 1855 it consisted of 5241 vessels; the united tonnage of which amounted to 528,964 tons, and the seamen to 28,038; an increase of 125,987 tons since 1851. This in a country of less than 1,500,000 inhabitants is a great stride, and is a further proof of its increasing prosperity. The repeal of the English navigation laws probably gave a considerable impulse to Norwegian shipping.

17. LITERATURE, ETC.

Literature in Norway is rather at a low ebb. The cause of this may be traced to the state of society, which is evidently unfavourable to great mental exertion; nothing is to be gained by it, and as intellectual labour follows the same law as bodily, where people are at their ease, and are not urged on either by want or by ambition, no strenuous efforts are to be expected, and the reading part of the public is so limited in numbers, that no pecuniary temptation is held out to the man of letters. It is true that Norway has produced several scientific writers of note, but all of them, in order to ensure a circulation for their works, have been obliged to publish them in the German language. In the lower departments of literature there have been several authors of merit, and numerous translations of foreign books, particularly English and German, are to be met with. Among their own writers, Holberg, Munch, Wessel, Welhaven, Wergeland, and several others, are always mentioned with distinction. At the University there are professors who are acquiring European names in astronomy, geology, and other branches of science. Norway can also boast of several artists of celebrity, but who, from want of encouragement at home, are chiefly settled in Germany.

The state of the public press is creditable to the country, and conducted with considerable talent. Almost every town possesses a newspaper, and the capital no less than six, besides a Penny Magazine and several monthly publications.

There are Norwegian theatres in Bergen and Christiania, and also a Danish theatre in the latter, where Danish pieces principally, and translations of French vaudevilles, are acted. There is a considerable collection published of *Norwegian national airs*, and some of the melodies are very charming. The constant theme of the most popular songs and favourite airs is *Gamle Norge* (Old Norway). "The Swiss Ranz des Vaches does not produce a more wonderful effect upon the Alpine shepherd than does this simple national allusion on the mind of the Norwegian."—*Crichton's Scandinavia*, vol. ii. p. 315.

NOTICE.

In the following Norwegian Routes the names of Stations and distances have been checked by the Government Road-book as far as it extends. For those which are not included in that book, Wallgorski's Map, and Roosen's, both published in Christiania, have been relied upon, as being considered the best and most likely to be used by travellers. But to guard against any alterations which may be made in the Stations, or inaccuracy of their names or distances, it is always advisable, on sending Forbud papers, to have them checked and compared with the *Lomme Reiseroute*, before sending them.

Distances in Norway will always be given in *Norsk* (Norwegian) miles, unless English miles be expressly stated.

Both in Norway and Sweden the heights of mountains, and levels of lakes in all the Routes, have been (with few exceptions) taken from Forsell's Map, in 8 sheets, published at Stockholm, and are therefore given in *Swedish feet.*—See "Measures," in Preliminary Information to the "Handbook for Sweden."

The asterisk *, prefixed to the names of Stations, denotes that good or tolerable accommodation is to be obtained there.

And the obelisk †, before the name of a Station, marks it as a "Fast Station;" that is, that horses are kept in readiness there; see pp. 5, 11.

T before the name of a station signifies a telegraph station.

Inland Steamers.

It may be mentioned that Steamers run on the Miösen ; Tyri and Hosfjord ; Kröderen ; Randsfjord, and probably on Tinsöen ; on Nordsöen and Hitterdals Vand, in Lower Tellemarken ; and Bandags Vand, in Upper Tellemarken ; and Storsöen in Österdal. The traveller is particularly requested to make every inquiry concerning their routes, before leaving for the interior.

Telegraph Stations in Connection with England and all Parts of the Continent.

Christiania, and all Stations on railway ; the frontiers of Norway and Sweden at Högen, Frederikshald, Frederikstad, Sarpsborg, Moss, Hölen, Dröbak, Hamar, Lillehammer, Gjövik, Dombaas, Drammen, Kongsberg, Svelvik, Holmestrand, Horten, Tünsberg, Vallö, Sandösund, Sandefjord, Laurvig, Frederiksvœrn, Brevik, Porsgrund, Skien, Langesund, Kragero, Risör, Tvedestrand, Arendal, Grimstad, Lillesand, Christiansand, Mandal, Farsund, Flekkefjord, Egersund, Stavanger, Skudesnœs, Kobbervik, Hougesund, Lervik, Bergen, Lœrdalsören, Aalesund, Veblungsnœs, Molde, Christiansund, Trondhjem, Espevœr, Kalleseid.

Railways.

There are now open lines from Christiania to Eidsvold, about 42 English miles ; Christiania to Kongsvinger, about 60 English miles ; Hamar to Grundsæt, about 22½ English miles ; Trondhjem to Stören, about 47 English miles.

ROUTES THROUGH NORWAY.

ROUTE 20.

LONDON TO CHRISTIANIA.

The most direct and cheapest route is by way of Hull, a distance of 500 English miles. A boat leaves Hull every Friday as soon after 6 P.M. as tide permits.

By leaving London by the Great Northern Railway about noon, Hull is reached in time to catch the boat for Christiania, which leaves the same evening. Berths can be secured, and exact time of departure ascertained, by writing to Messrs. Wilson and Son, Steam Navigation Company's Agents, Hull. Christiansand is usually reached on the Sunday evening, and travellers wishing to go round the coast by steam to Bergen (Route 25) had better land here. For Inns, see Route 24. The Hull boat proceeds on her voyage after a short delay, and usually arrives at Christiania on the Tuesday morning. Fares from Hull, 4*l.*; return tickets, available for the whole season, 6*l.* Fore cabin, 2*l.* 13*s.* 4*d.* The boats return on the intermediate Fridays.

There are, however, various other

modes of reaching Christiania. The quickest, after the one pointed out, is by Calais or Ostend to Hamburg, which can be reached in 36 hours from London, if the traveller be limited for time. Supposing the traveller to have arrived in Hamburg by 6 o'clock A.M. on the Saturday, he will be in time for the train from Altona to Kiel. At Kiel he can join the Christiania government steamer, which starts immediately after the arrival of the train, and arrives at Christiania on the Sunday night or early on the Monday morning. Christiania can be reached by this route between the Thursday and the Tuesday following, but not at a less expense than from 8*l.* to 10*l.*

By selecting this route, if the traveller is desirous of visiting Copenhagen, which will well repay the trouble and additional expense, he can take the steamer from Kiel to Korsör on the west coast of Zealand, and from thence by rail to Copenhagen. A Norwegian government steamer leaves that capital every Wednesday at noon, and arrives in Christiania early on the Friday morning, after stopping at Gottenborg for a short time *en route*. N.B.—*It has been deemed expedient to let the above remarks stand, for though the Norwegian boat runs now to Lubeck instead of Kiel, the old route will be used as soon as matters in Denmark have been readjusted.*

Those who do not dislike a sea passage will find it cheaper to go from London to Hamburg by steamer, and thence by rail to Kiel or Lubeck, as described; or by a steamer direct from Hamburg to Christiansand, and thence by some of the coasting steamers to Christiania.

For inland steamboat tables, and railway tables, make inquiries in Christiania.

Kiel to Christiania.

A Norwegian *steamer* leaves Kiel (vid. remarks in italics above) every Friday at 10 o'clock P.M. for Christiania, on the arrival of the train from Hamburg. Fare, chief cabin, 8 specie dollars. Average passage, 43 hours. On her return voyage she leaves Christiania on Tuesdays at noon, commencing on the 30th of March, and, after touching at intermediate ports in the Christiania Fjord, reaches Kiel on Wednesday evenings.

On clearing the pretty bay of Kiel, and entering the Baltic, after a run of about 40 Eng. m., the Great Belt is entered between the islands of Langeland on the W. and Laaland on the E., see Route 9. Proceeding up the Belt, the ship calls at Korsör on Zealand, see Route 8,* and at Frederikshavn in the north of Jutland. On leaving the Belt, the course taken leads nearly due N. across those portions of the North Sea which are known as the Kattegat and Skagerrack. During heavy gales in winter the seas here are terrific, and the loss of life and property, at times, frightful. On leaving the Skagerrack the ship enters the mouth of

The *Christiania Fjord*.—This magnificent fjord, by which most travellers approach Christiania, properly commences about Frederikstad, on the eastern side of the fjord, and Sandesund on the western side, where the steamer calls, and where passengers desirous of going round the coast can generally catch a steamer going westward to Christiansand. The length of the fjord is about 70 Eng. m. The rocks at the entrance of the fjord are numerous and rugged, on one of which, by name "Færder," there is a lighthouse. From Frederikstad the fjord gradually narrows till arriving at the small town of

* For Routes 1 to 19 see the "Handbook for Denmark."

Horten on the left, while on the opposite side is Moss. Horten is the Portsmouth of Norway; most of the government vessels are now built, repaired, or laid up in ordinary here. On passing Horten, the fjord spreads considerably, and soon becomes divided, the branch to the left running up to the large town of Drammen (see Route 24); the right to Christiania. This branch becomes very narrow at the small town of Drobak, where some new forts have lately been erected. Drobak is on the right, and the fjord then gradually widens to a noble expanse, studded with numerous islands. At the northern extremity stands Christiania. The voyage all the way up this fjord forms a moving panorama of lake scenery, unique in character, and of great beauty. Those who expect savage grandeur and picturesque outlines of the mountains and rocks on the banks of this fjord will be disappointed—they must be sought for in the Bergen and other districts to the W. and N., where they abound in perfection. Most of the islands and hills seen from the fjord are too round in form to be very picturesque—they are of granite and of gneiss, and for the most part covered with fir and pine trees from the water's edge to the summit, interspersed with patches of clearing, each farm being distinguished by its group of buildings. On the whole, the scenery of the Christiania Fjord is as lovely as its form and extent are magnificent.

The traveller, coming from Hamburg, will be probably much struck by the lightness of the nights in the months of May, June, and July, and the gorgeous sunset effects, which blend into those of sunrise without losing their brightness. Any one fortunate enough to steam up this fjord on a clear, still night in one of these months will be amply repaid for staying on deck all night and watching the glorious colours reflected on the water. The steamer's course is due north—towards the sun—the whole night, and there is probably no place in the whole of Norway, where sunsets are seen to greater advantage. Farther to the northwards, and nearer the Arctic circle, the sun, being but a little below the horizon, has generally too much power for the colours to be very gorgeous.

On the left, before reaching Christiania, numerous villas are seen; then the new palace comes in sight, with the Castle of Agershuus in the foreground beneath. Rounding the point on which this castle is built, the whole city, with its harbour, at once opens up. The ship now quickly reaches her moorings, and is speedily hauled alongside the quay. A Custom-house officer immediately comes on board, and if assured that the luggage contains no merchandise, a very slight search is made. Nothing can exceed the courtesy of the custom-house officials.

CHRISTIANIA.—*Inns:* The *Victoria Hotel* is by far the best, and is extremely well conducted. English spoken. There are, besides, the *Hôtel du Nord*, the *Hôtel de Scandinavie*, the *Hôtel d'Angleterre*, *Prinds Carl*, and the *Copenhagen Hotel*. English, French, and German spoken generally at all of them. None of them are distant from the landing-place, and if full, the masters can generally procure lodgings close by. There is an excellent restaurant at the Freemasons' Hall, and at Christophersen's, in Kongens Gade.

The *Post Office* (post-contoir), which used formerly to be on the northern side of the market-place, has been removed into Akers Gade. Show your card on asking for letters. The postage of a letter by the regular post to England is 1*s.* 5*d.*, and by Hull, 7*d.*; by the latter route, one-half must be paid on posting the letter, the other half in England on receipt. By the first route, letters can be prepaid or not, as is most convenient. Postage on letters all over Norway is 4 skillings, but within the town and its suburbs, 2 skillings.

The British Consul-General, Mr. Crowe, resides in Christiania. He and his son, the Vice-Consul, are most courteous and kind in giving information to travellers respecting any part of Scandinavia, or who intend to proceed to Russia, which perhaps they are better qualified than any one in the North to do.

Money.—See Preliminary information (§ 2). Circular or Bank of England notes are most convenient; the former have generally special agents, named in the letter accompanying the notes; with respect to the latter, advice is readily afforded at the Consulate, as to how they can be most profitably converted. Before leaving Christiania a good supply of change, or small money, *must* be taken. It is not to be obtained, except in large towns. The hours of business in Christiania are usually from 8 to 1. Coffee is taken on rising (and excellent it is all over Norway); déjeûner à la fourchette at 10, and dinner at 2. All classes take off their hats on entering a shop, or other place of business, and a foreigner will not meet with less attention for respecting this Scandinavian custom.

Christiania is the modern capital of Norway. By the census in 1855, the population was 40,000. This city was founded by Christian IV., close upon the site of the ancient city of Osloe, which, with the exception of the Episcopal Palace, and a few houses, was entirely destroyed by fire on the 24th May, 1624. Christian IV. named the city after himself, happening to be in Norway at the time on a visit to his newly discovered silver mine at Kongsberg.

Osloe was founded in 1058, by King Harald Haardraade, and in 150 years was, after Nidaros (now Trondhjem) and Bergen, the third city in the kingdom. Upon the union of Norway with Denmark it became the capital of Norway. Two kings, Christopher III. and Christian II., were crowned there. The Cathedral of St. Halvard was very rich; it was there that James VI. of Scotland and I. of England married Anne of Denmark, sister of Christian IV., in 1589.

The streets of Christiania are broad, and laid out at right angles. But few of the ancient and picturesque log-houses remain. Most have been consumed in the repeated fires to which the city has been subjected, and in consequence of which a law has been made which precludes the erection of wooden houses within the precincts of the city. Since the great fire in 1858 an immense improvement has taken place in the style and architecture of the houses, many of which are of noble dimensions.

This fire took place in April, by which 60 houses were destroyed, and 1000 people rendered houseless. It broke out in the Skipper Gade in the very centre of the town, and long defied the efforts made to extinguish it. The estimated value of fixed property burnt was 110,000*l.*, and about a similar amount of goods and moveables—in all about 220,000*l.*

The rapid strides that Norway has made in wealth and population since she became emancipated from the Danish yoke give abundant hope for the future. The population of Christiana alone has increased 30,000 since 1815. There is a genius and firm, quiet energy in the people, which, added to their patriotism, their ardent love of "Gamle Norge" (Old Norway), will overcome all obstacles of climate and geographical position. To the honour of the Government, they sent one of the ablest of the Norwegian advocates to France and England to inquire and report upon the law of evidence and trial by jury, with a view to the improvement of the criminal law of Norway. Let them adopt the same plan with their architects and civil engineers, furnish them with the means (which they do not possess) of seeing what has been done in other countries, and the public buildings and roads of Norway may be expected to keep pace with those of other European countries, provided sufficient grants and laws are made by the Storthing.

The chief merit of the *New Palace* over the very miserable old one in the heart of the town is its situation, which is very fine. Tickets to view the palace can always be procured; the hours of admission are from 11 till 7. From the roof an uninterrupted and splendid view is obtained of the city, the fjord, and the surrounding country.

The *Storthing House*, which was begun in 1861, will be a handsome building when completed. The site chosen is on an eminence at the beginning of Carl Johan Gade, facing the new palace.

None of the churches possess any particular architectural interest.

The *University* numbers about 500 students. The *Library*, containing about 200,000 volumes, admirably arranged, is well worth a visit. It is open every day in the week from 12 to 2, excepting Saturday and Sunday. The Librarian, Mr. Keyser, takes great pride in showing strangers over it. The education of the students is gratuitous, with the exception of a small entrance fee.

The *Collection of Northern Antiquities* is open every Monday and Friday, from 1 to 2. Though not extensive, when compared with that at Copenhagen, it nevertheless contains a variety of most interesting objects. Amongst them is a massive gold collar, and a number of other gold and silver ornaments found in the Agershuus district in 1834, which are supposed to have adorned a statue of Odin, and to have been hidden where they were found upon the introduction of Christianity and spoliation of the heathen temples. There are several articles here with Runic inscriptions upon them. Also a girdle and the knives used in the duel which prevailed amongst the lower classes in Norway till within the last 60 years. Each man began by driving his knife into a piece of wood; so much of the blades as were not buried in it were then carefully bound round with strips of hide, the men placed close together, face to face, the girdle buckled round their waists so that neither could get away from the other—their knives were then handed to them, and they fought it out. This mode of fighting was known as the "duel of the girdle." Here also are the crown, girdle, and frontlet, such as are still worn by brides in the Bergen district, at least such as are chaste, as the unchaste are not allowed to wear the crown at their marriage, and, therefore, to be married without a crown is the direst disgrace a damsel of that district can incur. The Museum contains a number of small rude statues in bronze of heathen gods, horses, &c. The authorities of the Museum find great difficulty in adding to this portion of the collection, as when any of these idols are found, the peasants usually refuse to part with them, believing they have medicinal virtues and healing powers, so strongly do the remains of idolatry still linger in the North amongst the lower orders—and it was just the same in Denmark. The specimens of weapons and ornaments in flint, bronze, silver, and gold are very interesting, and admirably classed. There are also some fine old swords, bits of armour, and wood carvings.

The *National Gallery* is situated in the University, and contains several pictures of the modern school. All of Tideman's are well worth looking at. His famous picture of the "Haugianer" was in the Paris Exhibition in 1855, and has great merit. Of landscape painters, Dahl, Gude, Fearnley, Frich, Cappelen, Eckersberg, and Muller, have their respective merits, and most of them have established a name in Germany. The Dusseldorf school is well represented. Nordenberg, whose compositions are in the same style as the Norwegian Tideman, and others, represent the Swedes.

The collection of old pictures is hardly worthy of remark: the best are some pictures of the Dutch school. It is open on Sunday and on Thursday from 12 to 2. Casts from some of Thorwaldsen's lovely works form a great and valuable addition to the gallery.

The *Cabinet of Coins* may be seen every Monday and Friday from 1 to 2, and the collection of models from 12 to 1.

The *Zoological Museum* is open on Mondays and Fridays from 12 to 2; but to those who wish for admission for any special purpose, four hours weekly are granted. The Museum contains some fine specimens of Scandinavian fauna. In addition to these there are the *Zootomical Museum*, open on Saturdays from 1 to 3; the *Collection of Minerals*, on Fridays from 11 to 12; the *Anatomical Museum*, on Saturdays from 1 to 3; the *Chemical and Metallurgical Laboratories*, to be seen every working day.

The *Botanical Gardens*, *Library*, and *Herbarium*, under the management of Dr. Fr. Chr. Schübeler, are open every day in the week. Dr. Schübeler has lately published a book on the Geographical Distribution of the Fruit Trees and Berry-bearing Shrubs of Norway, which gives some interesting information about the botany of Norway. (Vid. *Barnard's Sport in Norway*, p. 236.)

The different collections in the University are open for public inspection several days in the week, when a Professor usually attends, and with much kindness gives information with respect to the various objects to all who seek it. Should strangers be unable to attend on the public days there is not much difficulty in obtaining admission at other times.

The *Theatre* is a detached building, about the size of the Surrey Theatre in London, very neatly arranged and decorated; the performers are now mostly natives; the entertainments consist chiefly in vaudevilles, translated from the French, and operas; occasionally the legitimate drama is performed. The performances commence at half-past 6 and end at 10. The orchestra is good, and the theatre is altogether very respectably conducted.

Close to the theatre is the National Bank, the Army Depôt, and Freemasons' Hall; part of which is used as a restaurant. In it there is a ball-room, capable of containing 1700 people, which is used on all public occasions.

The *Castle of Agershuus* is situated on a slight eminence at the southern extremity of the town, and commands the entrance into the harbour; the ramparts, which are laid out in walks, form an agreeable promenade, and are much frequented by the inhabitants. The castle is supposed to have been built about the year 1302; the regalia of Norway and the national records are preserved within its walls. It was strongly fortified, and has withstood several severe sieges; the last was undertaken by Charles XII. of Sweden in 1716. A meadow on the opposite side of the fjord, which is visible from the fortress, is still called "Svenske Sletten" (Swedish Field), from being the spot where his army was encamped. Strangers are allowed to inspect the interior of the castle—a fine view over the fjord and harbour is obtained from the ramparts. On the western side of the keep are mounted two splendid brass guns, cast in 1620, and highly decorated with subjects in bas-relief; groups of barbarians fighting, admirably modelled and finished. These guns appear to be of Saxon or Bavarian workmanship, and are said to have been taken during the Thirty-Years' War by the Swedes, from whom they were again captured by the Norwegians, and have ever since been placed here. They are used to alarm the city when a fire breaks out. In the keep there is a small collection of old arms and armour, to see which application must be made at the "Artilleri Gaard." A large body of convicts (or, as they are here called, "slaves"), most of them very heavily ironed, are imprisoned in this castle, and worked in gangs. Here also, in a room or cage formed of thick iron bars, was immured for life Höyland, the Robin Hood of Norway. His vices were inordinate love of the fair sex and theft. His robberies were, however, always confined to the upper classes, while his kindness and liberality to those in his own rank of life rendered him exceedingly popular amongst them. His crimes never appear to have been accompanied with personal violence. He was a native of Christiansand, where he began his career. On being imprisoned for some petty theft, he broke into the inspector's room, while he was at church, and stole his clothes; these Höyland dressed himself in, and quietly walked out of the town unobserved and unsuspected. He was subsequently repeatedly captured and imprisoned in this castle, and as often made his escape. On one occasion he was taken on board a vessel just leaving the Christiania Fjord for America. Previous to his last escape, all descriptions of irons having been found useless, he was placed in solitary confinement in the strongest part of the basement of the citadel—his room was floored with very thick planks. Here he had been confined for several years when, one night, the turnkey said to him, "Well, you are fixed at last, you will never get out of this, and so you may as well promise us you will not attempt it." To this he only replied, "It is your business to keep me here if you can, and mine to prevent your doing so if possible." The following day, when his cell was opened, the prisoner was gone, apparently without leaving a trace of the manner in which he had effected his escape. After a repeated and careful search, on removing his bed, it was found that he had cut through the thick planks of the flooring. On removing the planks cut away (and which he had replaced on leaving the cell), it appeared he had sunk a shaft, and formed a gallery under the wall of his prison—this enabled him to gain the court-yard, from whence he easily reached the ramparts unseen, dropped into the ditch, and got off. No trace of him could be found. About twelve months afterwards the National Bank was robbed of 60,000 specie dollars, chiefly paper money, and in the most mysterious manner, there being no trace of violence upon the locks of the iron chest, in which the money had been left, or upon those of the doors of the bank. Some time afterwards a petty theft was committed by a man who was taken, and soon recognized to be Höyland. He then disclosed how he had effected his last escape, which had taken him 3 years of steady patient labour to accomplish: while others slept he was at work, and with a nail for his only tool. Having money concealed in the mountains he was sheltered in Christiania—disguised himself—made acquaintance with the porter of the bank—gradually, without his knowledge, took impressions of the various locks—made keys for them—and thus committed the robbery before mentioned. He carved beautifully in wood and stone, but latterly he was no longer allowed the use of tools, after which his sole occupation was knitting stockings with wooden pins. Twice during the day, while the other prisoners were not at work, he used to be allowed to leave his cell for air and exercise, and occasionally he got the amusement of a chat with the governor, by writing to him that he would disclose where the rest of the bank money was concealed which he did not get rid of while at liberty. At last he hung himself in prison in despair.

The *Steam-boat Office* is on the quay, and rarely open except in the morning. A printed list may be obtained there of the arrival and departure of the different steamers all round the coast and elsewhere. Care must be taken to ascertain at the office for what length of time the list may be relied upon, as alterations are made towards the end of the season. The *Passport Office* is at the corner of Raadhuusgaden, not far from the Hôtel du Nord.

Shops.—Most of the shopkeepers speak English. The best houses of business are in and near the Kirkegaden. At a corner of that street is I. W. Cappelen's book and music warehouse. It is the best for books, maps, and music; and for those intending to stay any time in Christiania, it may be convenient to know he also keeps a good assortment of pianos to let out on hire. A travelling map, and the small "Lomme-Reiseroute" (or Road-book), published by the Government, or "Bennett's Handbook," will be found useful, as they contain the routes of the inland steamers. Munch's map is the best, but is rather expensive. Roosen's is good, but minute, sometimes requiring a magnifying glass. It is in two sheets, price about 5 sp. d. Waligorski and Wergeland's is cheaper, but has not nearly as many places marked as Munch's or Roosen's. Keilhau's Amts Karter is the best geological map. For those bound to the far north Friis's map of Finmark cannot be too highly recommended. It can be purchased at Dybvad's in Östre Gade. Take care to ask for the *last* edition of the Road-book, as some of the stations are altered from time to time. Herr Cappelen speaks English, and is a most intelligent person. Lenow's, at the corner of Dronninggen's-gaden and Kirkegaden, is a shop for provisions, preserved meats, &c., and Duhrendahl's in Kirke Gade.

Carriages.—Mr. Bennett may be depended upon to supply travellers with carrioles or carriages. See page 10. The plan always recommended by Norwegians and others here, is to buy a carriole or other carriage; when this is done, and the purchaser wants to sell at the end of his journey, he may be sure his loss will be from 30 to 50 per cent. Those who are returning to Christiania, and only intend to remain a month or two in the country, will therefore do well to *hire* instead of buying. In this case the bargain should be for so much a day, or week, the lender to pay for any repairs requisite from wear and tear; the party hiring for those arising from accidental damage; and to have the option of purchasing, at a given sum, instead of paying for the hire, should he wish to do so, within a time to be named. This is very advisable in case the traveller should alter his route and not return to Christiania. The value, of course, depends upon the build and state of the carriage, and the time it is hired for. The price of a good light phaeton without hood, is about 20*l.*; a set of new double harness, with breeching, 3*l.* 10*s.*; a new carriole without springs costs about 8*l.*; with springs, 9*l.*; harness, 45*s.* The hire of a phaeton, with harness, for a journey of about a month, costs about a dollar a day; a carriole, from 1 to 1½ mark. If going a long distance, by all means buy new harness. Hames, padded with leather, being used instead of a collar, the same harness readily fits every horse, and is of the most simple description. Do not be persuaded to dispense with breeching.

Near the new palace there are some *Tea-gardens*, commanding agreeable views. A good band of German performers play there most evenings in the summer. Refreshments are supplied as in Germany; admission, 1 mark.

Society in Christiania is described as being particularly pleasant. Great hospitality prevails, and the upper classes are generally highly educated, and particularly intelligent and agreeable. Winter is the gay time here; and "a traveller, transported by the fairies some fine winter night across the North Sea from an evening party in Prince's Street, Edinburgh, to one in Prindsen's Gade in Christiania, would scarcely know, if deaf to the difference of language, that he had changed the scene."—*Laing's Sweden*, p. 360. "At a dinner party the gentlemen rise from the table and return to the drawing-room with the ladies, when the old Norwegian custom is generally observed of the family shaking hands all round with their guests." In addressing ladies here, as in Sweden, you will always be on the safe side to address the married ones as Frue (my Lady), and the maidens as Fröken. Madame and Jomfrue are the titles of the shopkeepers' wives and daughters.

Those who have time and inclination to cultivate an acquaintance with the language of the country will find it an excellent plan to board with some respectable family—this can readily be done, and upon very reasonable terms. It is not a difficult language for an Englishman to acquire, and a month or six weeks' assiduity will generally enable an intelligent person sufficiently to master Norsk for all travelling purposes.

The *Environs of Christiania.*—The botanical garden is about an Eng. m. from the town on the road to Trondhjem, and contains a good collection of plants indigenous to Norway and the neighbouring countries. The garden is tastefully laid out, and from its elevated position affords a fine view of the town and fjord.

The best views of the environs are obtained from *Frogner-aasen*, a point about 1500 feet above the fjord, from whence there is an extensive panorama of the country. In clear weather, to the westward, the snow-capped mountains of Valders and Tellemarken are visible; whilst to the eastward the view extends to the frontiers of Sweden. Lakes, islands, forests, villas, highly cultivated meadows, blended with wild scenery, present themselves on every side; in fact, whichever way you turn, new and picturesque groups and varied objects meet your eye; and the vegetation, except where the naked rocks protrude themselves, is so luxuriant, that did not the bright blue sky, and occasionally the keen atmosphere, contradict it, the traveller might well imagine himself in southern, instead of northern Europe.

The view from the opposite hill of Egeberg, which is about 400 ft. high, and rises close over the old town, is thus described by Von Buch:—"We ascended by numerous serpentine windings the steep height of the Egeberg; looking down from its summit what a varied view is seen! The large town at the end of the bay, in the midst of the country, spreading out in small divergent masses in every direction, 'till it is at last lost in the distance among villages, farm-houses, and well-built country houses. There are ships in the harbour, ships behind the beautiful little islands which front the bay, and other sails appear in the distance. The majestic forms of the steep hills rising in the horizon over other hills which bound the country to the westward, are worthy of Claude Lorraine. I have long been seeking for a resemblance to this country and to this landscape: it is only to be found at Geneva, on the Savoy side, towards the Jura mountains; but the Lake of Geneva does not possess the islands of the fjord, nor the numerous ships and boats sailing in every direction. Here the pleasure resulting from the sight of an extraordinary and beautiful country is heightened by the contemplation of human industry and activity."

Among the seats in the neighbourhood, Bogstad, the residence of the Countess Wedel Jarlsberg, stands pre-eminent, and is worthy of a visit. The drive to it, especially, is very beautiful. It is situated about 7 Eng. m. W. of Christiania. From the back of Holgerslyst, a summer cottage belonging to the Stadtholder, a splendid view is obtained of the fjord and castle of Agershuus.

There are several pretty drives in the neighbourhood of the town; one to Maridal Lake, distant about 5 Eng. m., affords some beautiful views; another to Ladegaardsöen, which is about 2 Eng. m. from Christiania on the southern road, and is a delightful retreat; the grounds are pleasingly laid out on a sequestered isthmus stretching into the fjord. This spot was purchased by the late king's father and given to the inhabitants for a public promenade. The views from it are charming, and it is much frequented. Numerous boats may be seen on a summer's evening, passing to and fro on the smooth surface of the fjord, and filled with gaily dressed visitors. A band of music plays regularly every evening; and there is likewise a good restaurant on the spot. A pleasant trip may also be made to Ringeriget, about 14 Eng. m. on the Bergen road: see Route 21. The drive to *Prinsdal*, about 7 Eng. m. on the Dorbak road, is picturesque. The road is cut on the face of the cliff overhanging the fjord, and is a very fine specimen of Norwegian engineering: see Route 36.

Some interesting ruins of a monastery have lately been uncovered in Hovedöen, an island lying about an Eng. m. S. of the castle. It belonged to the Cistercian monks, and appears to have been built in 1147, and dedicated to the Virgin and the Anglo-Saxon king, Edmund. The first monks came over from England; at the Reformation it was secularized, and the materials were used to repair the castle. It is of sufficient interest to attract visitors, and the excavations are still being carried on.

Steamers leave Christiania for *Copenhagen* every Saturday at 8 A.M., commencing on April 3. They call at Gottenborg on Sunday morning, and reach Copenhagen early on Monday. The same vessel leaves Copenhagen on Wednesdays at noon, calls at Gottenborg on the Thursday morning, and arrives at Christiania early on the Friday morning, touching at all the immediate ports in the Christiania Fjord. Passengers wishing to go to the westward can land at Sandösund, and proceed from thence by one of the numerous steamers, which touch there on their way to Christiansand.

The average passage to Copenhagen is about 42 hours, of which some are passed at Gottenborg. Fare, chief cabin, 8 sp. da. For *Kiel* the steamer leaves, as previously stated, every Tuesday at noon, calling at Sandösund also, and other places in the fjord, to take up passengers that may have arrived from the westward.

Many persons who visit Norway are contented with going up the fjord to Christiania, and seeing a little of the country around the city. Those who do no more than this can form no just idea of the grandeur of Norwegian scenery. Comfort, during a journey into the interior of Norway, will much depend upon attention to the preliminary information given under the head of "Requisites for Travelling," § 5.

Excursions from Christiania to the splendid Falls of the Glommen (Sarp-Fos) near Frederikstad, and to Frederikshald, where Charles XII. was killed. This delightful trip can be most easily and comfortably made. A steamer leaves Christiania three times a week at 7 A.M. during the season, for Frederikshald (where she arrives about 3 or 4 P.M.), calling at the several towns and places in the fjord *en route*, including Frederikstad. From Frederikshald a steamer likewise starts three times a week at 7, arriving at Christiania between 3 and 4 P.M. on the same day. The captain speaks English; fares exceedingly moderate, cuisine and wines good and very reasonable. Carriages are taken on board. A carriage can easily be obtained from Frederikshald to the falls. For description of Frederikshald and of the Sarp-Fos, see Route 36.

The scenery upon this short voyage is highly interesting; and up the Swinesund to Frederikshald it becomes most grand. This fjord is generally of enormous depth, and in parts so narrow as to afford scarcely sufficient room for two ships to pass, the granite rocks on either side rising almost vertically from the water, and towering up to a vast height, beautifully broken and intermingled with foliage of various kinds. There is a most picturesque view of the Fortress of Frederiksteen, from the fjord, shortly before Frederikshald comes in sight. The forms of the rocks, with the winding fjord in the foreground, and the fortress crowning the hill in the distance, make a charming subject for the pencil.

Those who may prefer making this trip entirely or partially by land, can hire a carriage in Christiania, and follow Route 36.

ROUTE 21.

CHRISTIANIA TO BERGEN OVER RINGERIGET, AND THE FILLE-FJELD.

The *Northern Road.*—Distance 49¼ Norsk miles, or 346 English. Tourists have the choice of two other roads to Bergen, Routes 22 and 23. By this road the journey to Bergen (exclusive of any excursions which may be made *en route* to the Voring-fos, &c.) takes from 6 to 7 days. The shortest and best route is to go by railway to Eidsvold, and thence by steamer to Gjövig. It will be well for the traveller to arrange his route so as to sleep the first night at Sköien, 3¼ m. from Gjövig, Relen the 2nd night, Nystuen the 3rd, and Lærdalsören the 4th.

The post goes twice a week between Christiania and Bergen, alternately by this and the South road, Route 22. Forbnd papers may be sent by the post for a trifling sum, which effects a considerable saving. Take care *personally* to ascertain at the post-office what day the post goes, and which road it takes. Inquire also in Christiania, if any steamer is running upon the Rands Fjord, which lies parallel with this road for about 50 Eng. m., and what the days are, on which it runs.

Many of the hills upon this road are very steep, so that if you take a 4-wheeled carriage, it should be of the lightest description. Gentlemen will find a carriole by far the best and least expensive conveyance in all respects, both upon this road as well as all others in Norway. The only 4-wheeled carriage proper for Norwegian travelling is a light double-bodied phaeton, holding 4 persons. A good stock of *small* money is essential, as change is most difficult to obtain *en route.* Meat or white bread will probably only be found at one or two of the stations, and the Norwegian plan of carrying a box or basket of provisions, wine, &c., should therefore be adopted.

The scenery upon this route may be divided into two districts, which are separated by the Fille-Fjeld. The views on the eastern side are of vast extent and great beauty; the mountains upon a grand scale, and foliage most abundant—the effects at sunset sublime. On the western side of the Fille-Fjeld, foliage is comparatively rare, the outline of the mountains and rocks more picturesque, and the whole scenery wild and grand in the extreme. *Mr. Barrow* says, and says truly, "that it would be endless to describe, or rather to attempt to describe, the ever-varied beauties of the face of nature exhibited the whole way from Christiania to Bergen."—*Excursions in the North of Europe*, p. 261.

On quitting Christiania the road passes close under the new palace, which is seen on the right. Splendid views over the fjord on the left. At Stabæk the old road to Ringerige turns off. Ours continues along a new *chaussée*, and passes through pleasing woodland scenery to

† *Sandrigen i Bærum*, 1¼, a pretty village on a branch of the Christiania Fjord. From hence our route continues along a new and excellent road to

† *Humledál i Hole*, 1⅜, pay for 2 m., but not returning. Near this station is an "Udsigt," or view, inaugurated by the Princess Sophie, in 1860, from which a lovely view over the Tyri Fjord is to be had.

* † *Vik i Hole*, 1⅞. The old station, Sundvolden, is passed on this route, from whence Kroghleven can be ascended. Guides and ponies can be readily procured here. The views to be obtained from the famed *Kongens Udsigt* are splendid, and should on no account be passed unseen, as they are the finest and most extensive in the south of Norway. Opinions differ as to which is the finest view. *Kongens Udsigt* (King's View) is about ¾ an hour's walk from Johnsrud, and on the *right* side of the old road from Christiania. *Dronningens Udsigt* (Queen's View) is much nearer, and on the *left* of the old road. The King's View is the most extensive.

From thence the eye wanders over mountains, fjords, rivers, and lakes, until it rests in the far distance upon the massive heights of the Gousta-fjeld, which, though 70 Eng. m. on the W., are distinctly visible in fine weather. One of the most interesting features of this sublime prospect is a mighty chasm, closed in on either side by walls of sandstone, which rise perpendicularly from the depths below, as if severed by some mighty convulsion. The best time to see the magnificent views from hence is at sunrise or sunset.

Although the Gousta cannot be compared to Mont Blanc and the snow-capped mountains that encircle their Alpine monarch, this view is by many considered fully equal to the famous descent from the Jura to the Lake of Geneva. It embraces two beautiful lakes, the Tyri Fjord and Holr Fjord, and also a magnificent and almost circular valley, surrounded by a chain of mountains, of which Krogkleven is a portion, all which is called Ringeriget, or Ringa Rege, after King Ring, one of the ancient petty sovereigns of Norway, whose dominion it was.

On returning to Sundvolden, where tolerable accommodation may be had, the road crosses the Steens Fjord, a branch of the Tyri Fjord. Sundvolden is but a short distance from Vik. About half way between Vik and the next station the south road to Bergen turns off, Route 22, and leads to the *Hönefos*, which lies a short distance

N. of our route. If not intending to return to Christiania by Route 22, this noble waterfall should now be visited by following that road to the Hönefos Station (1 from Vik), from whence there is a direct road back to our route at Klækken; dist. 1 m.

* *Klækken i Hougs*, 1½. There is a good inn here. Upon this stage the road commands exquisite views over the *Viuls Elv*, which flows from the Rands Fjord into the Tyri Fjord, and the former magnificent lake is seen upon the left, shortly before arriving at

† *Hadelands Glasværk*, ¾. Situated at the southern end of the Rands Fjord. The road between Klækken and this place is good. From hence the road continues for some distance along the eastern banks of the Rands Fjord, which winds N. amongst the defiles of the mountains for upwards of 50 English miles.

* † *Kittelsrud i Jævnager*, 1½. Between this and Thingelstad there is a good parish road which it is best to use, especially in winter.

† *Thingelstad i Gran*, 1, where there are only tolerable quarters. The road here is very hilly, and three hours, at least, should be allowed.

† *Smedshammer i Gran*, 1½. Good road, but a filthy station. Between Grinager-marken and Smedshammer, Route 27, to Trondhjem, turns off to the N.E., joining the road on the western shore of the Miösen at Kræmmerbakken, near which there is a very remarkable obelisk, for which see Route 28: for stations to Kræmmerbakken, see Rte. 27. From Smedshammer the route continues more or less close along the fjord, and commands extensive views over it and the surrounding mountains. Vast forests of fir and pine are seen as far as the eye can range. The frequent appearance of the snow-plough, lying by the roadside, serves to remind the traveller that the way along which he now rolls so merrily in his carriage will soon again become impassable, except for sledges. From Smedshammer one can drive to † *Röken-vigen*, 1, a stopping station for the steamers.

† *Nordre Sand i Land*, 1½. The road still keeps near the fjord, and the scenery becomes more grand. On approaching the next station a mountain torrent from a small lake on the E. is crossed, which makes a fine fall before it enters the fjord.

The road continues to command superb views over the fjord, and the mountains on either side become still bolder.

From *Nordre Sande* the scenery increases in picturesque grandeur, the mountains become of vast height, and for long distances quite perpendicular; the masses of fallen rock and *débris*, with abundance of foliage, add to the beauties of the scenery.

† *Bjornerud i Land*, 1½. Good accommodation and civil people. From hence a road goes off eastwards to Mustad in Vardal; thus to † * *Lien*, on the *chaussée*, between *Gjövig* and *Odnæs*, on the Rands Fjord, 1½ m., to † * Mustad i Vardal, ¾, to † T. Gjövig, 1½. The road from Gjövig to Sköien is excellent. The road from Hadelands Glasværk to this place is more or less along the Rands Fjord the whole way, occasionally commanding extensive views over it and the surrounding mountains, and occasionally shut in by vast forests of fir. There is trout and pike fishing in the fjord, the fish running to a large size; the shooting is also well spoken of in the neighbourhood of Eidsvold, and bears may at times be met with. The head of the Rands Fjord is now reached. "The fjord had gradually narrowed till it became reduced to its feeding stream, which we had to cross at a village called Tonvold over a wooden bridge of a singular and simple construction, thrown across a foaming cataract."—*Barrow's Excursions in the North of Europe.* This stream

is the Dokke. These Norwegian bridges are very remarkable. On each side of the stream a platform is levelled in the rock; solid pine trees are then laid close together with their ends towards the stream on these platforms of the width of the bridge, and extending about three feet over the river; across these, to the outer edge of them, other trees are laid—then another layer parallel with the first, and so on, layer upon layer, each two projecting an equal distance over the last, until the span between each side is brought to a sufficient contraction upon the level of the road. Trees are then laid across the span; rough planks across form the flooring; side-rails are fixed, and the structure is complete. In the mountain districts all the bridges are built in this primitive but substantial way. On passing this bridge the road is continued along the grand valley of the Etnedals Elv, which rushes onwards close along the roadside. This is said to be a fine sporting district—feathered game abundant, and many bears and wolves. Some years ago, a peasant near here, when asked if there were many trout in the Etnedals Elv, replied, that the people about here never caught any, but that "an Englishman had been there and put some queer-looking things like flies upon his line, and with them he took great numbers of trout." The fact is that angling is almost unknown in the wilder districts of the interior, as the peasants' time is far too valuable, during their short summers, to be spent in angling.

† * *Skoien i Land*, 1¼. Good road. This is one of the best stations in Norway. From hence one can get to *Finden in Land*, 1¾; to *Nös in Birid*, 1¾; and to † *Stokke in Vardal*, 1⅝.

* † *Tomlevold i Land*, 1⅞. Excellent fishing and shooting to be had all up this valley. Bears spoken of as very destructive in the neighbouring mountains. The Etnedals Elv is crossed just before arriving at

† * *Gravdalen i S. Aurdal*, 1¼. Pay for 2 m. A good station. Here one gets the first view of snow in summer. From Gravdalen there is now a new road up the hill, which separates the Etnedal and Bægna valleys; it continues part of the way down the other side, when it joins the old one, and descends very rapidly to Frydenlund. From this place a road goes to † *Kræmmermoen*, ¾ m., by Bangs Church. After passing for some distance across the mountain, from the summit of the western side a scene of wondrous extent and beauty is beheld. At the foot lies the noble *Strand Fjord* (1137 feet above the sea), winding along a deep valley, while some snow-capped mountains in the direction of the Hurungerne Fjeld rear their gigantic heads in the extreme distance. The road now rapidly descends the mountain into the valley of the *Beina Elv*, and continues to afford splendid views all the way to

* † *Frydenlund i N. Aurdal*, 1⅜, pay for 1⅝. Game is abundant about here. Road carried near the bank of the river, and then of the Strand Fjord, all this stage, near the end of which the *Dal Elv* is crossed From hence a road goes to *Spirillen*, thus: on the E. side of Bægna Elv to † * *Kræmmermoen*, 1½; to † *Throndhuus*, 1; to † *Sörum*, 2; *Næs in Aadal*, 2, from which place a road goes to * *Strande*, 2¼, † *Sömdalen*, 2½, *Hönefos*, 1¾ (p. 96). Excellent quarters at Kræmmermoen and Strande.

† *Fagernæs i N. Aurdal*, 1½. Glorious scenery, with the Strand Fjord on the left nearly all the way. The peasants about here are a remarkably fine race of people. Somewhat of costume also begins; the men wear very short-waisted jackets, with large silver buttons and very gay waistcoats and queerly shaped hats.

Some of the old men are highly picturesque, with thin white hair flowing down their necks, and each side of the face, surmounted by a faded red worsted cap.

† *Reien i Slidre,* 1¼. Good road, but a poor station. The horses in this district are excellent, and about half the price of those round Christiania. The staple food of the peasants is "gröd," a kind of Scotch porridge, made of carefully boiled oatmeal; mixed with milk it is very good and exceedingly nutritious.

"From Reien the traveller, if he be a good pedestrian, may venture with a guide upon a five or six days' excursion to the highest mountains in Norway, the Jotunfjeld (Giant Mountains), part of which are the rugged mountains of Hurungerne. The excursion is fatiguing, and not without danger, and should not be attempted except in settled fine weather. According to the account given by Professor Keilhau, the best plan is to ascend from the farm of Skrebberg in Hurum, towards the Ranhorn to Bitnhorn, which lies ¼ a mile to the north of the former; it is 5000 feet high; at the foot of this is the Sæter Châlet Hodnstolen, 3250 feet above the level of the sea. Crossing the bridge at the northern end of Vinstervand, you pass by Synshoin to Hestevoldsbolen, on the northern shore of the Alpine Lake Bygdenvand, where the Mugnafjeld takes its rise. Passing the high Hestekampen, and the valley of Langsidedal, you reach Bramboden and Bygdenvand; from thence you ascend to the extensive Lake of Tyenvand. On passing through Koldedalen (cold valley), you get a splendid view of the Skagastölstinderne; you then proceed through Morkakoldedal to Aardal, or Utnedal. In Helgedal there are some good châlets. From Utnedal you proceed down to Hegge in Slidre, where you rejoin the main road."

For description of pedestrian route over the fjeld from Aardal or Utnedal to Gudbrandsdal, see Viig, or Laurgaard, in Route 26.

This excursion may be made on horseback, for almost anywhere that a man can go a Norwegian horse will be able to follow. The Jotumfjeld lies to the N.W. of Ölken, and by taking the above Route this road may be entered again at Leirdalsören upon the Sögne Fjord. From Ölken the road continues to ascend along the left bank of the fjord. The Begna Elv is crossed a little way below the *Mjös Vand,* which is 1576 feet above the sea, and the road continues along the right bank of that lake for the next two stages. The scenery is wild and grand, the mountains very steep, with much underwood, which makes them a favourite resort for bears. Feathered game is also said to be very plentiful, and the fishing excellent. A fine waterfall is passed on this stage. The next station is

† *Stee i Slidre,* 1¼. The shooting about here is well spoken of; reindeer generally abundant; fair road.

† *Öilöe i Vang,* 1. The buildings here are grandly situated. There is now a capital new road between Öilöe and Thune round Qvamsklev which shortens the journey considerably. The scenery is of wondrous grandeur. Wolves are common about here, but are rarely to be seen except in winter. Even then they will generally avoid a human being, except pressed by great hunger, and there be several together. In the winter of 1840 a peasant, when sledging on one of the fjords not far from hence, was attacked by a pack of 6 wolves. Fortunately he had his axe with him, and his horse was a high-couraged animal, who fought most gallantly with his fore-feet, as the wolves sprang at his throat. Between them three of the wolves were crippled, and the time occupied

by the survivors in devouring them enabled the man and horse to reach a place of safety. Immediately blood is drawn from a wolf his companions fall upon and devour him.

† *Thune i Vang*, ⅞. The station lies ¼ Eng. mile from the road on the left. The road still continues winding along the face of the mountain a great distance above the lake. The buildings and costume become more picturesque. Soon after leaving Thune a horsetrack turns off to the left, and leads across the mountains into Route 22, near the *Ekre* station. A grand waterfall is passed on this stage.

† *Skogstad i Öie*, 1⅞. This station is picturesquely situated. Here the ascent to the Fille-Fjeld commences, and 3 horses are again requisite for a 4-wheeled carriage, be it ever so light. There is excellent accommodation to be had at Nystuen on the top of the fjeld, and Maristuen, a mile beyond, on the descent to Hæg. These houses are kept by two sisters, who vie with each other in civility and attention to the comfort of their guests. Their provender is unusually abundant and good, and the beds clean and comfortable. Charge reasonable. From Skogstad the road is fearfully steep in many places, but the grandeur and wildness of the scenery amply compensate for all the fatigue encountered. Vegetation becomes very scanty, and stunted birch and mountain willow almost the only trees to be seen. The wood of the mountain birch is beautifully veined, and extensively used in Norway for making ornamental and other furniture. The plateau of

The *Fille-Fjeld*

is attained some distance before arriving at

* † *Nystuen i Öie*, 1, pay for 1½, which lies between two ranges of mountains, 3170 feet above the sea. The trout at Nystuen are celebrated. They are from a small lake (the *Utza Vand*) at the foot of the post-house. It is the source of the Beina Elv, which eventually falls into the Christiania Fjord. A little distance to the W. of this place is the source of the *Leirdal Elv*, a small stream, which soon swells into a mountain torrent, and forms innumerable falls and cascades before it joins the S.E. arm of the Sögne Fjord at Leirdalsören. The road there from hence follows the windings of this torrent almost all the way.

In summer there are generally some Laplanders in charge of a herd of reindeer near Nystuen; sometimes they are to be met with in a wild state, there being abundance of reindeer moss on the Fille-Fjeld.

From Nystuen to Leirdalsören the character and costume of the people are peculiar, and totally different from those on the E. side of the fjeld. The women have fair hair, oval faces, and soft gray eyes; many of them are very pretty. Their dress is a tight boddice of dark cloth, buttoned up to the throat, and with long sleeves; cloth petticoat, generally dark green; buttons and ornaments of silver. The married women wear a white cap of very singular form. Those women who have had a child without being married wear a cap peculiar to themselves, and are called "half wives." The maidens wear their hair in a most becoming manner: it is braided with narrow bands of red worsted, and wound round the head—the Norwegian snood.

On leaving Nystuen, a new and admirably constructed road leads across the rest of the plateau. A pillar on the left marks the division of the districts of Christiania and Bergen. Soon afterwards the road rapidly descends the left side of a deep, picturesque glen, down which the infant Leirdals Elv bounds along. In some places the road is a great distance above the level of the torrent below; and it is scarcely possible to say too much of the grandeur of the scenery all the way from Qvame. The buildings of a Sæter (mountain pasture attached to a farm) are passed on the left, before reaching Maristuen. At night the cows, horses, goats, &c., are driven in, and, with their attendants, group round the fires which are lighted to keep off the bears and wolves. It is a wild and most picturesque scene.

* † *Maristuen i Lærdal*, 1¼. This comfortable post-house is beautifully situated, 2517 feet above the sea. The skulls of bears, nailed up over the door, evidence the skill of the Norsk sportsmen. One of these men had a narrow escape from a bear near here some time since. In hot pursuit of the beast, which he had lost sight of, the hunter was running down the rapid slope of a mountain, when, coming to a small patch of brushwood, he leaped over it, but had no sooner done so than, hearing a noise behind him, he turned, and had only just time to raise his rifle and draw the trigger, when the bear was upon him. Fortunately it seized the muzzle of the rifle, which, exploding at the same instant, blew its head to atoms.

From Maristuen the road keeps close along the banks of the Leirdals Elv, through a most magnificent pass; enormous masses of rock, in many places, fallen from the mountains above, add to the terrific grandeur of the scenery and one of the wildest districts in Norway is now entered, abounding in legend and romance. About midway to Hæg the road crosses the torrent, and soon after the S. road from Christiania, Route 22, is passed on the left.

*† *Hæg i Lærdal*, 1, pay for 1½; a fine waterfall near the station. On leaving here, caution the man who accompanies you on the stage from hence to stop at Borgund. The road continues rapidly to descend, the torrent thundering close alongside all the way. The falls and cascades which this stream makes between the Fille-Fjeld and the Sögne Fjord are most numerous, and afford fine subjects for the sketcher who delights in this kind of scenery. Some of the peasants' cottages are particularly picturesque. They are built of solid trees on foundations of rock, generally one story high; when more than that a gallery is made outside. The roofs are constructed with planks overlaid with birch bark, and then covered all over with turf. The vegetation upon these roofs is very luxuriant, birch and alder are commonly seen growing upon them; and they are favourite browsing spots for the goats. Shortly before reaching the next station, the church of *Borgund* is seen below the road a short distance off it to the left. It is one of the two oldest buildings in Norway, and should not be passed unseen. The keys are kept at the clergyman's, close by the church. This most singular and interesting edifice "seems to have been built in the 11th or 12th century, for the arches and the apse are semicircular, and it has all the characters of the style of a small German Romanesque church, so far as it can be imitated in wood."—C. T. N. It is of very strange fantastic design with carved wooden pinnacles, giving it almost a Chinese aspect, built of Norwegian pine, and protected from the weather by thick coats of pitch. The nave measures but 39 feet, the circular apse 15 × 54. A low covered way, about 3 feet wide, runs round the exterior of the body of the church. The belfry is of much more recent date, and stands some distance apart. Views of this church will be found in a work called "Ancient Norwegian Churches," recently published at Dresden and Leipsic, from drawings by Professor Dahl. A church somewhat like this

existed near Leirdalsören. It was sold to the King of Prussia, and is now erected in Silesia. See also the church at Hitterdal, near Kongsberg, in Route 23. The old road from Borgund to Leirdalsören was terrific, and several frightful accidents occurred. An admirably constructed series of zigzags now enables the traveller, with reasonable care, to descend the face of the mountain and reach the valley at its foot in safety. The scenery is wildly grand.

* † *Husum i Lærdal*, ⅞, pay for 1⅛. Some very bad hills on this stage. The road keeps the bank of the river almost all the way, and runs through a magnificent pass, at times so narrow that the road is blasted out of the face of the perpendicular rocks. In one place it passes through a cleft in the rock just wide enough to allow a carriage to pass. These rocks distinctly show that this road was formerly the bed of the torrent, which now flows 100 feet beneath, and that some mighty convulsion must have split the mountain ere the stream could have arrived there. In a narrow part of the pass the road is carried across the stream, a great distance above it. The views from this bridge both up and down the pass are very fine.

* † *Blaaflaten i Lærdal*, 1⅞. There is very tolerable accommodation here. The road continues along the stream, which here abounds with salmon. Numerous traps for them are seen, of the rudest and most picturesque kind. Habitations increase as the valley widens, and the land becomes good towards Leirdalsören. Before arriving at the village of Leirdal, a torrent from the south falls into the river, which is soon after crossed for the last time. Many of the bridges on this stream are very picturesque, and truly Norwegian, being entirely constructed of solid pine trees, in the rudest manner.

T. * *Leirdalsören i Lærdal*, 1. Excellent quarters. Everything very clean, and charges reasonable. Though not a fast station, there is seldom much delay in getting a boat-*skyds* to Gudvangen. As this Inn is much frequented, and it is small, beds should, if possible, be ordered a day or two in advance. This is particularly requisite in the latter end of September, when there is a large fair held here, which is attended by most of the peasants of the surrounding districts. Their costumes, particularly those of the women, are highly picturesque.

Leirdalsören is a capital place for head-quarters while making excursions in the neighbourhood, many of which are of the greatest interest. It is a small town, where most things which the traveller may require, such as provisions, &c., can be obtained. Boats may be had for making excursions on the noble Sögne Fjord, and its numerous branches; and guides, for shooting and other excursions in the mountains, where reindeer, as well as bears, are sometimes to be found; and feathered game, including woodcocks, is plentiful. Take nothing with you on an excursion from hence but what you cannot do without; the landlord at the inn will take care of your heavy baggage. Look well to your supply of provender, including some brandy. All present at the death of a bear or deer are entitled to share it equally, therefore make your bargain beforehand with those who accompany you, if you desire that it should be otherwise. And beware of entrusting a second gun, when loaded, to an attendant; promises not to use it will be forgotten if any large game is within shot, and after a long and anxious stalk, just as you are arriving within range of a splendid pair of antlers, a shot from your guide may spoil your sport. Instances of this have happened once or twice to English gentlemen.

Leirdalsören is the best starting-point from whence to visit some of the grandest Alpine scenery in all Norway, *Skagstöltind*, considered for some time to be the highest mountain in Norway, ; but it will be seen from the Amts Karter that *Galdhö-piggen*, in the Ymes Fjeld, is 423 feet higher. *Galdhö-piggen* is 8300 Norse feet above the level of the sea ; *Skagstö'tind*, 7877 ; and *Sneehætten*, 7300. See Viig, in Route 20, and Route 33. Also, the *Justedal* mountains, about 5 Norse miles N.W. of Leirdalsören. Carriages or carrioles must be left here, and the land stages traversed on foot or horseback. The Norwegian horses may be as safely trusted as the Swiss mules.

The *Route to the Hörungerne* is as follows : From *Leirdalsören* to *Solvorn*, 2½ m. by water; *Dosen*, 1½ do.; *Skjolden*, ¾ do. ; *Fortun*, ¼ ; a heavy ride. A bridle road goes hence to † *Röisheim in Lom* parish. The voyage to Skjolden takes from 10 to 12 hours. Vid. p. 186.

The *Glaciers of the Justedal.*—The way there is by water from Leirdalsören to Solvorn, in the *Lyster Fjord*, 2½, and thence on to *Rönneid*, 1½, good quarters; thence to *Myklemyr* in Justedal, 2 m., where horses and a guide to the glacier can be obtained, 2 m. There is a good inn at Rönneid, but dear. A very tolerable bridle-road leads up the valley, and the distance may generally be done in 4 hours, exclusive of stoppages. A guide is not necessary, for when once put in the way, the traveller cannot easily make a mistake. The track is along the bank of the Justedal River, running through the narrow winding valley of that name. Indifferent accommodation may be obtained in Krondal at the foot of the Nygaard Glacier. There is no station, but a lodging at a gaard is generally to be

had. At the Rectory some way lower down the valley the clergyman is most hospitable. "On leaving the Rectory and ascending the magnificent pass there for about 1 mile, you arrive at the finest of the glaciers, Nygaard. It is seen on the left ; and near to the glacier there is a farm where a peasant can be procured to act as guide. I found it impossible to walk on the ice without spiked shoes. The Justedal River flows from the glacier, bringing down with it vast quantities of detritus, which whitens the fjord for about two or three miles from the spot where it flows in. It took me rather more than six hours to ride from the Rectory to the glacier, as well as to inspect it and return. I slept at the Rectory, and rode back to Rönneid the next morning. I was told that the mountains could be traversed from the valley of Justedal to Lomb, on the Vaage Vand, N.E. of Justedal, and that the journey would take one day from the Rectory."—S. C.

The glacier of Nygaard, with a course of less than 4 miles, has a breadth of 1000 or 1100 yards, according to Durocher.

Beyond the Nygaard Glacier, farther up the Justedal Valley, there are other glaciers, and the stupendous mountain of Lodals-Kaabe, 6798 feet high, with its wild dreary scenery, is reached. "The glacier of Lodal is the largest in Norway, its estimated length being 5½ Eng. m., and its greatest breadth above 800 yards. This is Durocher's estimation."—*Forbes' Norway*, p. 224, which see for farther information on the glaciers of Norway. To the artist this region of the Justedal affords numerous subjects of the grandest description of Alpine scenery, many of the peaks of the mountains being covered with perpetual snow. The dwellings of the peasants in this wild region are few, and those of the poorest description.

Bears are often to be found in the neighbourhood of the Justedal, as well as reindeer in the Sögne Fjeld, upon the W., and feathered game is said to be abundant.

Routes from Justedal.—On returning to Rönneid the route can be varied by taking boat to Marifiæren—from thence ride 1 mile to Hillestad, and another to Nögeloien, where one of the steepest hills in Norway was formerly descended, but it is now converted into an excellent road; ½ a mile further, either on horseback or by water, leads to Sögnedalsfiæren, where there is good accommodation at the station-house. From thence back to Leirdalsören is 4¼ m. by water. To Gudvangen 4¾. And down the fjord to Bergen about 16.

Again from Nygaard, a little north of Justedal, a horse-track leads across the mountains to the *Faleidet* station, on the high road between Bergen and Molde, Route 24. Or, from Nygaard another horse-track leads along the bank of a torrent to the N.E., and, after crossing the ridge of the mountain, descends to the north, and passing the Lis Vand leads into a splendid valley, which opens into Gudbrandsdal at Laurgaard, in Route 26. Soon after passing Hörgven, and before coming to the head of the Vaage Vand, another horse-track leads due N. into the grand valley of Romsdalen. See Routes 30 and 38, on the high road to Molde. No one must venture on taking either of these tracks who cannot support fatigue and the roughest food and lodging. Those who can do so will be amply repaid. The following is a description of the scene from the mountains at the head of Justedalen :—

"Never shall I forget the view which then burst upon us; I can only compare it to some of the wildest I have seen of Lapland or Siberia, but it was still wilder and more desolate than those. A precipitous rock, or rather an abrupt mountain side, sunk beneath me, and far below, on my right, was a wide sea-green lake, bordered by snowy ridges and peaks which overhung its waters; and a cluster of small specks in the distance, which my guide told me were a herd of reindeer, added interest to the scene. In front rose the Lodals Kaabe, the loftiest mountain of the range, to a height of many thousand feet, between which and the point where I stood was a ravine filled by a huge glacier, and on my left was the vale of Justedal. The stream which rushes through it issues by cataract from the lake, which is, I believe, called Stug Sö."—*Milford's Norway*, p. 237.

For the *Sögne Fjeld*, see Route 38, from Leirdalsören across these mountains and others to Romsdalen.

The *Söjne Fjord.*—This enormous fjord runs upwards of 120 Eng. m. inland. It has several extensive branches, each of which has its own name; of these the Lyster Fjord and Aardals Fjord, upon the N. of Leirdalsören, offer a variety of interesting excursions to the lover of Alpine scenery; but it requires the exercise of some nerve to trust oneself across the fragile bridges and along the narrow footpaths, with apparently unfathomable abysses and roaring torrents below. Proceeding from Leirdalsören up the Lyster Fjord and its branch,

The *Aardals Fjord*, one of the dreariest mountain defiles is that of the Vettie Gielen. From Aardal you first proceed by the little lake of Aardalsvand about ¾ mile, then through the valleys of Fardal and Svarlemdal. Near Farnda, in the neighbourhood of the farm of Vee, there is a fine waterfall, issuing from Rosdal, a small lateral valley. About ½ a mile farther on is the farm of Jokle, where the stupendous defile, or mountain chasm, named Gielen, commences. Here also there is a considerable waterfall close to the farm. About ¼ mile from Jelde is the little valley of

Afdal, the waters of which, descending from the wild chain of the Hurungerne mountains, precipitate themselves in foaming torrents, forming sometimes a succession of waterfalls, at others extensive rapids. About ¾ mile from Jelde you come to the last farm in the Gielen, called Vettie. From this point excursions may be made to the still wilder scenery around the Jotumfjeld, but these must not be undertaken without an experienced guide.

The *Aurlands Fjord* is another branch of the Sögne Fjord. It lies to the S.W. of Leirdalsören, and separates into two large branches; that to the S.E. leads to the valley of *Flaam* and its waterfall, and is well worthy the attention of the contemplative or artistic tourist. The numerous Bautastones to be met with afford evidence of many well-contested battles having been fought there. Proceeding farther up through Kaardal to the farm of Kleven, you enter the wild and picturesque region of the Sverrestein, through which King Sverre, in the beginning of his reign, effected his hazardous and bold retreat toward Hallingdal and Valders. At Kleven the horse-track up the valley separates: one leads to the S.W., down the valley of the *Randals Elv*, and joins this Route again at Vossevangen station; the other runs across the mountains to the S.W., and commands splendid views over the Hardanger Fjord, the most N.E. branch of which, the *Ouse Fjord*, is reached near the Ouse. This is the most direct way to the Vöring-fos from Leirdalsören.

In the *Outer Sögne Fjord* the scene of "Frithiof's Saga" may be visited. Vangnæs, where good accommodation may be procured, is generally considered to be the Framnæs of the Saga, the birthplace and residence of Frithiof. In calm weather it takes about 8 hours to row from Leirdalsören to Vangnæs in a six-oared boat, and 12 to return. Balestrand is the site of the temple of Baldur, burnt by Frithiof. Near the church of Lekanger there is a Bauta-stone, 21 feet in height, called Baldur's stone. Some point this out as the birthplace of Frithiof.

The Sögne Fjord and its branches abound in waterfalls and cascades; the scenery generally is grand, but sombre. In all the tributary streams there are salmon wherever they can get up. There is good wild-fowl shooting on this fjord. Seals are also frequently seen here.

Route to Bergen continued from Leirdalsören.—A steamer runs from Bergen to Leirdalsören on Tuesdays at 8 P.M., and returns from Leirdalsören on Wednesday mornings. If it be not the steamer's day, those who desire to proceed by water to Bergen must hire a boat at Leirdalsören. There are water stations all the way, and the distance is about 20 Norsk miles. The stations from Leirdalsören are—Frævig in Leganger, 3 m. by water; Feljös, 1¼; Vangnæs, ½; Quamsö, ½; and Kirkebö, 2½, all by water. [From Kirkebö there is a route northwards to Sondfjord, where Route 24 (Bergen to Trondhjem) can be joined. Vadlem, ¾ by water; Sande, 1½ by land; Langeland, 1 ditto, on Route 24.] But if the traveller wishes to go to Bergen he must continue down the fjord from Kirkebö to Leervik, about 2 m., and there join Route 24. The time occupied by the voyage will of course much depend on the wind. At Leirdalsören, as well as all the other water stations in Norway, the boats are under the management of the station-master, so that each boat has its regular turn of duty. Carriages and carrioles have their wheels taken off before being embarked, and the same boat takes the passengers. There is no convenience whatever for embarking and disembarking carriages upon these fjords. With carrioles there is no difficulty, from their being so light, but 4-wheeled carriages occasion much trouble and delay, for fear of accidents in getting them in and out of the boats. Carriages are so seldom used here that the boatmen require much attention to prevent damage being done. These boats are furnished with a large sail; great care should be taken not to allow the sheet to be fixed, but to have it kept in hand, so that it may be let go instantly, as the gusts from the mountains are sudden and dangerous.

The passage to Gudvangen depends upon the wind, and averages from 6 to 12 hours. Look to the provender before starting, as there is nothing to be had *en route*. When sending a Forbud on these long water stages, so much depends on the wind that it is impossible accurately to calculate the time of arrival. The best plan, therefore, is upon the Forbud paper to order the horses to await your arrival, at whatever hour it may be, and state that they will be paid for accordingly. Without this precaution, they would leave as soon as their time was up.

About half-way to Gudvangen, on a bluff to the left, at the mouth of *Aurlands Fjord*, is Fronningen, a small village, at which the crew, if rowing, sometimes pull up to make an attack on their provision boxes. Too much cannot be said in praise of the scenery upon this truly grand fjord—the whole voyage forms a moving panorama of the finest description. In many places the dark mountains rise perpendicularly from the water to an enormous height, upwards of 5000 feet, and are very picturesque in form. Numerous waterfalls are passed, and the atmospheric effects are splendid. About midway up the Aurlands Fjord, a branch of it, the *Nærõens Fjord*, runs to the S.W. (which is our way), and the scenery increases in grandeur as the water narrows towards the head of the fjord. The boatmen will generally stop several hundred yards below the inn at Gudvangen, unless made to row up to it; they expect a gratuity of about 4 or 6 skillings each beyond their fare. The salmon and sea-trout fishing in Aurlands Elv are well spoken of.

* *Gudvangen i Aurland*, 4¾. Comfortable quarters. This place is situated in a very deep and dark narrow valley, closed in by mountains of immense height. Opposite the station, high up the face of the mountain, may be seen the *Keel-fos*, a fall of 2000 feet, but the body of water is small. Good salmon-fishing in the stream up this valley, and shooting in the mountains around.

Those who in coming from Bergen desire to proceed from hence direct to the *Justedal Glaciers* (see Leirdalsören) can do so. The distance by the water stations from hence to Rönneid is 7½ m. And hence to Skjolden, in Route 38, over the *Sögne Fjeld*, is 8 m.

Soon after leaving Gudvangen the road crosses the river, and continues along this most grand and picturesque valley till all further progress is apparently precluded by the mountain which rises abruptly at the head of it. This is, however, ascended by a long series of zigzags. A fine waterfall is passed on the left, and near the end of the stage a torrent is seen to the right, which makes a grand fall at its junction with the Gudvangen stream. The zigzags up this mountain, as well as those on the other side of Leirdalsören, near Borgund, were constructed by a Norwegian officer, Captain Finne, and they are works of which any engineer might be justly proud.

† *Stalheim i Vos*, 1½. Poor accommodation. The view down Nærödal valley from hence is very fine. Some little distance off the road, on the N. from this station, there is another fine waterfall of 1000 feet — the *Sevlefos*. This stage runs on very high ground much broken, and with a good deal of wood and heather, old

trees, and masses of rock, highly picturesque. Good shooting about here.

† *Vinje i Vos*, 1. During all this stage the scenery continues very fine. A lovely stream, near which the road runs all the way, is twice crossed. Just before reaching the next station a fine waterfall of considerable height is seen on the right; the water is separated into two falls, and then split into a succession of smaller ones, forming one of the most picturesque objects of the kind that it is possible to imagine. There is a curious old church close to the station which is worth seeing.

† *Tvinden i Vos*, ⅞. Still a succession of glorious scenery, but the mountains gradually become less wild, and more like Westmoreland. The beautiful Tvinden Foss should not be passed unvisited. Several small lakes are passed on the left, and the road, at length, descends into the lovely valley of the *Rundals Elv*, near the head of the *Vangs Fjord* at

† *Vossevangen i Vos*, 1. Good accommodation at Jersin's Hotel, or at Madame Schlambusch's. This is an excellent resting-place and starting-point, from whence to visit the Hardanger Fjord, and Vöring-fos, the Glaciers of the Folgefond, and the Östud-fos, and from thence going down the fjord to Bergen; or returning here and going on there by this Route. The Vöring-fos lies some distance from the head of the Hardanger Fjord, about 7 m. S.E. of Vossevangen. The Glacier of the Folgefond is about 6 miles nearly due S. of Vossevangen, and half-way down the Hardanger Fjord, on the left bank. The Östud-fos is on the opposite side of the fjord.

The distances by water in making these excursions are so long, and the stages practicable even for carrioles so few, that those who intend returning to Vossevangen will save much time, trouble, and expense, by leaving their heavy baggage and carriage, or carriole, there, and riding the land stages on horseback; the same is advisable even if they should go down the Hardanger Fjord, and return to Vossevangen by the direct road. Take care to replenish the provision basket before leaving Vossevangen.

The *Vöring-fos*.—The road there from Vossevangen is to the S.E. by way of *Vasenden*, 1⅜ m. by land, returning pay for 2¼; *Graven*, ⅛ by water; *Eide*, ⅛ by land. The steamer from Bergen stops here; *Ulvik*, 1⅛. Good station on the Hardanger Fjord. The road from Graven to Ulvik is very hilly, and had best be ridden over. Thence down the Ulvik Fjord, and up Eid Fjord to *Vik*, 1¼ m. by water. This can be done in one day from Vossevangen. The scenery, in a branch of the fjord which ends at Oss, should be explored. About half a mile beyond Vik, the Eid-fjord Vand is crossed to *Sæbö*, from whence the ascent to the Vöring-fos is commenced. From Vik to the Eid-fjord Lake is through a deep valley, shut in by towering mountains. Beyond the lake up to the Vöring-fos the road is only practicable for horses, which may either be taken across in the boat, or obtained, together with a guide (who is *essential*), at Longrei, or Sæbö. In any case much delay will be saved by sending Forbud from Vossevangen to bespeak horses, boats, and guide. From Vik to the fos is about 1¼ Norse mile.

"Some distance from the landing-place on the Eid-fjord Lake, the path becomes rugged, and, bending to the left, proceeds up the wild valley of Symendal, twice crossing in its course the rapid torrent by frail and unstable wooden bridges. It then reaches a very steep acclivity, which is ascended by a rough, winding, zigzag track, in some cases a mere staircase formed by blocks of gneiss, but which is practicable for the horses of the country. On arriving at the summit (probably 800 or 1000 feet above the valley), a moor is traversed for upwards of an Eng. mile, from which a fine view is obtained of the snowy *Normandsjökeln* (on the N.E., 5500 feet high). A deviation is then made to the left of the path, and a few minutes' walk across some marshy moss ground brings the traveller to the left bank of the river, and to the Vöring-fos; but the fall is so deeply seated in a narrow ravine, that the traveller is quite close to it before he is made aware of its proximity by the sound or other circumstances, and a stranger without a guide might possibly search for it in vain. The height of the fall is said to be 900 feet, and the descent of the very considerable body of water seems to be unbroken, but it is a difficult and perilous task to attain a complete view from the dizzy point where the spectator is placed. This point is about 100 or 150 feet above the *top* of the fall, but the cliffs on the opposite side are more than double that elevation above the commencement of the fall; so that if the height be rightly estimated, the precipices on the right bank must be 1100 or 1200 feet above the level of the river immediately beneath the fos. The rocks near the fall are so vertical, that there are no trees whatever on their faces, and it is only at a little distance that the occurrence of ledges on the escarpments admits of a sprinkling of birches. A descent to the bottom, which is a work of time and difficulty, does not repay the labour, as the view of the fall is partially obstructed by a projecting rock."—T. J. T.

The best view of the fall may be obtained from the cliff on the north bank, that is, the opposite side to the usual point of view. To reach this the river must be crossed above the fall, if there is a boat to be met with. There is sometimes one attached to a sæter.

Mr. Elliott, in speaking of the Vöring-fos, says, "The river falls perpendicularly, without a single contact with the rock, 900 feet into a valley scarcely broader than itself. The body of water is, perhaps, equal to that of the Handek in Switzerland. It is the highest waterfall in Europe (except that of Gavernie in the Pyrenees), and the *Lion* of Norway."—*Letters from the North of Europe.*

Mr. Everest visited this fall in the middle of March. He says, "It was now falling within a case of ice. Opposite the spot where I was standing extended a broad framework of icicles, reaching from the top to the bottom. It could not be less than 1000 feet high, green and glittering."—*Journey through Norway*, p. 257.

There are two other grand falls, which are scarcely known to tourists; they are a little to the N. of the Vöring-fos, namely, the *Skyttie-fos*, 700 feet high, and the *Rembledals-fos.* A small ridge of mountain lies between each of these falls. The streams from the last two unite, and flowing down Simedal enter the N.E. part of the Eid Fjord.

The time occupied in going from Vik to the Vöring-fos and returning must very much depend on the amount of fatigue the traveller can endure. For a good walker 3½ or 4 hours are sufficient to go in, and the same to return. The accommodation at Vik is not particularly good.

On returning from the falls, the way may be varied by making a détour to the S.E., ascending the mountains and returning to the Eid Fjords Vand by the valley of Hielmöe, where there are several smaller but beautiful waterfalls.

The *Vöring-fos to the Riukan-fos.* See the latter in Route 23.

The *Östud-fos* is in Steindalen, near the village of Vikör, on the N. side of the Hardanger Fjord, and opposite the range of the Folge-fond. In going from the Vöring-fos to the Östud-fos, the best plan is to return to Vik, and from thence go down the Hardanger Fjord to Utne, 2 m., and from there to Vikör, 2½. The fall is not far distant from the station. The Östud-fos is one of the most celebrated falls in Norway. "The height of the fall is 700 feet, and the volume of water immense. The water falls perpendicularly 400 feet upon a ridge of the mountain, from whence it foams in cascades over vast pieces of rock into the valley. I stood under the fall, upon a projecting piece of rock, and the mass of water, as it fell over the protruding ridge above, produced a beautiful rainbow. The view of the fjord from the mountain above the fall is splendid."—*MS. Journal*, W. H. B.

In going from the Östud-fos by the nearest way to Bergen, a horse-path leads up Steindalen and across the mountains to the head of Samnanger Fjord, a branch of the Björne Fjord, and, proceeding down these waters, Route 24 is entered at the *Hatvigen* station near Bergen.

The *Glacier of the Folge-fond.*—The ascent can be made either from Jondal, 1 m. from Vikör, on the opposite side of the fjord, or from Bondhuus, in the Morang Fjord, some miles farther down. Horses and guides to the glacier may be obtained either at Jondal, or at Bondhuus; and at the latter comfortable accommodation will be found at the farmhouse of John Bondhuus.

"The Folge-fond is the most important glacier-bearing field of Norway. According to Hertzberg, Smith, and Naumann, the highest portion of the fjeld falls short of 5460 Eng. feet, which seems irreconcilable with the statements of Hertzberg and Von Buch, placing the snow line only 220 feet lower. The dimensions of the snowy and icy surface are irreconcilable with the supposition of so small a height for its supply. There are several small outfalls of ice on the east side, of which the chief is the glacier of Buer, which descends to 1000 feet (according to Captain Biddulph); another, and smaller, is near the hamlet of Moge on the Sör Fjord. But the most majestic outlet by far of the icy surplus is on the south-west, forming the fine glacier of Bondhuus, which descends to within 1120 feet of the sea level."—*Forbes' Norway*, p. 221.

If desirous of crossing the peninsula of the Folge-fond from Bondhuus, go to Övrehuus, and sleep; thence pedestrians with a good guide can cross to Odde (Route 23) on the east side of Sör Fjord, in 4 or 5 m.

The *Hardanger Fjord.*—This unique and magnificent fjord and its branches, in addition to the scenery before described, abounds in cascades and waterfalls. The *salmon-fishing* is good on all the tributary streams to the Hardanger, where the fish can get up. Wild fowl of all kinds abound in the Hardanger Fjord, and woodcock, ptarmigan, &c., in the surrounding mountains. "It is curious here to see the pertinacity with which the skua gull (called in Norwegian tyv-fugl, thief bird) pursues the smaller kind of gull when they have caught a fish, hunt them till they drop it from their beaks, and catch it in mid-air as it falls. The skua gulls always feed in this way: they never fish for themselves."—*MS. Journal*, W. E. C. N. "Some of the best reindeer ground is to be found in the neighbourhood of the Hardanger Fjord, viz., at Vikor, Graven, Ulvik, and Kinservik." Bears are numerous in this Amt. "Properly prepared for the campaign, and able to devote plenty of time to it, the bear-hunter would, I am confident, find the mountains bordering the Hardanger Fjeld a noble field for operations."—*Sport in Norway.*

Route to Bergen continued from Vossevangen.—The road is carried along the N. bank of the Vanga

Vand, which resembles Windermere—the scenery becomes of a softer character, and numbers of waterfalls are seen in the hills, on both sides of the lake.

The road leads down a valley of lovely pastoral character, with mountains gradually rising on either side, and clothed with verdure to their summits; two small lakes are passed on the left, and the road then follows the windings of the *Rundals Elv*, which is here a large and rapid stream, abounding with salmon. It connects the lakes passed with that at Evanger, and eventually enters the Bergen Fjord.

* *Evanger i Vos*, 1¼. The accommodation is good; but the charges too high. It is rare to meet with instances of this description in Norway; here it is probably owing to the influence of rich yachting Englishmen coming from Bergen, and who are so unfair to other travellers as to pay whatever they are charged, and thus spoil the people. This station is beautifully situated at the head of the *Evanger Vand*. There is a delightful walk through the hills, directly opposite the house; the path will be readily found by walking round the head of the lake. Great numbers of salmon are taken about here with nets; this place is a depôt for them when dried; also for pickled herrings. Both are excellent. The Rundals Elv enters the lake close to this station. Trout run large, and are abundant in this stream.

Those who sleep at Evanger and desire to reach Bergen in one day, must start very early in the morning to do so. The time occupied by the journey is uncertain, as so much depends on the wind—under the most favourable circumstances it takes a long day, and, with a 4-wheeled carriage, fully 3 hours more must be allowed than with a carriole, so much time being occupied in getting it in and out of the boats, which is done by the main strength of the boatmen, there not being the slightest convenience for the purpose. Look to the provender you must have with you for the day, as the accommodations *en route* are wretched, except at the next station, Bolstadören.

The Evanger Vand is but a short distance from the most eastern branch of the Bergen Fjord, into which its waters flow: it is small, narrow, and winding, but the mountains around it are very grand—their rocky sides rise almost perpendicularly from the water, while thousands of stunted birch and pine cling wherever there is the smallest hold for their gnarled roots. The slopes of *débris* are occupied as little farms, the mountains above and around, in most cases, being so steep as to preclude all access to them except from the water. These habitations are fearfully dangerous, particularly in the spring, after a severe winter, when avalanches of rock come thundering down the mountains, sweeping everything before them. Instances of this kind have occurred in Norway, where a whole village has been swept away. On arriving at the foot of the lake, if ordered in time, horses will be in readiness for the ¼ m. by land, which forms the rest of this stage. The road is alongside a fine salmon stream, the last portion of the Rundals Elv, and which connects the Evanger Lake with the Bergen Fjord.

* *Bolstadören i Vos*, 1. ¾ by water. Good accommodation: salmon and trout fishing about here well spoken of. Those who are going to Bergen will do well to sleep here instead of at Evanger, as they will be more sure of reaching Bergen in one day. From hence a boat can be taken to Bergen direct, viz., to *Bernarstangen* 3 m. by sea, and thence to Bergen 3 m. The voyage is sometimes made in 8 or 10 hours. Pursuing the land route from Bolstadören, down the Bergen Fjord to the next land station, this

branch of it (the *Bolstad Fjord*) is narrow and winding, but the scenery sublime. No wonder that these dark and fathomless fjords abound in wild legends—they look the paralise of water-spirits. In some parts the mountains literally overhang the water.

Dalseidet i Haus, ¾ by water. When there is floating ice in Bölstad Fjord it is often necessary to go over Tisse Fjeld, about ½ m. Miserable station. It takes about 1 hour to get to

Dale i Haus, ⅞. Wretched quarters. A desolate spot, and not a dwelling to be seen. This stage usually takes six or eight hours, according to the wind. After proceeding down a small branch of the fjord the main line is entered and continued for the rest of the way—the mountains very grand the whole distance, and in numerous places rising quite perpendicularly from the water—the strata of many of them twisted in the most curious way. Numerous waterfalls are passed, some of them on a grand scale. No one can form a just idea of Norwegian scenery without visiting some of the sublime fjords on the west coast. Nothing would be more easy than to construct roads along them, but the cost would be enormous, as they must be chiefly blasted out of the solid rock, and will therefore in all probability never be made. Winter, as before observed, is the season when the natives travel; these fjords and lakes are then frozen, and traversed upon sledges with great rapidity. In the spring, when the ice becomes too thin to bear, it is tremendous work forcing a passage through in a boat, as is sometimes done. The boatmen in Norway pull slowly, but with great steadiness and surprising endurance. The large island of *Osterõen* forms the west side of the fjord, and not a single habitation to be seen upon it for a long distance—here and there a boat is moored; and looking up the mountain, peasants may be seen making hay on small patches of *débris* where the slope is so rapid that a single false step would plunge them into the fjord 1000 feet below them. Goats abound here. The eastern side is thinly scattered with small farms, and looks a fine shooting country. Game is said to be abundnnt. The mountains gradually decrease in height on approaching.

Garnæs i Haus, 2⅛. This stage runs over a fine broken picturesque moorland, with mountains looming in the distance. In fine weather, on the south-east the glaciers of the Folgefond are visible about fifty English miles distant. The scenery on this stage, in some places, much resembles Borrodale and other parts of Cumberland.

Lone, ⅞. Two bad hills on this stage, and, on the whole, an admirable example of the up and down road constructed by the Norwegian farmers, who appear always to prefer going over the crown of a hill instead of along its side. The scenery continues lovely, with bold hills and numerous coppice woods of birch and alder. The first view of Bergen is obtained from a hill about an English mile from the town, and the traveller should pause here to see it. It is beautifully situated, surrounded on three sides by mountains, and the fourth open to the fjord, with islands of lofty hills in the extreme distance. Numbers of neat villas, timber-built, and mostly painted white, are passed before arriving at the old entrance gate of the town.

T. BERGEN, 1⅛. (Here Route 24 round the coast is joined.)—*Inns:* Hôtel Scandinavie (Madame Friis) is very good, but generally full during summer. Rooms with 2 beds, 40 skillings; breakfast, 16 sk. each; dinner, 30; tea, 16. There are, also, several private houses where travellers are received; that said to be most frequented by the English is kept by a Mrs. Sontum; charges about 1 sp. d. per diem for board and lodging. Very comfortable lodgings are to be had at Mr. Pellot's, a confectioner's, at Madame Perreguard's, Skipperborger Hansen, and these houses have the advantage of being cheaper and quieter than the hotels. The Hôtels Scandinavie and du Nord are both on the high ground on the south side of the harbour; and in the street beneath, called the Strandgaden, running parallel with them and the port, is the *post-office;* near to which is the *steam-boat office*, and also the counting-house of Messrs. Alexander Grieg and Son, who act as agents to several of the London bankers, and will cash circular notes and bills drawn on letters of credit. Do not omit replenishing the purse with a stock of *small* money; it is difficult to obtain it except at the Bank, which is only open from 9.30 to 10 in the morning, or at the post-office. Mr. Alexander Grieg is *British Vice-Consul* here, and most kind and obliging to all who seek his advice and aid, which is highly valuable in this little-frequented but magnificent district. Those desiring to meet the steamer here, or at Christiania, should not delay going to the office to ascertain the times of departure, and arranging to leave this place accordingly. Should the office not be open, which it rarely is, except on the day the boat comes in, the manager may generally be found at the Bourse near the office. It travellers land or embark a carriage here, they should personally see to its being properly done, as the people are sadly clumsy, being little used to handle anything heavier than a carriole. There is a crane on the quay, for the use of which, in landing or embarking a carriage, a small fee is payable. Look over carriage and harness, &c., carefully, and have damages repaired. Trust not to others, but see to it personally, as Norsk workmen are slow, and require much looking after to keep them to their work.

Those who land here and want a servant, or to hire or buy a boat, or carriole, will do best in the first instance to apply to Mr. Grieg for his advice on the subject. Advertisements are very cheap, and often save much trouble in finding out what may be wanted. For information as to price of carrioles, &c., see Christiania, and preliminary information, "Modes of Travelling." Carrioles are somewhat cheaper here than at Christiania; horses considerably so.

The city of Bergen was founded in the year 1069 or 1070, by King Olaf Kyrre, who made it the second city in his dominions. Shortly after its foundation, in consequence of the advantageous position of its harbour, and the privileges given to the merchants of the Hanseatic League, who had erected a factory there, it became the first city in the kingdom. This pre-eminence it maintained down to the last few years; its trade is even now greater than that of Christiania: but as that capital, since the separation from Denmark, has become the seat of government, and also of the University, it has rapidly increased in trade and importance, while Bergen has remained almost stationary.

The population of Bergen is about 25,000; prior to the last war it was considerably greater.

Previous to the Calmar Union, Bergen was the theatre of several remarkable events. In the year 1135 King Magnus was taken prisoner in this city, and his eyes put out by Harald Gille, one of the competitors for the throne, who the year following was himself murdered in the same place. In the year 1164 King Magnus Erlingson was crowned here by the papal legate, and in the century following King Hakon and his son were likewise enthroned here. The plague which made such fearful ravages in Norway, first made its appearance in this city. In the years 1600, 1618, 1629, and 1637, Bergen was again visited by this dreadful scourge.* In the year 1665, during the war between England and Holland, the Earl of Sandwich pursued the Dutch under the command of Admiral van Bitter into the harbour of Bergen, but was obliged to retire, the Dutch being protected by the fortifications of the town. Several of the shots fired by the English are still to be seen in the walls of the fortress, the cathedral, and other places.

The English were the first who traded with Bergen; in the year 1217 King Hakon Hakonson concluded a treaty of commerce with England. This treaty is the more remarkable, as it is the first compact of the kind which England entered into with any foreign nation. The English continued to pursue the trade with but indifferent success until the year 1435, when they were driven from Bergen, and a monopoly granted to the Hanseatic League, who formed a large establishment here, and carried on a very prosperous trade until the middle of the last century, when the monopoly was abolished, and the port thrown open to all foreigners. In the year 1763 the last buildings belonging to the Hanseatic League were sold, and from that period the trade, being unfettered, has considerably increased.

The principal trade of Bergen at present is the export of stock-fish (dried cod), oil obtained from the livers of cod, and herrings. The take of fish on the W. coast of Norway may be judged of by the fact that Bergen alone usually exports about 2,000,000 specie dollars' worth of stock-fish; 20,000 barrels of cod-fish oil, divided into first, second, and third qualities; and from 400,000 to 600,000 barrels of herrings, which are chiefly pickled. The stock-fish mostly goes to the ports of the Mediterranean, the herrings to the Baltic, and the cod-fish oil to all parts of Europe. The cod are usually very fat when caught; they are immediately gutted, and the livers thrown into barrels; the oil which gradually rises to the surface is then skimmed off; this is of the first and purest quality, and called "blanc;" it is used for lamp oil and dressing and currying leather, as well as medicinally for consumptive and scrofulous cases; the second and third qualities, brown blanc and brown, are obtained by boiling the refuse, and used exclusively for dressing and currying leather. In the months of March and April, when the large square-rigged yachts (*Jægts*) laden with fish from Loffoden and Finmark arrive, the town presents a busy and animated appearance; the harbour is frequently crowded with from 600 to 700 vessels of 70 to 200 tons burden, besides larger foreign vessels waiting to receive their cargoes from them. There are two great arrivals of these Jægts in Bergen, one in spring, another later in the summer, when 100 or more come in at a time.

There are also some manufactories in the neighbourhood, but they are not of any note.

The fortress of Bergen-huus, which commands the entrance to the harbour, is irregularly constructed. It consists of three bastions and a ravelin towards the town, and three bastions and two batteries towards the sea; it was erected by Olaf Kyrre, the founder of the city, and, previous to the union with Denmark, was the residence of those Norwegian kings who made Bergen their capital. Prior to the introduction of artillery it was considered impregnable. On the opposite side of the harbour there is also a strong fort.

Previous to the Reformation Bergen contained 32 churches and convents;

there now remain but five, the Cathedral, Cross Church (Korskirken), New Church (Nye Kirken), the Hospital Church, and the German or St. Mary's Church; this last is the most ancient, and is spoken of by Snorro as existing in the year 1181; it is also the most interesting. This church is situated near the entrance gate on the N. side of the port, and is distinguished from all the others by its having two towers. The singing there is very good. The altar-piece is of high antiquity, and a very elaborate and fine specimen of the carving of the period at which it was executed. It is probably of Dutch workmanship. There are also several other fine specimens of carving. The font is a flying angel, carved and coloured the size of life, the basin held in the extended hands. This figure is lowered from the roof immediately in front of the altar. The pictures are numerous, but without excellence. The Cathedral is passed on the right on entering the town from Christiania. The Sacrament is administered there every Friday morning; there is much chanting in the service; the priest is dressed in a surplice and large ruff, and wears a rich and highly embroidered scarlet mantle over the surplice, with a large crucifix worked on the back.

The Cathedral school is a handsome new building near the cathedral. The poet Welhaven, and Dahl the artist, are natives of Bergen, and were both educated at this school. Holberg, the dramatist, and Ole Bull were likewise born here. There are also several charitable and scientific institutions in the town. The Hanoverian consul here is said to have a good collection of pictures.

The Gallery of the *Konst-Forening* (Art Union) is at the Cathedral School, and may be seen. It contains several pleasing specimens of native art. The best picture is by Jensen, now residing in Munich. It represents a Norwegian sea king endeavouring to save a Greek lady from being carried off. The figures are of the size of life and most carefully drawn; great truth and force in the expression of the heads, and the colour unusually rich and transparent for a northern artist. There are also some very pleasing landscapes by an artist named Duntze; he resides in Bergen, near the Hôtel du Nord; and those who desire to possess a souvenir of Norwegian scenery cannot do better than to purchase one of his pictures. His prices are very moderate; he excels in winter scenes.

The *Museum* comprises a collection of northern and other antiquities, which have been found in tumuli, chiefly in the neighbourhood of Voss, pictures, and a cabinet of natural history. The most interesting portion of the museum is the small collection of northern antiquities, comprising sepulchral urns, arms, &c. There are likewise some Runic inscriptions in a fine state of preservation, and a collection of about 3000 Norwegian coins, commencing from Hako the Good, son of Harald Harfager, in the 10th century. Hako was educated in England, by King Athelstane, and by his aid obtained possession of the throne of Norway. The lovers of antique furniture will be gratified with the sight of a most elaborately and beautifully carved oak bedstead of Dutch manufacture. Upwards of 200 years since this bedstead was brought to Bergen by a young English couple, just married. They settled here. The husband was unfortunate in trade, and soon after died, leaving his widow enceinte with her first child. Norwegian hearts warmed to the young mourner and her fatherless infant, and when they at length sailed for England the widow gave this only and valued relic of her happy days to a family here who had shown her the greatest kindness. Their descendants presented it to the museum, where it remains a token of British gratitude for Norwegian generosity. The pictures here are, with one or two exceptions, a vile pack of grandly baptised rubbish. It would be "doing the state some service" to burn them all with as little delay as possible; they are a disgrace to the town, and injurious to those who are induced to believe such trash models upon which to form a judgment in the art. The only picture here deserving notice is an elaborate specimen of the Byzantine school of the 11th century. It came from one of the churches in the Sögne Fjord, where it is said to have been placed by one of the sea kings, who brought it from Constantinople. This picture is in 8 compartments, representing the Persian king, Chosroes, carrying off the holy cross from Jerusalem; the Emperor Heraclius attacking and slaying him, recovering the cross, and replacing it on the altar, at which the dead are raised up from their tombs beneath. Considering the great age of the picture, it is in a good state. There is an inscription round each of the compartments.

The cabinet of natural history is somewhat rich in specimens of Norwegian animals and birds, particularly such as are found in the Bergen district; and also some good specimens of fish. Those of the bear and red deer, as well as the extensive tribe of feathered game, merit the sportsman's attention. The amiable and venerable master of the cathedral school, Herr Sagen, takes a great interest in this museum, of which he is a director. He points out with much satisfaction the skeleton of "my old friend," that is, a horse of the best Norwegian breed who served him faithfully for 40 years. In Norway and Sweden the horse generally attains a greater age, and retains his powers of usefulness many years longer, than in England. Pontoppidan, Bishop of Bergen, in 1751, published a folio volume on "The Natural History of Norway;" it was translated and published in London in 1755.

The theatre is somewhat smaller than that of Christiania. Here also the performers are Danes, and the pieces in general selected are those which have been played in the capital.

Bergen is a picturesque little city. The houses are mostly timber-built, painted red and white, each with its water-cask at the door for use in case of fire, from which Bergen, like the other towns, have several times suffered terribly. In 1488, 11 parish churches and the greater part of the town were consumed. One hundred and eighty houses were burnt down in 1855 in the west quarter of the town; and nothing, humanly speaking, saved the rest of the city but the broad market place, beyond which the flames were prevented from spreading. The streets are irregular, but, for the most part, well paved. The harbour is the great object of attraction. The fish market is held there on Wednesdays and Fridays, and should be visited. In point of language it is quite equal to our Billingsgate. Fish forms the principal article of diet here in summer, and it is fine, abundant, and cheap. Mackerel, 3 for an English penny, and a large halibut for 1*s.* 6*d.* In summer the port is usually crowded with vessels; there are generally two or three English yachts. The stock-fish boats from the N., before alluded to, are very quaint and picturesque; they will be readily distinguished by their high prows; the form of these vessels is of great antiquity. So prejudiced are the people who build and navigate these vessels, that they will not make the smallest alteration in their build or rig; they will not even avail themselves of the use of the windlass, and the huge square sail therefore still requires the same power to haul it to the mast-head as it did 1200 years since. They are clinker built, and with great breadth of beam, but are not adapted for sailing, except in smooth water. It has been erroneously stated that these Jægts are perfect models of those used by the old Norsemen in their piratical voyages. "Their *Drage* and *Orm* were long galleys, with one or more banks of oars."—H. D. W. The huge row of warehouses on the N. side of the harbour, several stories high, and running far back, are almost all filled with stock-fish; that is, cod-fish gutted, the head cut off, and dried, without salt. These warehouses once belonged to the Hanseatic merchants. They are very old and curious. Many descendants of these old Germans still live in Bergen, keeping up the language and customs of the fatherland, as much as possible, to this day.

There is a circulating library for native and foreign works, and one or two other good booksellers' shops near the cathedral. Travelling maps and the Government Road-book (Reiseroute) of stations and distances, &c., may be purchased there. The best jewellers' shops are in the Strandgaden; there may be seen the silver buttons and shirt studs worn by the peasants in the Bergen district; and also the crown and ornaments worn by the brides at their weddings. Travellers should endeavour to assist at a Bergen farmer's wedding; it is a highly picturesque and entertaining scene. Immediately the ceremony is over the house is thrown open to all their friends and neighbours, and feasting and dancing are kept up for several days. Each guest brings a present. The bride remains dressed in her crown and ornaments during all the merry-making; the crown is so constructed, that by withdrawing a pin it opens and falls from the head, and the gay doings of the wedding are at length ended by the bride dancing the crown off. Immediately she does so, the music is hushed, and the guests depart. The interiors of many of the peasants' houses in this district are extremely picturesque. The farmers make excellent, but clumsy, rifles, and are, many of them, splendid shots, killing ptarmigan with ball.

Tobacconists' shops are as common in Norway as in Germany. The Norwegians smoke to excess, and the constant use of tobacco in all ways renders some of them as objectionable in their habits as American backwoodsmen. Smoking at night in the streets is not permitted in any of the Norwegian towns.

Just outside the entrance gate by the German church there is a public garden, where an excellent band frequently plays in summer. The views from thence are extensive and beautiful.

There is an old custom still kept up by many families here, and in other parts of Norway, of sprinkling the leaves of trees before the house where a person dies; and the relations and friends of the deceased do the same before theirs.

"Many of the watermen about Bergen have peculiar dresses and customs, and form a class by themselves, like the Claddagh fishermen of Galway. They are called 'streels.' Accurate information about them is a desideratum." — *MS. Journal*, W. E. C. N.

The watchmen in Bergen are armed with a most formidable weapon called "the morning star." It is a globe of brass about the size of an orange (in which are fixed numerous spikes of iron of about ½ an inch long), mounted on a staff of about 4 feet. The Marquis of Waterford, when at Bergen, some years since, was nearly killed by a blow on the head given him by a watchman with his morning star.

The best general view of Bergen perhaps is from the entrance of the harbour. As you steam or sail in the town lies before you in a semicircle at the head of the bay, backed by two rocky cliffs separated from each other by a deep ravine.

Many of the villas about Bergen are beautifully situated, commanding lovely and extensive views; and the walks in the mountains which surround the town are charming. Some of these mountains, of which there are seven, lie quite near to the city, which makes its situation highly picturesque; but the altitude of these mountains, which is upwards of 2000 feet, renders Bergen very subject to rain, so much so, that it is calculated that the wet days here in each year average about 200. There are some horse-chestnut trees near Bergen, I suppose the northernmost place at which they are found; but the climate of Bergen, from its proximity to the sea, is quite mild, when compared with that of the country a very few miles inland.

From Bergen delightful sketching and sporting excursions may be made to the islands on the W. and N.W., as well as to the neighbouring fjords. Boats may be hired for the purpose, as also men who know the coast well, and can be relied upon. Most of the sailors speak a little English. Look well to the provender before starting. The islands abound in wild fowl—feathered game is abundant on some of them; and at times red deer and bears are met with there. The scenery of the outer islands, which are exposed to all the force of the ocean, is exceedingly wild.

The two grandest fjords near here are the Sögne and the Hardanger. The former lies about 7 miles to the N. The Hardanger is some 7 miles South of Bergen. For description of these fjords, and the fine waterfalls, and other objects in this neighbourhood, see previous part of this Route at Leirdalsören and Vossevangen. Also, Routes 23 and 24. Those who have a yacht and a tent with them may roam about these magnificent fjords, and remain wherever sport or scenery may attract them. It is still such comparatively unknown ground, that there is abundant room for enterprising tourists to strike out new routes and discover new beauties in these as well as many other parts of Norway. The costume of the peasant women about the Hardanger Fjord is very picturesque, particularly their Sunday dress, which they will sometimes put on to oblige strangers. Prints of Norwegian costume may be purchased at the booksellers in Bergen, also views of the town.

An *excursion* may be made from Bergen, which will combine the Sögne Fjord and the Justedal Glacier with the Hardanger Fjord and the Folgefond, and which may be done very comfortably within a fortnight. Go by steamer to Leirdalsören in the Sögne Fjord, taking care to arrange your plans to suit the day the steamer goes, thence to Justedal Glacier, visiting the head of the Sögne Fjord (see page 73). Return to Leirdalsören, or Gudvangen; from thence to Vossevangen, as described in this Route.

From *Vossevangen* cross the country to the Hardanger Fjord at Ulvik (see page 82), and across the water to *Vik* at the head of Eids Fjord. From hence the Vöring-fos may be visited. Returning to Vik take boat to *Utne* at the N.E. corner of the Folge-fond promontory.

Utne.—The best quarters in the Hardanger, reasonable charges, and a very central situation. The Folgefond can be ascended from here, by going to Bleyer, in 1 long day, returning to Utne at night. Thus:—boat to Bleyer, 3 hours; ponies and a guide to the glacier, 8 hours there and back; return to Utne, 3 hours. Take the ponies as near as possible to the edge of the snow. Observe the Alpine plants in this elevated region. If, however, you go to Odde at the head of the Sor Fjord, you must sleep there, or at Duttetun (see Route 23).

From Utne to *Vikör*, on the northern shore of the Hardanger, 6 hours by water, near which the Östud-fos should be visited. Here Route 23 may be joined, and Bergen reached in 11 miles; but if the traveller wishes to see the rest of the Hardanger Fjord (and it is well worth it), he should proceed in boat from Vikör first to

Bondhuus, 12 hours, at the head of a small fjord on the western side of the Folge-fond peninsula. The Folge-fond can be ascended from here, and it is better to do so from Bleyer or Odde in the Sör Fjord. From Bondhuus to

Rosendal, 8 hours by water, one of the most beautiful spots in the Hardanger. There is no Inn, but a lodging may generally be obtained. There is a beautiful valley leading up from the fjord, and a waterfall at the head of it; the baronial house is curious, as being one of the few manorial houses now left in Norway. It is a small stone building, erected in 1662. There is also a stone church of the early English architecture, containing the burial vault of the barons of Rosendal. The present owner of Rosendal is their lineal descendant, but bears no title, since the abolition of all titles in 1814. From Rosendal to

Teröen is 4 hours by water. Here the steamer touches, and travellers can proceed either northwards to Bergen, or southwards to Stavanger and Christiansand, as they have made their plans. Care should be taken before leaving Bergen to ascertain the exact time of the steamers calling at Teröen. So much of this excursion is by water, that a carriole would be a useless encumbrance, and it may be doubted if one could travel from Vossevangen to Ulvik. It is therefore better not to buy one, but to trust to the conveyances of the country. Provisions must be taken. The distances are by time, and depend therefore on the wind. At each station, before dismissing your boat, ascertain if another is to be had. If there is none, you must bargain with your former men to be taken on. The boats being seldom watertight, have some sticks or branches put underneath your luggage to keep it out of the wet.

On leaving Bergen.—Remember that towns are scarce in Norway, and, therefore, if going to linger in the country, think well before starting of what you are likely to want, and provide accordingly. Above all, forget not a supply of *small* money. For *Steamers* up and down the coast, which call here, see Route 25.

Those who wish to shorten the journey from Christiania to Bergen can go by rail from Christiania to Eidsvold Terminus, and from thence by steamer to *Gjövig* on the western shore of the Miösen (see Route 26). From Gjövig to

† * *Mustad*, 1¼ by land.

† *Lien*, ½.

† * *Sköien*, 1½. Where this Route is joined, page 72. Passengers can book themselves and their carrioles from Christiania to Gjövig, which will be a saving of expense, and a day gained in time; but they will miss Ringerige, and exchange the wild scenery of the Rands Fjord for the tamer beauties of the Miösen.

ROUTE 22.

BERGEN TO CHRISTIANIA, BY LIERDALSÖREN, THROUGH HALLINGDAL AND HEMSEDAL.

The *South Road.*—Distance 45¼ Norsk m., or 315 Eng. As to sending Forbud papers by the post, see Route 21. After leaving Hœg for Christiania the horses are generally better upon this than upon the North Road, and where the loss of a short time at each station is not an object, a Forbud need not be sent, as the station-masters have horses of their own, which they will usually furnish in about a quarter of an hour, upon being offered the "halvanden;" that is, 32 skillings per horse per mile, as at country fast stations. But this plan, which saves half the price of the Forbud horse, should not be relied upon.

This Route is the same as 21, till arriving at Hæg, where the ascent to the plateau of the Fille-Fjeld begins. There the road branches off to the S.E., and ultimately again joins Route 21 at Vik, about 4½ miles from Christiania. There is much difference of opinion as to the scenery upon this road, some persons considering it finer than that over the Fille-Fjeld, and others not nearly so fine; but however that may be, by following Route 21 to Bergen, making the excursions therein described to the chief objects of interest on the Sögne and Hardanger Fjord, and, returning by this road, the tourist will have traversed some of the grandest scenery in Norway. Or, instead of going direct to Christiania, by diverging from this road (as directed at (p. 95), the silver mines at Kongsberg, the Riukan-fos, and the town of Drammen can be visited *en route*.

From Bergen to Hæg includes 16 stages, 4 of which are by water, in all 20⅜ Norsk m. For particulars of accommodation at the station-houses, and the scenery and excursions on the way there, see Route 21. Do not forget a supply of provender, and plenty of *small* money.

Travellers who wish to go by land from Bergen to Trondhjem can either go by R. 24, or else by R. 22 to † *Hæg;* from † *Hæg* to † *Skoien* by R. 21; from †* *Skoien* to † *Lien i Land*, 1⅜; † *Mustad i Vardal*, ⅞; *T.* † Gjövig, 1¼; † *Stokke i Vardal*, 1; † *Grytestuen i Birid*, 1⅜; *T.* † Lillehammer, 1⅛; vide R. 26.

* † *Hæg to Christiania.*—The first stage is a very long one, through exceedingly wild and grand mountain scenery; a very steep ascent up zigzags great part of the way. At Breistölen half way on this stage the traveller has to rest ½ hr. Soon after leaving Hæg the road crosses the Leirdalsören River, as it comes thundering down from the Fille-Fjeld, and is then carried up the deep valley of a picturesque stream, which flows from the *Eidre Vand.* The highest part of the mountains is attained soon after passing this lake. The scenery here is grand, but of the most desolate character. A small lake is soon passed upon the right. This is the source of the *Hemsedal River*, whose waters flow S.E., and eventually fall into the Drammen Fjord. The road is now carried along the valley, down which the Hemsedal River flows to

* † *Bjöberg i Hemsedal*, 2¼. Pay for 3⅜ going west. Good accommodation. This is a "fast station;" that is, from the 15th of October to the 14th of May, 4 horses, and from the 15th of May to the 15th of October, 6 horses, are kept in readiness for the use of travellers, and for which the additional charge must be paid. On leaving Bjöberg the road rapidly descends; the Hemsedal River being close on the right all the way.

† *Tuff i Hemsedal*, 1⅛. Pay for 2¼, but for 1⅞ going west. Tolerable accommodation. For making out a Forbud on this part of the road from Hæg to Tuff over the Hemsedal Fjeld time must be allowed for the ascent from Hæg to Bjöberg, and vice versâ the traveller coming *from* Christiania must allow for the ascent from Tuff to Bjöberg. Near here on the N.E. is the *Skogshorn* mountain, 5007 feet high. Road still follows the left bank of the Hemsedal River, now become a splendid stream. The scenery along this noble valley is most grand and picturesque, and par-

ticularly so from hence to the village of Gool, beyond the Roe station.

† *Ekre i Hemsedal*, 1¼. From hence a horse-road branches off to the N., through a wild mountainous tract abounding in lakes and torrents, to Thune, on Route 21. Upon this stage the scenery increases in grandeur, and the road, descending tremendous hills, crosses the river near.

† *Löstegaard i Gols*, 1. A short distance from Löstegaard the noble Hallingdal is entered at the village of Gool, and then turns E. Near Gool the Hemsedal River is crossed, close by its confluence with the noble Hallingdals *Elv*, where it makes a splendid fall. The bridge here is worthy of notice. The descent continues very rapid during almost all this and the next stage, the road being near the river all the way.

† *Haftun i Gols*, ¾. Pay for 1¼ going west. Indifferent accommodation. The Hallingdal River is crossed about midway on this stage, to the right bank, down which the road is carried for several stages. From Haftun a road goes to † *Sundre i Aal*, 2¼ (rest ½ hr. at Ellefsmoen), *Neraal*, 1¾; *Hammerböen*, ½.

† *Næs*, 1¼. Good accommodation at Landhandler Meidells. The road here is 556 feet above the sea, and the descent becomes somewhat less rapid. The Hallingdal River flows through the *Bremmen Land*, upon this stage. The scenery continues very fine. About ¾ m. beyond Næs there is a footpath leading up to a farm-house, where a fine view down Hallingdal may be had. In winter the road from Næs to Hamremöen is on the frozen lake, and in summer it may be travelled over in a boat, but this plan is not recommended. If wished, one can go hence by boat to Sorteberg.

† *Islandsrud i Næs*, 1. Bad quarters. Close upon the S. of this place the summit of the *Eggedals Fjeld* is 4230 feet high. This fine range of mountains extends from Næs to Green.

† *Aavestrud i Flaa*, 1½. The road still follows the windings of the stream on its left bank. Soon after leaving Aavestrud the river runs through a small lake, and, on clearing it, flows but a little way farther before it enters the noble Krören Fjord.

* *Gulsvig i Flaa Annex*, 1¾. Good accommodation here; the people particularly civil. The house is some little distance off the road to the left, and is beautifully situated near the head of the fjord, which is only 303 feet above the sea. A steamer runs three times weekly on the Kröderen lake. This is an excellent place to stop at for a few days; the scenery around is very fine; fishing good, and shooting well spoken of. Bears are frequently met with near here. From Gulsvig the road is very hilly; it is carried along the left bank, and commands splendid views over the fjord.

Sorteberg i Krydsherred, 1¾. Pay for 2. A very hilly stage going westwards, requiring nearly 3 hours. When the ice on the Kröderen can be sledged on, which is generally the case from Christmas to the middle of April, travellers going west should order horses to meet at Stavnæsodden instead of Sorteberg.

* *Hamremöen i Krydsherred*, 1¼. Good road, but hilly. House beautifully situated near the Kröderen Fjord, on which a steamer runs daily.

The silver mine at *Kongsberg and the Riukan-fos* can be visited by taking the road which turns to the right, a little distance from Hamremöen, upon this stage, and leads through Haugsund to Kongsberg. The road keeps the bank of the river almost all the way to Haugsund, where it turns S.W. across the country to Kongsberg. Scenery beautiful all the way. The distance from Hamremöen to Kongsberg is 4 stages—viz., † *Præstegaarden*, 1¾; *Krona*, 1; † *Haugsund*, 2¼ (allow ½ hr. to rest at

Bjerndalen); *Kongsberg*, 2. At Haugsund, Route 23 is entered on the way to Kongsberg.

On leaving Hamremöen, after passing the road to Kongsberg on the right, our Route quits the fjord, turns N.E., and becomes very hilly.

* † *Hövland i Lunder*, 1¼. Upon this and great part of the next stage the scenery is fine, and the road turning S.E. leads down the deep valley of the *Sognedals Elv*.

* † *Veme i Hole*, 1.

Hönefos, 1. Road still continues hilly—scenery picturesque. The fine waterfall of *Höne-fos* is passed near the junction of the *Beina Elv* with *Vials Elv*, which flows from the Rands Fjord. On crossing the Vials Elv our route soon after joins the northern road to Bergen, Route 21, at the village of Norderhoug. This village is celebrated in Norwegian annals. In 1716 the Swedes invaded Norway, and a party of about 200 horse were quartered at the priest's house and those adjoining it. He was ill and helpless at the time, but his wife plied the Swedes with drink, and contrived to send one of her servants to advise the officer in command of a small Norwegian force in the neighbourhood, who immediately marched, attacked the Swedes, and took or killed almost all of them. Good trout-fishing.

† *Vik*, 1. From hence to Christiania, as in Route 21. There are only 3 stages, together 4¼. Bear in mind the magnificent views at *Krogkleven* (see p. 71), if not already visited.

ROUTE 23.

CHRISTIANIA TO BERGEN THROUGH DRAMMEN, KONGSBERG, OVER TELLEMARKEN, AND THE HARDANGER.

Distance 55¾ Norsk m., or 388 Eng.

This third route to Bergen cannot be travelled in a carriole farther than Gugaarden, at the foot of the Hougljfjeld. Travellers, therefore, who intend to go to Bergen will do well not to purchase a carriole, but to trust to the conveyances of the country, as far as Gugaarden. From thence to Odde, at the bottom of the Sör Fjord, the journey must be made on foot, or on horseback. If the latter, the traveller will do well to make a bargain at each station, "fjeld miles" being loosely calculated. Passing, as this Route does, through the celebrated districts of Tellemarken and Hardanger, it commands some of the very grandest scenery in Norway, so much so that it is considered by many travellers superior to that over the Fille-Fjeld, Route 21. The valley, before reaching Seljestad, and that of Gronsdale, before reaching Sör Fjord, are sublime, and the views from the fjeld above, before the track descends into them, among the finest in Norway. But these districts are so wild, and so thinly inhabited, that, with the single exception of those at Drammen and Kongsberg, all the station-houses are very inferior, and those in Tellemarken wretched. None but the hardy—those capable of enduring very considerable fatigue and the roughest food and lodging—should follow this road farther than Kongsberg and the Riukan-fos. Tourists prepared to face these difficulties will be most amply rewarded by the grandeur of the scenery, and the picturesque dwellings of the people and their costumes, all which are but rarely seen by any travellers, from the want of good roads and accommodation. To the true lover of nature in her wildest mood, the artist, the angler, and the sportsman, this line of country has very great attractions, which are increased by their freshness as well as their novelty.

Tellemarken begins a few miles W. of Kongsberg; excellent general shooting is to be had in this district, and its large and numerous lakes and their tributaries abound in trout and a variety of other fish.

Look well to Route 21 for hints prior to leaving Christiania; see page 70. After passing Kongsberg, even a carriage or carriole would be an incumbrance and expense, and it will be found much the best plan to perform the land stages on foot or on horseback. A carriole can always be bought in any town when wanted, and horses are easily hired at the mountain stations, as elsewhere. A *diligence* runs between Christiania and Drammen.

As far as Drammen all the stages are "Fast Stations;" that is, horses are kept in readiness; for which an additional sum is payable to that charged at the ordinary stations; see Table under head 6 "Preliminary Information." No Forbud is therefore requisite before Drammen. There is no post going to Bergen by this Route.

On leaving Christiania the road passes close under the new palace, and beautiful views of the fjord are obtained for some distance.

† *Sandvigen*, 1¼.

† *Ramsborg i Asker*, ¾. A Town stage from Christiania: good road. About half way between Christiania and Næs the Bergen Routes, 21 and 22, turn off to the N.W. The road then gradually leaves the fjord and turns S.W. through a hilly country covered with fir in all directions.

† *Gjellebæk i Tranby*, 1¼. Pay for 1¾, but returning for 1¼. Upon this stage Paradise Hill is crowned; from its summit there is a most extensive and splendid view of the valley of the Drammen, the town and the fjord. The road then descends into the highly picturesque valley of the *Leir Elv*, crosses that stream, and soon after joins the bank of the Drammen Fjord, along which it continues into the town.

T. ‡ DRAMMEN, 1¼.—*Inns*: Hôtel Scandinavie is considered the best; besides this, there is the Hôtel d'Angleterre, and one or two others. English spoken at the first two. Drammen is beautifully situated at the mouth of the noble river of that name, at its junction with the fjord. The lakes, torrents, and rivers, which are tributaries to the Drammen, are almost innumerable. Many of them rise in the mountain ranges of the Hardanger, and even farther north. They afford ample occupation for a host of anglers, as they abound in trout. Old Izaak Walton rests beside his loved and lovely "Silver Itchen," whose attractions he so well described. May some lover of the "gentle art" do equal justice to the Norwegian waters. *Salmon* cannot get higher up the river than Haugsund, on account of the *fall* there; in the pool beneath it the best fishing is to be had. Though not in much repute as a salmon stream, the Drammen may be worth trying in the early part of the season.

Drammen contains about 12,000 inhabitants; it is divided into three districts, Bragernæs, Strømsø, and Tangen, and consists principally of one long street, running along each side of the river, and connected by a handsome bridge. The chief trade, like that of all the towns on the eastern coast, consists in the export of timber and deals to France, Holland, and Great Britain, and no less than about 40,000 tons of shipping are annually employed.

From Drammen there is a road to Ringeriget (Route 21), by Nordal, along the Eastern bank of Holsfjord and Tyri Fjord to Sundvolden. The road followed is a very fine specimen of engineering, being in many places built up of solid masonry, for 50 or 60 feet on the side of the fjord. The scenery for 20 or 30 miles is very picturesque, and the *coup-d'œil*, when you first catch sight of the Ringeriget Valley, with its extensive sheets of water, is very striking. From Drammen *to Nordal* on this road is 1¼; to Enger, 1; thence to Sundvolden on Route 21 is 2¼ along the Holsfjord.

From Drammen to Kongsberg there are two roads, one on each bank of the river. Our route is by that on the left bank. It keeps close alongside the stream, through lovely scenery all the way to the next station. A small steamer runs several times a day between Drammen and

†*Haugsund i Eker*, 1¾. (Town stage.) Bad accommodation, though the place is populous for Norway. *To join the Road to Bergen* from hence the road continues up the left bank of the river, which it crosses at Vikersund, above the junction of the Snarum Elv, and then keeps up the valley of that river till it joins Route 22, at *Hamremoen*. For distances, &c., see that Route, p. 95.

Continuing our route from Haugsund, the road crosses the Drammen by a new iron bridge, and, crossing some steep hills, descends into the valley of the *Lauven Elv* shortly before reaching

T. † KONGSBERG, 2. There is a good *Inn* here, kept by Christiansen, near the smelting works. Population about 5000. The town is beautifully situated on the river Lauven, and near it to the W. the *Jonsknuden* mountain rises to an elevation of 3054 feet, from whence the view over Kongsberg and the valley of the Lauven is very fine.

Kongsberg to Skien.

From Kongsberg a road goes S. to Skien, Porsgrund, and Brevig on the Christiania Fjord. The stations are † Tinnœs in Hitterdal, 2½, pay for 3¼ m., resting 1 hour at Jerngruben; thence †Sæm or Lysthuus in Hitterdal, ½ m.; and thence by steamer to Skien. *Another road* by land all the way from Tinnœs is *Söjaarden*, 1½; Farvolden, ¾; Söboden, 1¼; † *Ulefos*, 1⅜, pay for 1⅞; † Bergan, 1¼, pay for 1½; † Fjœrestrand, 1, pay for 1¼; † Skien, ½, pay for ⅝. Total, 7¼ m. From Skien to Porsgrund is about 1 m. farther. A steamer runs on the Nord Sjo every week-day, except Tuesday and Thursday, from Fjœrestrand to Tangen, near Tinnœs, in about 6 hours, generally starting early from Fjœrestrand, and returning the same day. Hoier's Hotel at Skien is very good.

Kongsberg is celebrated for the rich silver mines belonging to the State, which are situated about a mile from the town. Hexahedral cobalt pyrites are also found here. During the last few years these mines have produced a considerable annual profit. By application through the innkeeper to the directors of the mines, a permission to view them is readily obtained.

The church at Kongsberg is a large brick building, and is one of the handsomest in the country. There are also in the town a mint, a manufactory of arms, the government powder-mills, and the smelting works for reducing and refining the silver ore, and manufacturing cobalt, as used in commerce. Specimens of the silver, of the cobalt pyrites, and of the various stages through which they pass, until the exquisite blue used in painting is obtained, can all be purchased here.

"The rock at Kongsberg contains native silver and sulphuret of silver, with copper pyrites, iron pyrites, and blende, disseminated through it; that is to say, in certain ranges of the strata from 1 to 60 fathoms broad. This is called the Fahlbaand. The dip of the strata to the E. is from 50 to 80 degrees. The rock in the whole mountain is mostly gneiss, with layers of mica slate and hornblende slate. The vein does not bear silver when it leaves the Fahlbaand; 100 lbs. of the rock in the Fahlbaand contains never less than ¼ oz. of silver. The veins also become metalliferous as they cease to run parallel with the cleavage of the felspar in the gneiss."—*Everest's Norway*, p. 279. The principal mine is said to have been discovered in 1623 by a peasant boy, named Grosvold. It was first worked in 1624 by Christian IV., and is about half a Norwegian mile from the town on the high road to Tellemarken. On the way to the mines the stamping and roasting houses are passed. The principal entrance to the mines is through a level commenced in 1716 by Frederic V.; this is tolerably broad and lofty, and is nearly 2 English miles in length; from this level you descend by 38 perpendicular ladders, of the average length of 5 fathoms each, a very fatiguing task, and then find yourself at the bottom of the shaft, and are rewarded by the sight of the veins of native silver. From this mine was obtained the famous mass of silver, about 6 feet long, 2 feet broad, and 8 inches thick, which is now in the Museum of Natural History at Copenhagen.

When at Kongsberg, an excursion to that fine waterfall the *Larbrö-fos* should be made. It is about a mile up the Lauven, above the town. The Lauven is a fine-looking salmon stream. See Route 25. A road turns off from Haugsund, the last station, to Ringeriget. From Haugsund to † Krona, 2½, resting ½ hr. at Bjerndalen. Krona is an excellent station; † Hollerud, 1¼; Egge, ½; Hönefos, ½. See Route 22. From hence you can join Route 21 at Vig, crossing Queenbergsund not far from Hönefossen, which in spring and autumn is worthy of a visit, from the great body of water which falls over it.

Kong[illegible] to Numedal. The route to Numed[illegible] as follows:—

To *Sve[illegible]sund*, 1½; *Gjellerud*, ½; * *Rostad[illegible]*; *Stjernæs*, ¾; * *Möjen*, 1½, ferr[illegible] over.

Bjor[illegible]sund and Mornsund. Strö n-sien, 1½, good new road.

**Skjö ine*, 1¾; *Liverud i Opdal*, 1. [From Liverud one can also ride to *Hröiterud i Opdal*, 2; to *Kjö iaas i Dagelien*, 1½.] *Björkeflaaten i Opdal*, 1½; *Flaaten i Opdal*, ¾, principally on horseback.

The scenery in the neighbourhood of Fennebu Fjord is extremely beautiful. Fair accommodation at Opdal, and good opportunities for shooting and fishing. Only a bridle-road from Flaaten.

Kongsberg to the Riukan-fos.

This celebrated waterfall, in itself worth the journey from Christiania, is upon the Maan Elv, which flows from the Mjös Vand into the Tind Sjö. It is a little to the N.W. of the Gousta Fjeld, which lies N.W. by W. of Kongsberg. There are 3 ways from Kongsberg. *First road*, dist. 12 Norsk m., or 84 Eng. By the post road upon this Route, see below, to Tinnæs, 2½, pay for 3½; Lysthnus, ½; Tinoset, 3, at the foot of the *Tind Sjö*. Vide under *second road*. N.B.—It is advisable to take a boat all the way from Tinoset to Haagenæs. From hence the Riukan-fos is about 1 m. more. The best resting-place is Dal, but it is not very good. Dal is frightfully abused by some travellers, and equally lauded by others. The fact is there is a Jomfru of superlative excellence, but all the other people in the house are an awful set. She at times is away, hence the difference of the reception met with. By starting early from the former place, Dal may be reached on the second day from Kongsberg. The two great attractions upon this road to the Riukan-fos are the falls of the river from the Tind Sjö, between Tinnæs and Sœm, and near the latter the interesting antique church of Hitterdal. Provisions should be taken from Kongsberg, and when ladies are of the party plenty of wraps for the water passage on the lake, which usually takes about 5 or 6 hours if the wind be tolerably favourable. To see the Riukan-fos, and ascend the Gousta Fjeld to advantage, 5 days should be allowed for the journey from Kongsberg and back there, but it may be done in 4. In making this excursion, it is essential to send a Forbud, that no time may be lost in waiting for horses or boats, and that the best accommodations may be prepared at the stations, which are miserably poor. *Second road*, dist. 8¾ Norsk m., or 62 Eng. This is the most direct way for *men* to take, "and decidedly the best."—W. West. From Kongsberg, keeping up the river immediately beyond the Laebrö-fos, a by-way leads up the valley of *Jonsdal Elv*, by *Moen*, 1, to * *Bolkesjö*, 2. There is tolerable accommodation here. From the hill above this station there is a fine view of the Gousta Fjeld and the mountains of Tellemarken. Thence *Kopstand i Gransherred*, 1¾; *Tinoset i Gransherred*, 1; *Aasloen i Hofvin*, 1½ by water on Tinsö. Agree at Tinoset for skyts to Sanden; *Sanden i Mæl*, 2 by boat. From Sanden take skyts to Dal, 1, or make an agreement to take you to Riukan and back. *Third road*, dist. 10¼ Norsk m., or 72 Eng. From Kongeberg to Bolkesjö, as in the above way, 3 m. Thence to Folseland, 1¼ (where there is decent accommodation to be had), and Tinoset, 1½. Between these two places there is a ferry to be crossed. Leave carrioles there, and proceed, as in first road to Dal and the Riukan-fos, 5¼. From Bolkesjö one can also take "Skyts" to Graver i Hovind, thence by boat across the lake to Saud, ¾ m. Graver is a clean station. The scenery upon the Tind Sjö is mountainous and grand, and it abounds in waterfalls. Bears are at times found upon its banks, and the general shooting is well spoken of. The difference of level between this lake and that of the Mjös Vand, just above the Riukan-fos, is 1275 feet, which the river Maan therefore descends in the short distance between these two lakes. It is expected that **there will be a steamer** on Tinsöen **this summer.**

Dal. **- The accommodation here is improved, and is the best to be obtained near the Riukan-fos.** At Ingolfslund, 1 Eng. mile **nearer the** fall, it is wretched in the extreme. Dal is therefore the only place to rest at while visiting the grand scenery about here, and where horses and guides, both for the fall and also for the Gousta Fjeld, may be obtained.

The *Riukan-fos.*—"About 5 Eng. m. beyond Dal the path contracts, so as no longer to admit a road by the side of the river, and we began to ascend. Above us were heights and streams roaring down from them; below, the *Maan* foaming over the rocks. Many a waterfall did we pass this day, which in other places would have been a theme of wonder, but was here without a name. At last we saw a light cloud of vapour resting on the side of the hill. The atmosphere around was clear, but it remained stedfast like the spirit of the waters; this was the Riukan (Reeking). We left our horses at a small plot of ground, which afforded room for two or three sheds, and then had more than a mile to go on foot along a goat's track, for the valley had now become nothing more than a great cleft in the rock. We crept forward, however, sometimes on a narrow ledge of the bare slate, nearly perpendicular; at others, clinging to the bushes of birch and fir, till the falling river opened upon us. It comes from the distance tumbling down a slope, and distorted by the rocks that oppose it, till it reaches the spot where they separate, and shoots into the depths below. It appears as fine and fleecy as white wool or cotton; and though the vapour obscures everything near it, yet in looking over the cliff you can discern shoots of foam at the bottom like rockets of water radiating in every direction. A low sound and vibration appear to come from beneath one's feet. As I hung half giddy on the steep, and turned my eyes opposite to the mountain mass that breasted me, its black sides seemingly within a stone's throw, and its snowy head far in the clouds above, my thoughts involuntarily turned to Him at whose bidding it upsprung. I long gazed upon this wonderful scene, which seemed like the end of the world. It still floats before me like a dream."—*Everest's Norway*, p. 30.

Estimates of the height of the Riukan-fos are various; the most probable is about 900 feet. The body of water is very great.

"There is a legend connected with this fall. It is called 'the Mari-Stien'—that path over the mountain, on the brink of the precipice of the Riukan, which even at this day the traveller treads with fear, and which was discovered by a young maiden strong in the courage of love. It was by this path that the beautiful Mary of Westfjordalen went with light and fearless step to meet the friend of her childhood, Ejstein Halfoordsen. But the avarice of her father separated them, and Mary's tears and prayers prevailed upon her lover to fly, to escape the plot formed by a treacherous rival against his life. Years passed, and Mary was firm in her constancy. Her father died; Ejstein had, by his valour and nobleness, made his former enemy his friend; and after their long separation the lovers were to meet again never to be separated. Ejstein hastened by the shortest way, the Mari-Stien, to meet his beloved. Long had she watched for him. She saw him coming, and his name burst from her with a joyful cry. He saw, and rushed to meet her, but fell, and the Riukan whirled him into its foaming depths. For many years after this, a pale form, in whose beautiful eyes a quiet madness spoke, wandered daily on the Mari-Stien, and seemed to talk with some one in the abyss below. There she went till a merciful voice summoned her to joy and rest in the arms of her beloved."—*Frederica Bremer's Strife and Peace, or Scenes in Norway*, p. 17.

The *Gousta Fjeld* may also be conveniently ascended from Dal. The summit is of a singular wedge-like form, the highest point being 5688 feet. The view from this mountain is of enormous extent, particularly towards the E., where the eye ranges over the magnificent district of Ringeriget, as far as Krogkleven, on the Bergen road, Route 21, a distance of 70 Eng. m.

From Dal to Kongsberg.

If returning to Kongsberg, there are two roads by which the route can be varied. First, by taking the horse-track, which leads from Dal up the left bank of the Maan, through Ingolfslund, and Vaa, to Holvik, at the foot of the Mjös Vand; and from there crossing the Maan, and taking another horse-track through the mountains (a long stage of about 2¼ m.), to Foseim, and entering the road to Kongsberg, near *Mælandsmo*, 7 m. from Kongsberg. By this way from Dal to Kongsberg is about 14 m. The *second* is by another horse-track, which crosses the Maan between Dal and Ingolfslund, passes along the foot of the Gousta Fjeld, and then to the E. of several small lakes, through Böen and Oystul, down the valley of the *Skange Elv*, and entering the road to Kongsberg at the *Mossebo* Station, dist. 5¾ m. from Kongsberg (see this Rte.) By this way it is about 11 m. from Dal to Kongsberg.

Dal to Bergen.

From Dal there is a horse-track up the valley to Holvik, across the Maan, and along the end of the S. branch of the *Mjös Vand* to Guardsjord, thence across the *Totak Vand* to Kosthveit, and entering this Route at *Jamsgaard*, 18 m. from Kongsberg; or it is possible to get a boat on the Totak Vand, and proceed up to its head at Odegarden, which is about 1 m. from Gugaarden, 3 m. farther to the West on this road to Bergen. But this route must only be attempted by pedestrians, and they must expect to rough it. It requires two long days to go from Dal to Gagaarden by this route; bad quarters are to be expected, and there is sometimes a difficulty in getting a horse or horses necessary to carry the knapsacks, provisions, &c. In crossing from Holvik to the other branch of the Mjös Vand the track leads over the shoulder of Bosnuten, from the top of which there is one of the most extensive views in Norway. The horizon on the W. and N.W. is bounded by the wall of the Hardanger Fjeld: in the foreground the lovely Mjös Vand winds north-westwards into the heart of the mountains; while to the south a line of peaks extends from Lie Fjeld, on the East, to the hills beyond Vinje on the West. By this route the pedestrian will, perhaps, see more of the real character of the wilds of Tellemarken, than by following the regular track from Kongsberg to Jamsgaard; but he must be prepared for much discomfort, and further, he will miss the church of Hitterdal, though, if he intend to visit the Fille-Fjeld, he may see one of the same character at Borgund. Some time is saved also by not returning to Kongsberg. From Dal to Jamsgaard is about 6½ m.

The *Riukan to the Vöring-fos.*

Those desirous of going the most direct way to Bergen from the Riukan-fos can take the Vöring-fos *en route.* In a direct line it lies about 9 m. N.W. of the Riukan-fos; but the country is so mountainous, and the track consequently so circuitous, that by the following way it is fully 17 N. m., or 119 Eng. The best route, though the longest, is to follow the route from Dal to Bergen (see above).

Let those who take it beware of attempting short cuts, unless so advised by their guide; nothing is more deceptive or dangerous in such a tract and country as this is. After leaving the Tind Sjö there are no regular stations all the way to the Vöring-fos, and the distances between those places where any food or shelter is to be obtained are very long; and when such places are arrived at the accommodations are miserable. It is therefore essential to take food for this journey, and it should only be attempted on horseback. The way from Dal is down the valley of the Maan to the Tind Sjö, and across it to Sjöthveit; or turning off at Mœl near the lake, and keeping round the W. end of it to Mareim, near the village of Tind, and then continuing round the lake to Sjöthveit. From here the track leads through Luraas to Skaalebö up the valley of the *Osboigd Elv.* Continuing from Skaalebö the track crosses the mountains of the *Tessung Fjeld* into the wild valley of the *Björnedals Elv,* on entering which, at Björkeflaaten, our track turns up the valley, and keeps to the W. through Flaaten, and across high table land, barren and desolate, to Nybu, a short distance N. of the *Haarteigen* mountain, 5700 feet high. From Nybu the track keeps to the N.W. through Maurset to the *Vöring-fos.* For description, see page 82.

As this way is very seldom traversed, even by the natives, great care should be taken not to start without a guide who is well acquainted with it. And it should not be attempted except in summer, as the habitations are so wide apart that it would be highly dangerous to be caught in a snow-storm. When snow is upon the ground the tracks are exceedingly difficult to distinguish, even by the most experienced guides, and wolves become very daring. Above all, let those who value their safety in this vast and desert region beware how they attempt to traverse it without *local* guides. Mr. Forester and Captain Biddulph are among the few who have crossed this part of the fjeld, but by a slightly different route. They seem to have taken their departure from the head of Mjös Vand, shaped their course N.N.W. to Normands-Laagen, a desolate lake, near which the highest point seems to have been reached, where the streams began to flow westwards towards Hardanger. They followed one of these down to Eidafjord. This was in 1849. They published an account of their tour on their return, "Forester's Norway in 1848 and 1849." Their route was as follows:—From Dal to Vaagen on the Mjös Vand, 4 m.; Kevenna, a farm at the foot of the Hardanger Fjeld, 4 m.; Laagen Vand, 6 m.; Sæbö, in Eidfjord, 5 m. The Vöring-fos is about 1 m. E. of Sæbö.

The *direct Route to Bergen continued.*—From Kongsberg a road leads down the valley of the Lauven to *Laurvig*, and other towns upon the Christiania Fjord. See Route 24. Our road keeps along the right bank of the river for some distance, and then turns off to the W. up the valley of the *Kauberbergs Elv.* This is a long and very hilly stage. About half way upon it the Tellemarken District is entered, alike famous for its wildness, its poverty, and the picturesque costume and appearance of the peasants, who, with the interiors of their smoke-dried houses, afford a great variety of subjects for the pencil.

† *Tinnæs i Hitterdal*, 2½; pay 3¼, and rest 1 hr. at Jerngruben. A short distance from hence a road is passed on the left, which leads S.E. to the town of *Skien*, see p. 98. The stream from the Tind Sjö is then crossed, which makes some picturesque falls near the road; and the *Hitterdals Vand* is seen upon the left.

• † *Lysthuus i Hitterdal*, ½. Tolerable accommodation here. It is a lovely spot. From hence a by-road leads N. to Bamleköse, 1, and Tinoset, 2. This is the water station at the foot of the Tind Sjö, on the way to the Riukan-fos. From Lysthuus our road keeps W. up the lovely mountain valley, Hitterdal, beside the *Hjerdals Elv.* The village of *Hitterdal* is a short distance from Sœm, on this stage. Examine its most ancient and interesting wooden church. It is one of the oldest in Norway, and of the same period and style as that at Borgund, on the Bergen road, Route 21; and like that it is included in Professor Dahl's work of the ancient Norwegian churches. Mr. Ferguson, in his "Illustrated Handbook of Architecture," page 933, after regretting the destruction of the wooden churches of Saxon and Norman times, says:—"The largest of these now in Norway is that of Hitterdal. It is 84 feet long by 57 across. Its plan is that usual in churches of the age, except that it has a gallery all round on the outside. Its external appearance is very remarkable. It is more like a Chinese pagoda, or some strange creation of the South-Sea Islanders, than the sober production of the same people who built the bold and massive round Gothic edifices of the same age." Mr. Ferguson suggests that the panels may once have been adorned by Runic carving, which, as they decayed, have been replaced by plain timbers, detracting much, of course, from its original appearance.

† *Mossebö*, 1¾. The road still continues up this wild and picturesque valley, with the torrent on the left all the way to the next station. About ½ m. beyond Bamble, the old station ¾ m. from Lysthuus, another by-road is passed on the right, which leads to Tinoset on the Tind Sjö; and still farther on another branch of the same road is also passed. The *Skangs Elv* crosses the road on this stage.

From Mossebö hence a horse-track leads N. to the Gousta Fjeld and Riukan-fos. Our Route still keeps up Hitterdalen.

† *Mælandsmo i Hjertdal*, 1½. A fair station. The scenery throughout this stage is magnificent; the isolated

mountain masses give a peculiar charm to the landscape. A short distance onwards the road crosses the Hjerdals Elv, and then turns S.; soon crosses the *Svarte Elv*, and, after a very hilly stage, descends into the valley of the *Flodals Elv*, near the *Flad Sjö*.

† *Nordgaarden i Sillejord*, 2¼. This place is in the heart of the Tellemarken. "The women of this district wear a red jacket, a black skirt, trimmed at the bottom with yellow, and a short vest, fastened by a ceinture where the jacket ends, and hanging in loose plaits for some inches below. A coloured handkerchief, tied round the head, floats in the air behind. The sides of the stockings are prettily worked, and the shoes are ornamented with large buckles, or star-shaped pieces of leather. The costume of the men is something like that in which Charles XII. is drawn, or that of the combatants in Spanish bull-fights:—a short jacket of some decided colour; a waistcoat striped, and very gaudy; dark breeches, with a streak of red running down both sides, and across the front; worsted stockings well worked; broad embroidered gaiters; large knee-buckles, and shoes embroidered like the women's. Both sexes wear a profusion of silver lace and trinkets upon their persons."—*Elliott's Letters from the North of Europe.*

From Nordgaarden there is a road S.E. to the town of Skien, in Route 24. From Nordgaarden one can also go through Nissedal to Arendal; to † *Moen i Hvideseid*, 1⅝; *Lönnemoen i Vraadal*, 1¼; † *Bakken*, 2; † *Tvedlsand i Nissedal*, 2; *Oi*, 1⅜; *Posser*, 1⅝; *Simonstad*, 1¼; *Mosberg*, ¾; † *Ubergmoen*, ⅞; *Brække*, 1⅛; *Arendal*, 1¼. On leaving Nordgaarden our road again keeps S.W. up a steep valley, with a torrent on the left, and then across the N. end of the *Broke Fjeld*, descending the mountains near the head of the *Rör Fjord*. From Nordgaarden there is a road to the Bandags Vand to † *Moen*, 1⅝; where the steamer on the lake touches. The days from Dal are Monday, Wednesday, and Saturday, reaching Strengen in about 6 hours; the boat returns on Tuesday, Wednesday, and Saturday, corresponding with the boats on the Nord Sjö. The bear and wolf are met with here at times, and a considerable variety of winged game. The lakes about here are large and numerous and the trout fine and abundant.

Berge i Brunkeberg, 1⅜. Another very hilly stage leads across a range of mountains S.W. to the village of Hödalsmo, where it again keeps W. to

Mogen i Hoidalsmo, 1½.—*Excursions to Copper Mines near Valle.*—From Ofte a road leads S. to Trisæt, 1¼, on the magnificent Bandags Vand. The view from Trisæt is splendid. Close by on the west is the church of Laurdal. From hence crossing to the S. bank of the Vand to Bandagslid the road continues over uninteresting country to Lillestuen, 3 m., and Moland on Tyris Vand. Accommodation bad, and horses are difficult to procure on this road. From Lillestuen there is a road to Arendal on Route 24. A horse-track also turns off to the W., and crosses the mountains to Sæterdal, which it enters a little to the N. of Valle, in the neighbourhood of which are some copper mines. By this route in fine weather, some beautiful views are obtained of the wild mountains of Sæterdal and Vatnedal. From Valle a station road runs S. through splendid scenery to the large seaport town of Christiansand, Route 24. From Valle another track leads along the bank of the beautiful Otter River, passing the Roe Vand on the left, through Bylke, and up Vattendalen to Suledals Vand, which is crossed to Gautetun, and our road to Bergen is reached at the Röldal station. This excursion from Mogen to Röldal is about 23 m. From Valle to Bykle the track crosses the celebrated Byklestigen (the Ladder of Bykle), a path formed by logs of wood driven into the rock, and covered with sand. Here the ascent of the Hardanger range commences, but is very gradual.

The *direct Road to Bergen continued.*—From Mogen a horse-track leads N. to the Totak Vand to the Riukan-fos. Proceeding to Bergen our road passes over a steep, desolate mountain to

Sundeli i Vinje, 1¼. From hence another track leads N. to the Totak Vand. Crossing the stream from that lake the road keeps up a steep valley past *Vinje Vand* to

Jamsgaard, 1¼. Here a track between the Borte Vand on the S.W., and the Totak Vand and Riukan-fos on the N.E., crosses. To the W. another track leads towards the Bukn Fjord, on the sea-coast, and the town of Stavanger in Route 24. On leaving Jamsgaard the road leads up a steep and grand mountain valley of the Hardanger range, and the stage ends at the *Grunge Elv*.

Tofsland, 1½. The *Trete Vand* is passed on this stage, and the scenery becomes more and more wild, desolate, and mountainous. The *Venemas Elv* is crossed near

Midtvedt i Haukelid, 1½. Here the post-road ends, and the route is no longer practicable for a carriole. This place lies at the foot of the Houglifjeld. It should be remarked, that in Norway, the name "Hardanger Fjeld," is not known. Hardanger, like Tellemarken, is the name of a district, viz., that tract lying along the eastern bank of the Sör Fjord. A track between the Suledals Vand on the W., and the head of the Mjös Vand on the N.E., crosses here.

The boundary of Tellemarken is passed near the mountain of the *Solfond Nap*, which is seen close upon the N., and the plateau of

The *Houglifjeld* is attained. After crossing this plateau the road rapidly descends into Röldalen, and the stage ends by the lake of that name. The scenery upon this stage is of the wildest character, but the mountains are mostly too round or flat to be very picturesque in outline.

Horre i Rödal, 6. From hence, and also a short distance N., there are bridle-tracks, S.W. to the Hyls Fjord, and on to *Vigedalsören*, where the high road is entered between Stavanger and Bergen, Route 24. The distance from Röldal to Vigedalsören is about 10 m.

Just before Röldal our route leads N. by a steep ascent, and after crossing the ridge on passing a small lake, the road enters the deep picturesque valley down which its waters flow.

Seljestad, 2. The bridle-track from hence keeps down the valley of Grönsdal all the rest of the way to the Sör Fjord. *Skare*, 1 m.

* *Hildal*, 1. From hence the track keeps by the W. bank of the *Sandven Vand* (or the lake may be crossed in a boat, ¾ m., which will save some time), and, passing through the village of Odde, reaches the water station at the head of that splendid arm of the Hardanger, the *Sör Fjord*. The scenery all the way from Röldal here along the deep valley of Grönsdal is of the grandest description, the vast range of the Folge-fond lying on the W., and that of the Hardanger on the E.

* *Bustethun i Odde*, 1. Hence there is a steamer weekly during June and July to Bergen. From thence the ascent may be made to

The *Glacier of the Folge-fond.*—The highest point is between Sauge and Regne Nuten, and is estimated by Professor Esmark to be upwards of 5000 feet above the level of the sea. See Route 21. From hence in clear weather the view is glorious over the Hardanger Fjord and range of mountains to the E. Instead of returning to Odde, the traveller can proceed from Bondhuus on the west side of the glacier down the fjord to the fertile barony of Rosendal, a smiling oasis in the midst of stupendous and barren mountains. It lies to the S.W., near the bank of the Hardanger Fjord.

On quitting Rosendal, and going on to Sandvik 1 m. S., tourists can there embark, and proceed up the fjord to Vikör on the N.W. bank, visit the *Ostud-fos*, and go on to Bergen through Steindalen and Haalanddal. See Route 21.

The *Hardanger Fjord*, see also Route 21. Be provided with some provisions before starting on these long water stages, and a bottle of brandy for the man will facilitate matters.

From *Odde* the scenery down the Sör Fjord is grand in the extreme. The valleys leading from it to the E. abound in fine scenery and picturesque waterfalls. From *Bustethun* to

Helleland, 2. On the E. bank from hence the Voring-fos may be visited, by proceeding to † Vik, 2¾, up the Eid Fjord. See Vossevangen, Route 21.

Continuing down the fjord from Helleland the next station is

* *Utne*, 1, on the W. bank. From *Utne* to † *Vik* is 2 m.; and from *Utne* to † *Hagestad* in Ulvik, 1½; and from *Utne* to *Eide i Graven*, 3 m. From thence, rounding the N.E. foot of the Folge-fond, the Hardanger Fjord is entered; the scenery continues of grand Alpine character to

Vikör, 2½, on the N.W. bank of the Hardanger Fjord: near here is the *Ostud-fos*, see Route 21, which for its height is perhaps the most picturesque of all the great Norwegian falls. From Vikör to

Jondalsören, 1, across the fjord; from here the Glacier of the Folgefond may be ascended; or farther down the same side of the fjord at Bondhuus. From Jondalsören down the fjord the scenery continues most grand, and abounds in waterfalls.

Gjermundshavn, 2.

Huse, 1¼, on the high road from Stavanger to Bergen, Route 24, and only 7 m. from the latter.

ROUTE 24.

CHRISTIANIA TO HAMMERFEST AND THE NORTH CAPE ROUND THE COAST BY LAND.

Distances.

	Norsk.		English.
Christiania to Christiansand	32⅝	or	227
Christiansand to Stavanger	25⅝	,,	177
Stavanger to Bergen .	18⅞	,,	133
Bergen to Molde . .	39⅜	,,	275
Molde to Trondhjem .	20½	,,	143
Trondhjem to the Namsen	18⅞	,,	132
The Namsen to Hammerfest	83⅝	,,	584
Hammerfest to the North Cape	13	,,	91
Totals . .	251⅜		1762

There is now steam communication every week between Christiania and Hammerfest, and this route is little used, except over small portions, where the traveller may wish to disembark from the steamer, and rejoin it again at some other point. The descriptions of the towns are therefore for the most part given in Route 25.

The only carriage to be taken upon this route is the carriole, and even that it would be better to sell at Stavanger if it be intended to pass any time in exploring the scenery upon the Hardanger or Sögne Fjords. When required, another can easily be purchased, either in Bergen or elsewhere. The carriole can be taken in almost any boat, but of course entails additional trouble and expense.

With the exception of those on the E. side of the Christiania Fjord, this route comprises almost all the towns in Norway, and consequently is of much importance to those who may be travelling for commercial objects.

The water stages are numerous, and often very long. Most of the stations upon them are good, particularly N. of Trondhjem; but meat and white bread can but seldom be obtained, except in the towns. The tourist should therefore, if possible, never be without a small supply of provisions—such is the custom of the country. For the water stages a keg of water, with a drinking-cup, waterproof cape, or coat, and stout boots, are essential to comfort. A bottle of brandy and some tobacco as presents to the men occasionally are also advisable.

When sailing, never allow the sheet to be fixed, but always see that it is kept well *in hand*, as squalls from the mountains are frequent, and at times very dangerous, if this be not most strictly attended to. A good supply of *small* money must not be forgotten.

From the town of Frederiksværn to that of Ekersund, and again from the town of Stavanger to the N. Cape (with very few exceptions), there are regular water stations all the way; so that those who desire it may make almost the whole journey in boats. Nearly the whole length of coast from S. to N. is protected by a reef of islands, and it is between them and the mainland that the water stages usually run; the sea being there quite still, however rough it may be outside. Some of these islands are large, and contain red deer. Occasionally a bear may be met with. Quantities of wild-fowl frequent most of them, particularly N. of Trondhjem.

Christiania to *Christiansand.* Dist. 32⅞ Norsk miles, or 227 Eng. From Christiania to *Drammen*, as in Route 23, dist. 4 miles. There are two post stations in Drammen; one on the east side (Bragenæs), and one on the W. (Strømsö), where horses can be ordered.

† *Östre i Sande*, 1. An excellent new road.

† *Revaa i Sande*, ⅞. Good level road. Hence to *Eidsfos Ironworks*, 1 m. From Revna one can go to *Skien* thus: to *Fogstad i Hoff*, 1¼; *Schjerven i Laurdal*, 1⅝; *Hole i Laurdal*, ¾; *Hancvold i Laurdal*, 1¼; *Överbö i Slemdal* (no longer a station), 1⅜; and to *Skien*, 1½.

T. † *Holmestrand*, 1⅛. Hotel, Madame Becker's, well spoken of. This small town is chiefly supported by ship-building. The rocks overhanging the water here are particularly fine: and the birch, beautifully intermingled with the dark fir, gives an agreeable variety to the foliage. From Holmestrand a road goes to Kongsberg thus: to *Fogstad*, 1⅛; *Goveröd*, ½; *Treten*, 1⅜; *Vinæs*, ⅝; *Volden*, 1; *Kongsberg*, 1½. [From Holmestrand a road diverges to Svelvig and Drobak. The stations are—† *Odegaarden*, ⅝ m. by water; † *Svelvig*, 1⅝, hilly stage; † *Klokkerstuen*, ⅞; *Dröbak*, 1½, crossing the fjord from *Slottet i Hurum*. It is, however, far better to go by water to all these places on the fjord by steamer, wherever possible.]

Excursion to Horten. From Holmestrand a road to the E. leads by †*Bruseröd*, ⅝, and †*Horten*, 1½. For description, see Route 25.

From Horten there is a road which joins our route at Fyldpaa by Kjær, 1⅛. Fyldpaa, ⅞. Close to Borre church, between Horten and Kjær, there are several tumuli, dating probably from the period when there was a royal residence there.

Direct Route to the North Cape continued from Holmestrand.

† *Sollerö:l i Undrumsdal*, 1⅜. Rather hilly on leaving Holmestrand.

* † *Fyldpaa i Sem*, ¾. From hence a road S.E. leads to *Tönsberg*, ½ m. This town is beautifully situated, facing S.W., at the head of a small fjord, and, though now of little note, was formerly one of the largest in Norway, and indeed for a long period was the only town in the southern division of the kingdom. Previous to the Calmar union, it possessed 10 churches and monasteries, and a fortified castle called Tönsberghuus.

In the year 1536 it was totally destroyed by fire, and since that period it has been unable to recover its former importance. Of its 10 churches but 1 remains, and scarcely any traces exist of the site of the castle. About half an English mile from Tönsberg is "Jarlsberg," the seat of the Counts Wedel Jarlsberg. It was formerly the property of Count Griffenfeld (Schumacker), the favourite but unpopular minister of Frederic III., who, after long basking in the sunshine of royal favour, was exiled for a period of 18 years to the dreary fortress of Munkholm in the Trondhjem Fjord. The *Vallö Salt Works* are upon the Christiania Fjord, ½ m. from Tönsberg; the steamers for the capital and the districts to the east and west call there.

† *Sörby i Stokke*, ⅞. From this place to Tönsberg, 1½ m.

† *Haukeröd i Sandherred*, 1. On the S. of this place, ½ m. dist., is the little town of *Sandefjord*, which is situated at the head of a deep bay, and has lately risen into the dignity of a bathing-place, being much resorted to during the summer by the inhabitants of Christiania. It is well spoken of for rheumatic complaints.

T. * † LAURVIG, 1¼. There are two respectable hotels here. For description, see Route 25. From Laurvig a road goes to Kongsberg thus: to *Gjone*, 1½; *Odberg*, 1⅛; *Hanevold*, 1; *Hole*, 1¼; *Skjerven*, ¾; *Teeten*, 1¼. See under Holmestrand.

The town of *Frederiksværn* is ⅜ of a mile from Laurvig on the S. *Inns* wretched. This place is a station for the royal fleet, and the seat of the Naval Academy. Many naval officers, with their families, reside here, which makes the society pleasant. "The hills about this town might well make any one a mineralogist. The beautiful crystals of iridescent felspar that shine in them are seen at a distance of several yards."—*Everest's Norway*, p. 23. The view of the town from the water is very picturesque.

Route to the North Cape, continued from Laurvig.—The formation of the coast here renders a considerable détour requisite in this land route. Those who wish to proceed at once to the westward may save some hours and several miles by taking horses to Helgeraaen, 1¼, from thence proceed by boat across the fjord to *Langesund*, ¾, and there again take horses to Udgaarden, 1½. Steamers run from Langesund to Skien, calling at Brevig, and Porsgrund. The next station is at

† *Vasbotten i Bruslangnæs*, ½. Good road from Laurvig.

† *Lanner i Eidanger*, 1¼. From Lanner a road to the N.W. leads into the Bergen road, Route 23, through the town of T. † *Porsgrund*, ½ m. It is a place of some trade, and contains two small churches. The Amtmand (principal civil officer) of the province resides here. On the N.W. of Porsgrund, and on the way to the Bergen road, likewise the town of Skien, ¾. This is the largest town in the province of Bratsberg, and one of the most ancient cities in Norway; the church is a respectable brick building, there are several sawmills in the town, and a considerable export trade to England and France is carried

on. Between Porsgrund and Skien are the ruins of an old Catholic chapel.

From Skien the road passes along the South side of the Nord Sjö, at the head of which the road divides; the right runs through a splendid pine forest, and enters Route 23 near the Tinnæs station, on the way to the celebrated Riukan-fos, or the town of Kongsberg, distant 10½ m. from Skien; the left enters the same Route on the way to Bergen at the Nordgaarden station on the Sillejord Vand. See page 104, Route 23. A steamer runs from Fjærstrand at the South end of Nord Sjö to the North end of Hitterdals Vand, near Tangen, Route 23. There is another steamer on Bandags Vand. The scenery upon the upper part of the Nord Sjö is grand, and the costume and dwellings of the peasants, in that wild part of Tellemarken, are highly picturesque. The fishing and general shooting to be had in Tellemarken are also well spoken of. The trout and other fish are fine and plentiful in the lakes and streams which abound in this district; and the bear, wolf, and a variety of winged game are said to be numerous in the mountains. Some of the peasants are capital shots; they generally use only the rifle; bore very small.

Route to the North Cape, continued from Lanner.

T. †BREVIG, or *Stathelle*, 1⅛. A hilly stage from Lanner. This is a small town built on the point of a promontory in the Langesund Fjord. It contains about 2000 inhabitants. The scenery about here is bold and fine. On leaving this place the fjord is crossed by a ferry of about ⅛ an Eng. m. to the little town of *Stathelle*, from whence a road leads to the small town of *Langesund* at the mouth of the fjord, distant ½ m. From Stathelle the stage continues to

† *Rönholt i Bamble*, 1¼, a very hilly and heavy stage from Stathelle. From Rönholt one can go to T. Kragerõe thus: to *Breviystrand*, ¾ m. by land, and 2 m. by water; the boat should be ordered to meet at Udgaard. Kragerõe is a small place famous for the goodness of its oysters. Near here, in the island of Langõe, there are some iron mines.

† *Tyrand* and *Hægland i Sanikedal*, 3. A very hilly stage from Rönholt. Hence to Kragerõe is 1¾ m.

† *Holte i Gjerestad*, 1¾. Ascent for half of this stage, the rest descent. From hence the small lake of *Gerrestad* is crossed near the Osterriisöer iron-works.

† *Röd i Gjerrstad*, 1¼, pay for 1⅜. Now a tolerably level road; there is a bridge over Holtsund. Close here a road to the East leads to the town of * *Osterriisöer*, 1⅛, pay for 2, or 1 m. by water all the way. This is a small place, and only known as one of the many harbours of refuge on this coast. Continuing from Röl, the next station is

* † *Angelstad i Holt*, 1¼, pay for 1⅜. The first part of the road from Röl is very hilly. At Næs, ⅛ m. W. of this, there are the most valuable iron mines in the country. And on the coast ¾ m. S. is the town of *Tvedestrand*, a little place from whence iron is shipped, which is produced at Næs, ¼ m. From Angelstad to Ubergmoen 1 m., from whence one can proceed to Övre Thelemarken, see p. 104. Continuing from Angelstad the next station is

† *Brække i Östre Möland*, 1¼.

† *Blödekjær*, 1⅛. Hence a road goes to T. ARENDAL, 1 m. See Route 25.

Lærredstredt i Oiest, ⅜. This is only ⅛ of a m. from Arendal.

Bringsværd i Fjære, ⅞. A short distance from hence a road leads S. to the coast at the small town of *Grimstad*, ⅛ m. It has little foreign trade, and is chiefly supported by ship-building. Continuing from Bringsværd, the next station is

Landvig, ⅞. From hence to Grimstad it is also ½ m. by another road E.

† T. *Lillesand*, 1⅝. This place is beautifully situated upon the coast and sheltered from every wind. It was formerly a town of some importance, but is now one of the smallest in Norway, all its trade having been removed to the neighbouring towns of Arendal and Christiansand. There is a good inn kept by Jomfru Guldbrandsen. A short distance from the road, between Tingsaker and this town, on the left, is Moland church, where there is a lofty Runic stone. Continuing from Tingsaker our route quits the coast, and runs inland to

Trede i Birkenæs, 1⅛. An excellent road from Lillesand.

Aabel i Birkenæs, ½, pay for ¾. Near here the *Topdals Elv* is crossed. It was here that Mr. T. W. Lassels, of Liverpool, killed 216 salmon, and rose 465, as related in his published account, between 30th June and 19th July, 1841, weighing 2145 lbs., the largest being 30 lbs. "Salmon go up to Boen Foss. A part of this river is owned by an Englishman. It abounds with fish, but they are generally of small size, and of poor quality."—*Sport in Norway.*

"Tempora mutantur."

The artist will find ample occupation on its banks.

From *Aabel* to *Knarrestad*, ½, whence in summer one can go by steamer to Christiansand.

From Aabel the river is crossed by a new bridge, and the road winds round the Topdals Fjord to

† *Kostöl i Tred*, 1⅜.

T. CHRISTIANSAND, 1⅛. — *Inns*: Ernst's Hotel, Britannia Hotel, and Scandinavia Hotel. For description of Christiansand, see Route 25.

Excursions.—Three miles up the Torrisdals Elv there is a fine fall, *Hel-foss*. The road is along the bank of the river through a grand pass; and the salmon-fishing near Hel-foss is well spoken of. "The fishing on this river belongs to Consul Vildt, a Swiss gentleman, who will probably give leave. A small payment will have to be made. Good fishing at Vigelund, where there is an excellent station."—*Sport in Norway*, p. 61.

To the *Hardanger Fjord*.—From Christiansand the most direct road to this magnificent fjord is through some of the most beautiful scenery in the S. of Norway. But this route must not be taken excepting by those capable, as well as willing, to incur much fatigue and the roughest accommodation at the station-houses, most of which are miserably poor. The road leads N. through Sætersdal by a succession of lakes and rivers, and passes numerous waterfalls and cascades. As carrioles can only be taken part of the way, that is, to Ryssestad, or Rige, it would be the best and cheapest plan to make the journey on horseback.

The distance to the Hardanger Fjord is 34 m.

The stations are from Christiansand to—

Mosby, 1 mile.

Hommoen, 1⅛.

Raiersdal, 1.

Hegeland, 1¼.

Moi, 1⅛. Heavy road.

Fahret, ⅞.

Guldsmedmoen, 1⅛. Here you cross the Otteraaen.

Langerak, 1.

Aakhuus, 1⅜. Heavy road.

Froisnæs, 1⅛. Here you again cross the Otteraaen by a new bridge.

Langeeid, 1⅛.

Ryssestad, 1¼. Between these stages you again cross the Otteraaen to

Rige, 1⅜.

Biorneraae, 2⅛. The last stage you have to leave your carriole, and take to the saddle, as there is only a riding road. A few years ago some copper mines were being worked in Sæterdal, which are said to have been productive, and to have been discontinued solely on account of difficulties experienced in the reduction of the ores; at any rate, for want of unanimity and capital among the proprietors, the works were discontinued. The best accommodation is at Fabret, Langerak, Fröisnæs, Rige, but at none of them is it over good. If the wind is fair, a water skyds on Kile Fjord or Bygland Fjord saves time. A level road, and uninteresting scenery, till Byggland; thence very fine. From Valle, a horse-path leads to the N.E., to Route 23, at *Ofte*. From Björnerna a horse-path leads to Bykle, 1½; Vatnedal, 2; Breivik, 1; Jordbrekke in Soldal, 3; Gautetun, by land ¼, and by water ½; Botten, 2; and Röldal, 1. Here Route 23 is joined. "It is said that ages ago in the remote past, some Scotch families found their way into Sæterdal; and that in time they became so intermixed with the Sæterdal peasants, that all indication of their foreign extraction became obliterated." . . . "The Sæterdal peasant has an innate horror of water, and washes himself properly only every Christmas."—*Barnard's Sport in Norway.*—Bears are said to be numerous in Sæterdal, while game abounds.

Christiansand to Stavanger.

Dist. 26¾ Norsk m., or about 180 Eng. "The first half of the road, as far as Oldestad (beyond the Eye or Eide Station), is of extraordinary beauty and interest. Here the great Scandinavian chain of mountains dips into the sea, and the road passes it by crossing the valleys and ridges at right angles. As the hills are very rocky, the valleys much interspersed with lakes and arms of the sea, and as the abundant wood is of a more varied character, owing to the milder climate, than is common in these Northern regions, and as all the features of the landscape are of moderate size, there is an endless variety of the most pleasing objects, and the traveller passes for 70 or 80 E. m. through a series of the most charming scenes of rock, wood, and water, which pass before his eyes with a rapidity of succession and prodigality of beauty that would perhaps be difficult to match in Europe.

"The latter half of the road is of a very different character, being for the most part over a wild dreary moor, with little of interest. About Haar the road is actually taken over the sea-beach below the level of the high tides. Towards Stavanger every now and then may be seen one of those large unhewn upright stones which have given so much occupation to antiquaries."—C. T. N.

From *Christiansand*, hilly road, with the exception of the first ½ of a mile. Between Christiansand and the next stage the Sögne River is crossed, in which there is good fishing.

† *Lunde i Sögne*, 1¾. Between this stage and Mandal you are ferried over the Trys Fjord.

† *Vaine i Holme*, 1¾. Hilly road.

T. * † MANDAL, 1¼. The river Mandal flows through the centre of this small town, which is of little note, excepting as a harbour of refuge. The salmon-fishing is spoken well of, and the shooting is also good, black game and woodcocks being abundant.

† *Vigeland i Valle*, 1¼. Tolerable road.

† *Fahret i Lyngdal*, 2¼. From this stage there is a good road to Farsund, 2 m.

Tjomsland i Lyngdal, 1. Between these you cross the bridge that has been thrown over the Lyngdals River, where the ferry formerly was. From this station to the N. a station road leads up the picturesque valley of that river to the head of the *Lynge Vand*. There the station-road ends, but a horse-track continues N. over the mountains to Brokkebod, on the *Baads Vand;* there the track separates, leading to Valle in Sœtersdal on the E., and to the head of Lyse Fjord on the W. The accommodations on this route are rude in the extreme, but it has great attractions for the angler and lover of wild mountainous scenery.

Rörvig i Fedde, 1½. Hilly road. Between this and Fedde you are ferried over Fedde Fjord, ¼ m., for which you pay a Sound due, and not the regular Skydts payment.

Fedde, ½. The Qvinna flows into the fjord ¼ m. N.E. of this place. It affords some good fishing, and fine mountain scenery. There is a station-road up the valley for 2½ miles.

T * *Flekkefjord*, 1¼. Hilly road. A small town, containing about 3000 inhabitants, and carries on a considerable trade. The harbour is good. One can go by boat to this place from Fedde, 1¼ m.

Sirnœs i Bakke, 1¾. Hilly road. About ¼ m. from this station you cross a very pretty chain bridge which has been thrown over the Seri River.

Nysted, or *Moi i Lande*, 1½. Between Sirnœs and Moi one can go by water ¼ m. The road passes the so-called Tronaas. From Nysted there is a road to Soggendal, viz. :—*Midland*, 1½; *Hauge*, 1½; *Soggendal*, 1¼. From Hauge you can go to Egersund, viz.:—*Ougendal*, 1½; *Svanœs*, 1; and *Egersund*, 1.

Eye in Hœskestad, 1¾. Good level road.

Refsland, ¾. Ditto.

Svalestad i Helleland, ¾. Good road. From Svalestad to Egersund it is 1¼ m. From Svalestad you can likewise go by the following road to Stavanger, viz.: † *Birkrim*, 1; † *Bue*, 1¼; *Aalgaard*, 1¼; † *Skeiene*, 1¼; *Stavanger*, 1½. This road, though shorter, is seldom used, as it is very indifferent.

Slettebö i Egersund, 1. Level, good road. From this station it is only ¾ m. to Egersund.

Hegrestad i Egersund, 1. Level, good road, with the exception of a few hills near Tegnsbrid.

Hölleland i Ogne, ¾. Hilly road.

* *Haar i Varhoug*, 1. Level, good road. First-rate night-quarters.

Hobberstad i Varhoug, ¾. Ditto.

Ree i Time, 1½. Ditto.

† *Skeiene i Höylands*, 1¾. Ditto.

T. STAVANGER, 1½. Ditto. 60¾ from Christiania. Good inn kept by Olsen, and by Madame Jespersen.

From Stavanger there are numerous excursions well worth the attention of the traveller. In addition to those exploring the minor branches of the Stavanger Fjord, and their various tributary streams (all having their falls and cascades), by taking boat from Stavanger to Holle, 4 m., and thence up the Lyse Fjord to its head at Lyse, about 4 m., a horse-path leads from thence to Valle in Sœtersdal. (See Christiansand.)

From Stavanger also the grand scenery on the Hardanger Fjord may be explored *en route* to Bergen. The way there is by the water stations, across the vast *Bukke Fjord*, thence to the N.E. up one of its branches, the *Sands Fjord*, and E. to the head of *Hyls Fjord* at Hylen, along Suledals Vand to *Röldal* (page 105, Route 23), and in the immediate vicinity of the finest part of the Hardanger Fjeld. From Stavanger to the Hardanger Fjord by this road is about 19 m. For particulars of the scenery on the Hardanger Fjord, see Routes 21 and 23.

At Hougesund (one of the stations on the coast in going to Bergen by water), the gravestone of Harald Haarfager, the first king of all Norway, may be seen. At least so it is called, and the popular belief here is, that he was buried there. But that such was not the fact appears more than doubtful, as by another account the place of his interment is stated to have been "one of his manors in Drontheim;" and that "near the spot a magnificent heathen temple was erected, which was standing in the days of Snorro."—*Dunham's History of Norway*, &c., vol. i. p. 183, who cites *Harald Harfagre's Saga*, c. 45.

Route to Bergen by open boats.—Those who prefer going on from hence to Bergen by water can do so, and the following are the stations. Dist. 16 m. Fieldöen, 1½: Forresvig, 1¼; * KOPERVIK, 1—this is a very small town on the Island of Karm; * Hougesund, 1 (mentioned above as to King Harald Haarfager); Lyngholmen, 1¼; Tjernagelen, 1; * Mosterhavn, 1; * Folgeröen, 1; Engersund, 1; Bækkervigen, 1; Ostre Hagholm, 1; Bukken, 1½; Bergen, 2.

Stavanger to Bergen.

There are so many water stations on this route, and so little that is interesting by the land stages, that the tourist is advised to take the steamer direct to Bergen. But failing to meet it, and continuing by the *land* route, dist. 18¾ Norsk m. (10¼ of which are by water), or 133 Eng., the first 6 stages are by water.

Gangenæs, 1; on the large island of *Rennisöe*.

Judeberget, 1; on the island of *Findöe*.

Ramsvig i Sternerö.

Nerstrand, 1.

Vigedalsoen, 1¾.

Træd, ¼. From hence the next 3 stages are by land.

* *Ölen*, ¾. At the head of the *Ölen Fjord*. From this and the two next stages there are water stations all the way, should it be desired not to continue the land journey. From *Ölen* there is a new road to Hougesund—viz., to *Smedevig*, 1½; *Hvidenæs*, 1¼; *Hougesund*, 1¾.

Etneöen i Etne, 1; or by water, 1. The road from *Ölen* is heavy.

Lecknæs, ¾ by land, pay for 1¾; by boat 2 m. From hence the mouth of the *Mattre Fjord* (a branch of the Bommel Fjord) is crossed.

Excursion to the Hardanger Fjord.—From the Mattre Fjord that of the *Aakre* branches off and winds away to the N.E., amongst the snow-clad mountains of the *Folge-fond*. The scenery becomes very grand towards the head of the Akre Fjord, near Fjœre, from whence a horse-track leads to *Seljestad*, on the way to the Hardanger Fjord; Route 23. Those desirous of taking this wild route had better proceed to the next station (Ölfernæs), from whence to Seljestad is about 7 m., and to the Hardanger Fjord at Odde, 10 m. These routes should not be attempted without a guide. For travellers who are upon this part of the coast, this is the best route for exploring the grand scenery of the Hardanger Fjord, as it enables those who take it to traverse the whole fjord and enter the road to Bergen again at its mouth, without going over any part of the way twice. For particulars of the scenery, see Vossevangen in Route 21, and Odde in Route 23.

The next station is

Olfernæs i Skonevig, ¾. From hence the next 2 stages are by land, round the foot of the Folge-fond.

Vahlen i Eid, ¾.

Helvigen i Kvindherred, 1. (From hence to Bergen there are water stations all the way, should it be desired not to continue the land journey.) This station is on the S. side of the *Hardanger Fjord*, and is a good point from whence to explore its beauties. From here the fjord is crossed to

Huse i Kvindherred, 1¼. Thence by land to

Sundfjord i Strandvig, ¾. From here the *Strande* Fjord is crossed to

Særvold i Strandvig, 1¼. Thence by land to

Ufteitu i Fuse, ½, pay for 1. Here

Björne Fjord, a branch of the Strandle Fjord, is crossed to

Hatrigen i Os, ½; and the next 3 stages into Bergen are by land.

Osören or *Indre Moberg i Os*, ½.

† *Nedre Sandven i Fane*, 1¼.

T. † BERGEN, 1½. For *Inns*, and description of this city, see Route 21.

Excursion to the Sögne Fjord (see Leirdalsören, Route 21). The scenery along the coast, between Bergen and this fjord, is not very picturesque; there the best plan is to follow Route 21 from Bergen to *Leirdalsören*, at the head of the fjord. From thence to visit the Fille-Fjeld, the glaciers of Justedal, &c., and then drop down the fjord, rejoining this route at the *Leervik* station near the coast, or one of the places where the steamer calls to the N. or S. of the entrance of the fjord.

A steamer runs from Bergen to Leirdalsören, on Tuesday evenings, returning on Wednesday mornings.

Bergen to Molde.

Dist. 39⅜ Norsk m., or 275 Eng. This part of the route comprises the most picturesquely grand scenery in the country. The coast scenery upon the line taken by the steamers, between Bergen and Trondhjem, is comparatively very uninteresting to that by land after passing the Sögne Fjord. All who have time, and can bear the fatigue, are therefore strongly advised to take the land route. It is practicable for carrioles, but horseback or foot would spare much trouble, and be preferable, except taking a longer time. There are 15 fjords to be crossed; the scenery upon most of them is superb, and but little known to tourists. They may perhaps be told, even by respectable persons in Bergen, that it is scarcely possible to pass this way, but let them not heed that.

Most of the land stations are poor; some provisions should therefore be taken, and brandy for the boatmen. These men are generally careful and skilful, but, when sailing, the greatest care should be taken never to allow the sheet to be fixed.

There are two modes of getting from Bergen to the N. side of the Sögne Fjord; one entirely by boats, and the other partially by land. Should the wind be fair, the water route will be the best to adopt, as the scenery by land is not only uninteresting, but the roads and stations are wretched. The stages by water are—

Bukken i Sund, 2½; Alveströmmen i Hammer, 2; Kiilströmmen, 2½; Skejerjehavn i Eivendvig, 1½; Sognefest i Eivendvig, 1½; Leervig, 1⅜; in all, 11½ m. Steamer to Leervig will save much trouble.

The stages by the *land* route are—

Rödland i Hammer, ⅜, pay for 1. Heavy road.

Horvig i Hammer, ⅜, pay for 1. Here the *Oster Fjord* is crossed to

Isdaal i Hammer, ½ by water and ½ by road.

Næse i Hosanger, 1⅜. Here a small bay is crossed to

Hundven, ½. The station is some little distance from the landing-place.

Fanebust i Lindaas, 1½. Here the *Mas Fjord* is crossed, and the stage continues by land along the foot of the steep mountains to the *Steens-fjeld* on the E. to

Steene i Evindvig, 1½. ½ m. by road and 1 by water.

Eid (or Elie), ½. Thence by water to

Haveland, 1½.

Rutledal i Brekke, 1. From here the *Sögne Fjord* is crossed to

T. * *Leervig*, 1½, and the scenery becomes magnificent. From hence the next 4 stages are by land, through most grand mountain passes and very fine wild scenery.

Systad i Hyllestad, 1.

Skaar i Hyllestad, 1.

Flekke i Ytre Holmedal, 1½.

Dale i Holmedal, ¾. This station is on the S. side of *Dale Fjord*, the scenery upon which is most beautiful. To the E. the grand range of the *Justedals* mountains is seen. From Dale our route is by water up the fjord to

**Eidevig i Holmedal*, 1¾. There is good accommodation to be had here. From hence the next 4 stages are by land.

Langeland i Holmedal, 1.

Förde i Förde, 1, from Förde to Langeland pay for 1¼. This station is at the head of the *Förde Fjord*, where a fine stream, affording some excellent fishing, falls into it.

From hence our road turns E. up a beautiful valley. Two fine cataracts fall into a small lake passed on the left.

The road continues to wind up the valley through very fine scenery and a splendid forest of pine trees. Rest a quarter of an hour on this stage.

* *Nedrevasenden i Jölster*, 1¾. Good quarters. This station is at the foot of the Jölster Vand, a small but beautiful lake, surrounded by lofty mountains. The stage from here is by water to the head of the lake at

Skei, or *Ovrevasenden*, 1½. The scenery upon this stage is of the grandest description. The road winds through a deep and narrow ravine, in mountains of enormous height, and rising perpendicularly in many places. The *Justedals* range is upon the S.E., the highest parts of which are estimated at 7000 feet. The huge masses of rock fallen from above give a vast air of desolation to the scene up this grand ravine.

Förde i Bredheim, ¾. From hence the *Bredheim Vand* is crossed to

Reed i Bredheim, 1½. This place is charmingly situated amidst splendid scenery. From hence the glaciers of the *Justedals* mountains are visible.

From Reed the road is carried up a very steep ascent, commanding splendid views of the Justedals to the S.E., and of the long-peaked range of the *Lang Fjeld* to the E.

Moldestadt i Bredheim, ½.

* *Udvigen i Indvigen*, 1. Beautifully situated on the margin of the *Indvig Fjord*, the most E. branch of the *Vaags Fjord*. It would amply repay the lover of Alpine scenery to explore the numerous tributary lakes at the head of this grand fjord. The sportsman would have a good chance of finding a bear or two there, besides small game and reindeer in the mountains. From Udvigen the Indvig Fjord is crossed to

Faleidet i Indvigen, 1. Higher up the head of the fjord, from Taaning, a horse-track leads E. through the mountains by Vange Vand into Gudsbrandsdalen, at the *Laurgaard* Station, Route 26. And from Oldören, at the head of this fjord, another horse-track runs S. through some of the wildest country in Norway, by Justedal to the head of the Sögne Fjord at *Leirdalsören*, in Route 21.

From Faleidet, along the coast, the next stage is by land to

Kjosebunden i Horningdals, 1½. The scenery continues to be very wild, and of great beauty and grandeur, during this and the 4 subsequent stages.

Grodaas i Horningdals, ½ by water, or ¾ by land. This station is near the head of the *Horningdals Vand*. Good shooting here. From hence the road winds up a grand valley by a steep ascent to

Haugen, ¾. At the end of this stage the road descends to

Thrunstad i Sunebren, ¾. From this place Aalesund can be reached by another route, perhaps one of the wildest and most picturesque in this part of Norway, by branching off by a cross road to the N.W. to Öie, a wretched station. The road is bad, the most of it being only fit for riding or walking. From Öie across the fjord to Sæbö, a lovely row of ¼ m., and thence down the fjord to *Svartebæk*, 2½ m., and Aalesund, 1 m. The mountain scenery on this route will well repay the trouble.

Hellesylt, ¾. This station is at the head of the most S. branch of the *Stör Fjord*, and close by these is a very grand cascade. Hence one can go by steamer to Aalesund. The scenery upon this fjord is exceedingly fine, and the costume of the peasants about here very picturesque. From hence by water down the fjord to Slyngstad it is 2¼. But there is another route by water to

Ljöen, ½. And thence by land to

Helstad, 1½, and

Slyngstad, ¾. From hence there are stages to Relingden, 2¼, and Sylte, ¼ m., near the head of the N. branch of the Stör Fjord; and from Sylte a horse-path leads across the mountains of the Lang Fjeld to the *Nystuen* Station, in Romsdalen, Route 30.

Continuing down the fjord from Slyngstad the scenery gradually becomes less bold to

Andam i Örskoug, 1¼; thence by road to

* *Söholt*, ¾ by land, on the N. side of the fjord, and an excellent station.

Excursion to Aalesund, from Söholt.—The first stage is partly by water to *Sorte*, 1¼; *Röduet*, 1½.

T. * AALESUND, 1½. This town is small, but very picturesquely situated, and the views from it of the distant peak range of the Lang Fjeld, on the S.E., are exceedingly grand. Although of recent date, this place already carries on a considerable trade with Spain and Italy, chiefly in cod fish. The harbour is admirably sheltered, particularly the inner one, which is quite secure in all weathers. The vessels from hence have adopted the new mode of fishing for cod, invented about 20 years since. Long nets with a large mesh, and about 7 feet deep, are sunk to the bottom of the sea where the cod feed; several of these large nets are joined together; the fish become entangled in the nets, and in this manner 1000 are sometimes taken at a single haul. Good quarters at Spörck's Inn. A steamer goes hence to Hellesyldt and Larsnæs from the beginning of June to the end of December.

The country about here abounds in historical associations connected with the ancient history of Norway and her sea kings, and the legends are numerous and interesting.

About 1 Norsk mile W. of Aalesund is the small island of *Gidskö*, formerly the residence of one of the most powerful families in Norway. The remains of the old family chapel are still visible.

A little to the S. of Aalesund was the Borg, or Castle of *Hrolf Gangr*, or Rollo the Walker, "so called because he was so tall and robust that no Norwegian horse could carry him." He was the conqueror and founder of the Duchy of Normandy, and ancestor of our William the Conqueror. After several years' hostility with the French, their sovereign, Charles the Simple, opened a negotiation with Rollo, which terminated in his embracing Christianity and being baptized as Robert; and thereupon Charles gave him Gisele, his natural daughter, in marriage, and invested him with the Fief and title of Duke of Normandy, A.D. 912. The followers of Robert also embraced Christianity, and settled in Normandy. Upon Robert's investiture, part of the ceremony of the homage to be done by him upon the occasion consisted in his kissing the king's foot. This the herculean conqueror was too proud to do, and was therefore allowed to appoint a deputy, but he proved to be as haughty as his master. Upon Charles raising his foot to be kissed, the bold Norseman raised it still higher, and threw the poor monarch on his back, amidst the suppressed laughter of the assembly.—*Dunham's History of Norway, &c.*, vol. i. p. 311.

The *Steamers* between Christiansund and Trondhjem call here in going both up and down the coast. For the road from Aalesund to the grand valley of *Romsdalen*, see Route 30.

The neighbourhood of Söholt is very picturesque. The road upon this stage crosses the peninsula between Aalesund and Molde.

† *Hellingsgaard*, 1¼. Poor quarters.

* *Vestnæs*, 1. Tolerable accommodation. From hence the Molde Fjord is crossed in about two hours to

T. * MOLDE, 1½. For description of this town, see Route 30, up Romsdalen, which splendid valley should, if, possible, be visited from hence. This is another place of call for the *Steamers* up and down the coast.

Molde to Trondhjem.

Dist. 20 Norsk miles, 140 Eng. Almost all the stations on this route are bad. Provisions must be taken. Nearly the whole of the first 3 stages from hence are along the N. bank of the *Fanne Fjord*, a branch of the Molde, through pleasing scenery, by

* *Lönsæt*, 1. Probably a horse may be hired from Molde to Angvik, 4⅞, which will be a convenience, as the stations are "slow."

Eide, 1. Poor inn. On this stage will be seen a mountain called *Stole*. It is on the S. side of the fjord, of extraordinary form, and said to be about 3000 feet high. — *Everest's Norway*, p. 207. From Eide a road branches off to Christiansund, viz., *Foræth*, ⅞, *Gimnæs*, 1¼, *Christiansund*, 1½, by water; or from Gimnæs to *Fladseth i Fredö*, ⅞, by water, to *Bolgen*, ⅞, by land, *Christiansund*, ½ m. by water.

Istad, ⅞.

Hægeim, 1. From here another road branches off to Christiansund, viz., to *Taarvik*, 3¼, to *Findseth*, 1, where it joins the route from Eide, see above.

T. CHRISTIANSUND, 1⅞. This town is built upon 3 islands, and forms almost a circle round its beautiful landlocked harbour. In entering from the sea, not a vestige of a house is to be seen until the narrow passage between the islands is passed, when this irregularly built town is at once opened up like magic. The three islands are named Kirkeland, Nordland, and Inland, and so irregular is the ground upon them, that scarcely any two houses stand exactly on the same level. They are all of wood, and, as usual, covered with red ochre. The population is about 4000. The trade of the town is fast rising in importance. It consists chiefly of stock-fish exported to Spain and Italy. Fresh fish are also cheap and abundant here—fine cod of about 4 lbs. each for 1*d*. English. The *Steamers* up and down the coast call here. On the S.W. of Christiansund is the large island of *Averöen*, at the N. extremity of which (half a mile distant from Christiansund) is the village of Bremnæs, near which, in the mountain overhanging a farm, there is a remarkable cavern.

Route continued, from *Hægeim*. The scenery again becomes romantic and beautiful, and, towards the end of the stage, the long S. branch of the Saluup Fjord comes in sight. It is called *Tingvold Fjord*, and the scenery upon it is very grand, particularly towards the head, where it penetrates amongst the mountains of the Dovre Fjeld. There also the *Sundals Elv* falls into it. This grand stream takes its rise in the Dovre Fjeld, some miles S. of the celebrated mountain of Sneehætten (Route 26), and throughout its course abounds in falls, cascades, and magnificent scenery; in the lower parts of it the fishing is good.

Angvik, 1, on the W. side of the

fjord. From hence to the head of it at Sundalsören there are 4 stages; in all 3¾ m.; and from thence, up Sundalen, there is a carriage-road to the village of Opdal near the *Övne* (or Aune) station, Route 26. Total distance, Angvik to Övne, 9¾. The shooting in Sundalen and its neighbourhood is fine.

From Angvik the Tingvold Fjord is crossed to

* *Bakken*, ½. This stage is across the hills to

Bolseth, ½. From hence there are two ways; the 1st, and which perhaps is the more preferable for scenery, is by water to * Surendalsören, at the mouth of the *Sura Elv*, 2 miles, and thence by land to Honstad, 1. The second and more direct from Bolseth crosses the

Hals Fjord (another splendid branch of the Salaup Fjord, and abounding in magnificent scenery) by water to

Stangvik, ½. Thence by land to

Aasen, 1¾. Midway on this stage the road enters Surendal at the village of Rannes, and there joins that from Surendalsören. The salmon and trout fishing about here and up this beautiful valley is good.

* *Honstad*, ½.

* *Grammen*, 1¼.

Holte, 1½. Poor inn.

Garberg, 1. About half way on this stage a by and nearer road on the left leads to Trondhjem, and joins our route again at the Fandrem station. The stages upon it are—from Garberg to Langseth, 1; Moe (where there are copper works), 1; by ferry over Ökla Elv and Fandrem, 1. Excellent salmon-fishing at Langseth; but most of the fishing on the Ökla is taken up.

The *Orkla Elv* (which affords tolerable *salmon-fishing* at times) is crossed near

† *Kalstad*, 1½. From hence a station-road runs up the valley of the Orkla, and enters Route 26, near the *Bierkager* station, 3¼ miles dist. See stations there, p. 152. From Kalstad the next station towards Trondhjem is

* † *Gumdal*, 1¾. Pay for 1½. There is a copper mine near here.

* † *Fandrem*, 1½. From hence a station-road leads to the large Island of Hitterem on the N.W., 7½ miles distant. The shooting to be had there is highly spoken of. See environs of Trondhjem. Some steep hills, commanding extensive and beautiful views, are passed upon this and the next stage. From Fandrem the road proceeds by a heavy stage to

* † *Orkedalsören*, ½. Good trout-fishing.

* † *Eli*, 1¼.

† *Saltnæssanden*, 1. There is another road from Fandrem to this place, viz., to † *By*, 1, and † *Saltnæssanden*, 1½. By both routes the stages are heavy. On this stage the *Gula Elv* is crossed by a ferry; the scenery upon this river is very bold and picturesque—the salmon-fishing good; the best is up the stream about Rogstad. Saltnæssanden is upon the S. branch of the Trondhjem Fjord.

Esp, ¾. About midway on this stage our route joins the Christiania road, Route 26. From Esp there is an excellent new road to

TRONDHJEM (or Drontheim), 1½. For inns and description of this city, see Route 26.

Trondhjem to the Namsen and Fiskum-fos.

Dist. 18¾ Norsk miles, or 132 Eng. to Hund at the mouth of the Namsen; 23¾, or 166 Eng. to Fiskumfos. A small steamer plies from Trondhjem to Levanger twice a week throughout the year. Inquiry should be made about this in Trondhjem. From Trondhjem to the North Cape, with very few exceptions, all the stations are good. The next town upon our route is Levanger, about 50

English miles. Leaving Trondhjem on the E. side, the road continues near the S.E. bank of the vast Trondhjem Fjord and its branches, through a rich, fertile, and highly cultivated district, but much broken with hills and masses of rocks. The road very steep in many places. Numerous little landlocked bays are passed, which are highly picturesque. The lateral valleys, each with its river, are fine, and afford ample occupation for the angler. The stages are—

* *Haugan*, 1⅛. The Stordals Elv is crossed by a bridge at Helle. Stordal is the largest of the lateral valleys on this side of the Trondhjem Fjord. It runs about 60 Eng. m. up the country, and its beautiful stream abounds in trout. *Salmon* are also caught in it.

* *Sandfarhuus*, 1⅛. The road from Haugan here is new, and exceedingly good. Travellers going *North* should order horses here, those going to *Trondhjem* at Helle. It was here that in 1612, during the war between Christian IV. of Denmark and Gustavus Adolphus of Sweden, and after having made an ineffectual attempt upon Trondhjem, Colonel Mönnichofen landed with a portion of the Scotch and Dutch troops he had raised for the service of the Swedish King. From hence he marched up this valley without opposition, seized upon and permanently annexed to Sweden the two provinces Jemtelande and Hergedalen; and then moving upon Stockholm, relieved Gustavus Adolphus from a most critical position, and enabled him to arrange advantageous terms of peace with Denmark. The rest of Colonel Mönnichofen's force, led by Colonel Sinclair, landed in Romsdalen, and were destroyed by the peasants in Gudbrandsdalen. (See Route 26.) From Sandfarhuus a station-road leads up the valley, as far as Mœraker Hytte, 4¼ m. [The stations are Björngaard, 1½; Lillefloren, 1½; Reinaa, 1; Mœraker, 1; which is a good-sized village, with some iron-works near the foss.] From Mœraker a horse-path is continued across the mountains into Sweden, near to the station at *Stad*, on the way to Stockholm, Route 64,* and which saves a very considerable distance, instead of going through Levanger, for those who have no carriage.

From Sandfarhuus a very hilly stage leads to

Forbord, 1.

Vordal, 1, pay for 1½. A hilly stage to

* *Hammer*, ¾. Very hilly.

† *Nordre Skjerve*, ⅞.

* *Levanger*, 1. Here the scenery is very lovely. There are very comfortable lodgings in Levanger. This town is built on the E. shore of the *Værdals Fjord*, a branch of the Trondhjem Fjord. In 1846 nearly all the houses were destroyed by fire. It is one of the few towns lying north of the Dovre Fjeld. "The houses," says Mr. Laing, "are remarkably good and clean; the little parlours, the kitchens and pantries, are like those in an English maritime town; but the streets are unpaved and frightfully dirty; horses and carrioles are so general among the country people, that the comfort of the pedestrian is little attended to even in considerable towns, such as Trondhjem; while all that relates to driving, such as bridges, covered drains, and watercourses, is kept in excellent repair even on unfrequented cross roads." The harbour of Levanger is the most sheltered of all the inlets in the eastern coast of the fjord, and is consequently a great place of resort for fishing vessels, and forms "a sort of commercial outport for the trade of Trondhjem." The

* For Routes 60 upwards, see "Handbook for Sweden."

Swedes, too, come across the field in great numbers when the snow has set in, and made the transport of heavy goods practicable in sledges. This fjord affords, in reality, by far the readiest communication with the sea for all the northern parts of Sweden as well as Norway; in addition to being quite as near as the gulf of Bothnia, the fjord is never impeded by ice, and is consequently navigable at all seasons. Two large fairs are held yearly at Levanger, one in December, the other in March; and so fully aware are the Norsemen of the great importance of this situation for commercial purposes, that several of the mercantile companies at Trondhjem have establishments here. Nothing could be more interesting than to witness one of these fairs, held on the very extreme frontier of the civilized world—to see the Laplanders and the natives of Finmark from their unfrequented mountain homes come hither to exchange the produce of the chase for the few luxuries of civilized life of which they know the use or the value.

Some distance from Levanger the road separates; that to the right turns off to Stockholm, Route 33, up the beautiful valley of Værdal, and joins Route 64 at the frontier; ours keeps to the N. across Værdal. Its fine stream, the *Væra Elv*, is passed by a ferry. The fishing in this river is not very good, but the scenery along its banks is lovely. The best trout-fishing is to be had towards the head of Værdal. On this stage the soil becomes very good, and the country less rugged. Cultivation extends in all directions up the country over hill and dale, and luxuriant crops are produced, including hops.

Holme, 1½. Here the Værdals Elv is crossed. From Holme one can also go to Steenkjær, thus:—viz., to *Strömmen*, 1½; *Korsen*, 1; *Steenkjær*, 1. It is a good road, though rather hilly. From hence a road leads E. to the village of *Stiklestad*, which is celebrated in Norwegian history as being the place where St. Olaf was slain in battle, 31st August, 1030. Snorrow gives a different date, which has been proved erroneous. A cross marks the spot where Olaf fell, and the Antiquarian Society have also erected a pillar there. After being raised to the throne upon the express pledge that he would not disturb the people in their civil rights, or interfere with their religion, Olaf subsequently attempted to force Christianity upon them. His tyranny and atrocious conduct to his subjects at length drove them into rebellion, and he was compelled to quit the country upon its invasion by Canute the Great, who was thereupon proclaimed king, A.D. 1028. Aided by forces raised in Sweden, Olaf subsequently attempted to recover the throne of Norway, but was met at this place by the army of Canute, and, after fighting with great bravery, was slain, with most of his kinsmen and followers. Such was the conduct and fate of the man whose remains, when canonized, are stated to have performed all sorts of miracles, and to whose shrine at Trondhjem pilgrims flocked for centuries from all parts of Europe!

The church at Stiklestad is of stone, and very ancient. The entrance gate is a round Saxon arch with peculiar fillet ornaments similar to those in the transept of the cathedral at Trondhjem.

The late king, Bernadotte, visited this place in 1835. What must have been the feelings of this monarch, as he stood on the very spot on which, at the same hour of the same day of the month (3 P.M. 31st August,) 805 years before, King Olaf was slain by his subjects? Bernadotte stood on the little eminence surrounded by the descendants of the very peasants who fought and vanquished that prince; their priest, aged 82, gave the king his blessing on this very spot. In human existence there have been few such incidents. The king was sensible of it, and with peculiar good taste, went first to the mansion of the old priest previous to visiting the spot where King Olaf fell.—*Laing's Norway*, p. 386.

Proceeding from Holme the next stations are—

Röske, 1.

* † *Steenkjær*, 1⅝. There is generally a small steamer plying from here to Trondhjem and back, calling at Levanger, which the traveller will do well to inquire about in Trondhjem. Here the stream from the noble *Snaasen Vand* enters the Trondhjem Fjord, and the salmon-fishing is very good.

Immediately on crossing the river a station-road turns N.E. along the N. bank of the Vand, and enters the road upon the Namsen 9½ m. distant, at the VIE station, some way up the river, and near the best part for angling. The stations on this road are—*Föling*, 1; *Qvam*, 1; *Ryg*, 1; *Hammer*, ⅝; *Sem*, 2 m. by road, or 1¼ by water; *Home*, 2½. Towards the end of this stage the Namsen is crossed by ferry to *Vie*, 1.

The Snaasen Vand is a beautiful lake; it extends nearly 40 Eng. m. from N.E. to S.W., emptying its waters by the Snaasen River into the Trondhjem Fjord. Few persons who have read Victor Hugo's "Hans of Iceland," will be disposed to leave this interesting lake unvisited. Reindeer said to be plentiful hereabouts.

From Steenkjær the country becomes very hilly, with vast forests of splendid pine trees.

Ostvig, 1¼. Upon this stage the last portion of Trondhjem Fjord is passed. A heavy stage to

Elden, 1⅛.

Overgaard, 1, pay for 1⅜. At the end of this stage a small branch of the *Namsen Fjord* is crossed to

Bangsund, 1¼, pay for 2.

* *Spillum*, 1. Here there is a ferry across Bangsund, which, in good weather takes ½ hour. From this place, near the next station, the far-famed *Namsen Elv* is crossed. This and the Alten in Lapland are esteemed the two finest salmon streams in Europe. From this place one can be set over to Namsos, ⅜ m. by land, and ⅛ m. by water over Strömbylden's ferry.

Hund, 1½. Skage ferry across the Namsen is passed. This place is about 1⅜ m. from *Namsös*, where the coasting steamers touch (see Route 25, p. 141), at the mouth of

The Namsen River.

From Hund to Namsös there are two roads, one on the right bank of the river all the way, rather hilly. Another rather longer, but less hilly, which crosses the river below Hund to the left bank, and recrosses it near Namsös. This is certainly an easier road, but no advantage in point of time is gained, owing to the delay at the two ferries.

From Hund up the river a station-road runs parallel with the stream to the N.E. for about a mile, where the road separates; that to the N. continuing to Kongsmoen, at the head of the Folden Fjord, upon the coast. The other continues up the valley of the Namsen, by *Haugan*, 1; *Vie*, 1¼, on the right bank. There is now a good new road to Fosland.

Fosland, 1. At Midtaa, a small stream joins Namsen; the river now turns northwards, through a narrow and picturesque gorge with precipitous banks. The road now climbs a steep shoulder of the hill, obliging the traveller to follow his carriole on foot for about an English mile.

Fiskum, 1¼. This is a small village a short distance from the fos. Here the station-road ends, but from hence a horse-track continues up the rest of the valley, and, crossing the hills, enters that of the Vefsen Elv, terminating at Vefsen upon the coast. The scenery upon this route is in parts very fine, and the falls of the Namsen and some of its tributaries highly picturesque. At Fiskum the height of the fall is about 150 feet, and the body of water is very great.

A camp of Lapps (Laplanders), with their herd of reindeer, may usually be met with on taking a guide and keeping up the valley of the Namsen. The Lapps are a despised race amongst the Norwegians, whose feeling towards them is very much akin to that of the people of the United States to persons of colour.

Mr. Milford's account of his visit to a Lapp camp is graphic and interesting. In the latter end of August, 1841, he left Ekker, upon the Namsen, in company with a schoolmaster, whose duty it was to instruct the Lapps in reading and writing during the summer months. A Lapp guide also accompanied them. Some miles beyond Fiskum-fos there is another splendid fall of the river, and the scenery generally is described as exceedingly wild and grand. After 5 days' journey up the valley they arrived near the camp they were in search of.

"In the evening we crossed some barren mountains; and our guide (the Lapp) desired us not to fire at a pack of ptarmigan which got up close to us, lest we should disturb the reindeer, as he said every moment he expected to find his countrymen. Soon after, as we were walking in single file and keeping perfect silence, he stopped suddenly, and, pointing with his finger, directed our attention to some smoke just seen through the twilight, curling up the side of the opposite hill. The man's manner and attitude were quite dramatic, and we had the satisfaction of feeling that our object was about to be attained. He now tied up his dog, and ran off, evidently much rejoiced at the idea of rejoining his wife and family. He was also anxious to inform his countrymen who we were, and what brought us here, as he had some fear lest they should take alarm, and move off with their herd. He soon returned, and at the same time we saw a large number of reindeer being driven up the valley to their quarters for the night, by a man and a boy, accompanied by a dog, whose occasional bark seemed to keep them under perfect control. Upon our arrival we found the encampment consisted of two circular tents, built of poles joined together in the centre, in the form of a cone, with cloth stretched over them. The door of the larger one was so low and small that we had some difficulty in crawling in. The whole scene was highly picturesque. Each tent was occupied by a Lapp family; every member of which gave us a most kind reception, and, heartily shaking us by the hand, at once offered us a share of their tent. We thankfully accepted their hospitality, and soon found ourselves lying on skins before a large and cheerful fire. The inmates of the tent comprised three generations; namely, a middle-aged man and his wife, with four children and an old grandmother. The tent was made of coarse dark cloth, and the outside of it was covered with turf; around the inside were hung cheeses, bladders, dried gut of reindeer, guns, and various other articles. The chief part of the smoke escaped through a large opening at the top, but enough remained painfully to affect our eyes, and to give the copper countenances of the Lapps a shade as dark as those of Indians. The second family, who occupied the smaller tent, consisted of our late guide, Peter Johansen, his wife, and two children; they soon came to pay us a visit. His wife and daughter had light hair and fair complexions, and were pleasing in appearance. His son, a fine intelligent boy, although under ten years of age, took his turn with the men in watching the reindeer during the night. The little fellow was dressed in his best clothes, entirely made of skins, with a girdle round his waist, and had such a protuberance in front as to give him the appearance of being stuffed, and greatly to excite laughter. He wore his knife in its case behind, and several small ornaments by his side; thus forming a complete Lilliputian Lapp in full costume.

"We were soon presented with a large bowl of reindeer milk, which is much richer than that of the cow, and has a delicate aromatic flavour, resembling the milk of the cocoa-nut; but I found I could not take much of it with impunity, as it was more like drinking cream than milk. They also boiled for us a reindeer ham, which we found so good, that, upon taking our departure next morning, we were glad to add it to our store of provisions. It has a wild flavour, and is quite equal to our park venison.

"The old grandmother was as shrivelled as a mummy, but the other two women were by no means ill-looking. Their dress was of dark woollen cloth, with silver ornaments in front, as well as in the girdle round the waist, to which sewing implements were suspended. These ornaments were in good taste and well finished. This smart costume was put on in compliment to us. The dress of the men consisted of leather coats, and tight trousers of the same material, with reindeer-skin boots. All the females smoked; and the old woman seemed more pleased with having her pipe filled with tobacco from England than with anything else we gave her. Some lucifer matches were also highly prized by them; and they expressed no small astonishment at the manner in which they were ignited. We regretted we had no fish-hooks, which they inquired for. The head of the family (Johan Nielsen) was a grave, sedate-looking man; decision of character and intelligence were marked on his fine countenance. In reply to the questions I put to him through my interpreter, he said they were happy in the enjoyment of their wandering pastoral life; that they confined themselves to the mountainous ridge which separates Norway from Sweden; that they had been in their present encampment eight days, and intended to remain a fortnight longer, when they would move onwards for a change of pasture for the reindeer. He told me that in summer they conduct these animals, which constitute their wealth, to the elevated parts of the mountains, and in the winter to the level country. His herd consisted of about 300, and it appears that a family requires nearly that number for its support. These Lapps, although 'dwellers in tents' all the year round, are in many respects far from being uncivilized. They strictly observe the Sabbath, the best reader of the family officiating as priest, and going regularly through the Lutheran service. Occasionally they attend the church of the nearest village on the frontier of Sweden.

"Our companion, the schoolmaster, is employed by the missionary society, and twice in the course of every summer visits the Lapps for the purpose of instructing them. He stays for three weeks on each occasion, and divides his time between the different families who are encamped many miles apart. This man told me that all the children could read, write, and say their prayers. The Lapps have but few wants, and appear perfectly satisfied; having no bread, they subsist almost entirely on the produce of their herds, with the occasional assistance of fish and game. We saw no other description of food whatever, neither have they any candles; and when we required additional light, one of the women took a firebrand in her hand and held it up for us. On one occasion we wanted to pour some of their delicious milk into our small keg of flakel; in an instant they very ingeniously made a funnel of some of the birch bark which hung round the tent. The sun and stars are their only clock. They had no spirituous liquors of their own making, but it is well known that they are greatly addicted to inebriety, when they go down into the valleys of Sweden or Norway. Both Nielsen and Johannsen were great hunters, and were frequently absent from the encampment for many weeks together, in search of bear, seals, and game.

"It was nearly midnight before our interesting conference was brought to a close. At length Nielsen asked us in a civil, I might almost say in a polite manner, whether we felt disposed to sleep. To this we assented; and when all was quiet, I surveyed with no little interest the scene around me. Our host lit his pipe, by way of a soporific, laid down his head on his hard pillow, and comfortably puffed himself to sleep. One of the children coming in late, the old grandmother lifted up her large reindeer covering, and inclosed the young herdsman within its ample folds. It was a fine night, and we felt no inconvenience either from heat or cold. We were, however, as closely packed in the tent as negroes in a slave ship. I slept soundly notwithstanding.

"We rose at five o'clock, and after breakfasting on the flesh and milk of the reindeer, went up the hill to see the animals themselves. The whole herd was brought together for our inspection; they had sleek skins, and were in the finest condition imaginable, many of their branching antlers being of immense size, and covered with the softest velvet. We were informed that they suffered more from heat than from cold. Neilsen's eldest boy, a fine youth of 16, now threw a species of lasso round the horns of one of the deer, and the process of milking the herd began. They yield a very small quantity of milk, but this is made up for by the richness of its quality. They are remarkably quiet and gentle, and the Lapps are almost as fond of them as of their children.

"After purchasing some skins, horns, and lines which we saw the women making from strips of the sinews of the reindeer, by chewing the ends and twisting one piece on to another till it was of sufficient length, we bade adieu to the Lapps.

"Very little is known of the origin of these honest, simple, and hospitable people; they are considered by some to be descended from aboriginal Norwegians; but by others they are supposed to have sprung from a colony of Finns, although at the present day they are very unlike that race. From the earliest times they have led a nomade life. Their movements, however, are chiefly regulated by the quantity of moss (*Cenomyce rangiferina*) in the different localities essential for their reindeer, and which is more abundant in Sweden than in Norway; but the temperature of the former country is found to be too mild for these animals, who require the bracing air and eternal snows of the latter to preserve their health. The moss can flourish only amidst snow, and in a uniformly low temperature; without the moss the reindeer would perish, and on their herds entirely depends the prosperity, nay, the very existence of the Lapps. It is this animal which supplies them with clothing, food, the means of locomotion, and of maintaining whatever else their simple habits require. No other climate will suit these animals; the experiment of introducing them into Scotland has invariably failed.

"The milk of the reindeer is highly valuable; its flesh also supplies a nutritious food during a great part of the year; its sinews are made into thread and cord; its horns into spoons and other domestic utensils, and its skin furnishes the main portion of the Lapp's dress. This animal bears a great resemblance to the stag, but is rather smaller. The females are driven home morning and evening to be milked, and yield about the same quantity as a she-goat.

"The reindeer moss grows almost everywhere upon these mountains in great abundance; this vegetable, which after a long continuance of heat and drought appears withered and dead, immediately recovers new life from the rain. Dry and valueless as it looks, it is a most important gift to this wild region, for it is the chief support of many thousands of reindeer on the barren summits of the mountains through all the severity of the winter. The deer remove the snow with their feet to the depth of 5 or 6 feet to get at this food, and they cannot thrive nor even live without it for any length of time."—*Milford's Norway*, c. 8.

The general *shooting* up this grand valley of the Namsen is good, and it becomes better as the Swedish frontier is approached. The bear, lynx, and glutton are at times met with, besides capercailie, woodgrouse, and an abundance of ptarmigan. The woods and forests are of vast extent, and contain splendid pine trees; they also abound with the yellow molteberry, raspberries, red currants, and strawberries of delicious flavour.

Salmon-fishing in the Namsen. Namsen is considered the best salmon river in Norway. Fish attain an immense size, but it is idle for travellers to expect permission to fish there. English gentlemen have been in the habit of going there regularly for fishing for the last 12 years, and all the waters are held as strictly upon leases, as the rivers of Scotland, or Ireland. Salmon cannot get higher up the river than Fiskum Fos. The fishing begins at Haugan, but it is very indifferent so low down, except for a short time quite early in the season, or after an extraordinary flood. The three most choice fishing stations are Fiskum, Godtland, and Ekker Ferry, comprising in all about 6 to 8 Eng. m. of water, with comfortable room for 6 rods, 2 at each station. There are good quarters to be had at each of these places, and the charge for food, lodging, and attendance averages about ½ a dollar, 2*s*. 3*d*. a day. Boats are used for fishing in this river; each boat has two men, who are paid two marks, about 1*s*. 9*d*. each, besides which they expect the salmon not wanted for the angler's own use, and which is divided between the 3 stations. Above the Fos the trout-fishing is excellent.

"That distinguished fisherman, Sir H. Parker, killed on this river a salmon of 60 pounds weight after a little more than an hour's battle. It was caught on a No. 6 or 7 hook; wings, two golden tippets dyed crimson, sprigged with mallard, teal, golden pheasant, and Argus pheasant; horns, blue macaw; head, black; body, claret hog's wool; tag, red mohair; ribbed gold twist. On the same day he bagged 9 others, one of 40 lbs., one 30 lbs., one 18 lbs., one 15 lbs., and the rest from 8 lbs. downwards."—Vid. *Barnard's Sport in Norway*, p. 28.

The season here varies a little, but it is comprised in the 3 months of June, July, and August; the finest part is usually about the end of June to that of July. Four English gentlemen who were here for 2 months in 1841, each killed 1000 lbs. weight of salmon. Their largest fish weighed 47 lbs. In fact, it appears that at the proper season the river is so abundantly stocked with fish, that success becomes a matter of certainty. Neither is there much science required here to kill from 100 to 150 lbs. of salmon, grilse, and trout in a day, as, fishing from a boat, all the most likely places can be got at; and when a heavy fish is hooked it can easily be followed up or down the stream. The *Kobbe* (seal) is very troublesome in the Namsen, at times. A glimpse of a seal clears the river of the fish in an instant; they are stupefied with fear, and seek for shelter in the deepest holes and other hiding-places, which no fly, be it ever so tempting, will induce them to leave, until their much dreaded enemy has disappeared.—*Milford's Norway*, c. 4.

The *Steamer* between Trondhjem and Hammerfest calls at Namsös at the mouth of the river on her way both up and down the coast. (See page 141, Route 25.)

From the *Namsen to Hammerfest*, by Boat.

The following stations are inserted for the use of travellers by open boats. The steamers touch at more stations, and sometimes different to those named. It is presumed that travellers, for any distance along the coast, will make use of the steamers; and that the names of the boat stations given here will be sufficient for those who make short excursions, either along the coast, or to and from the steamer to any point where they may wish to land. Printed lists of the stations, at which the steamers touch, and of the days and hours, are hung up on board, and are so easily understood, that it has been thought useless to transcribe them; the more so, because the times, and even stations themselves, are liable to change, as the nights lengthen in the autumn. These printed lists may be obtained in Christiania.

The scenery on the first and second day from Trondhjem is not very striking: the cliffs and rocks are round-topped, and insignificant. *Rouches montonnées*, Professor Forbes terms them, rounded by the action of ice. North of the Arctic Circle, however, the cliffs become more peaked, and assume grander forms. If fortunate enough to have a fine day in crossing Vest Fjord, where the steamer stretches over to the Loffodens, the traveller will see one of the finest sea views in the world. On the S.W. there is the open sea: on the W. and N. the sharp-pointed peaks of the Loffodens rise nearly perpendicularly out of the water: covered, where not too steep, with snow almost to the water's edge, till quite late in the summer. Huge, rugged rocks they are as you approach them; their tops like extinct craters, which have fallen in, now filled with snow. Later in the summer, as the snow melts, numerous miniature waterfalls pour down over the sides of the cliffs, and at the bottom patches of green and a few fishermen's huts begin to be seen, till at length the steamer creeps in through a narrow passage to the fishing station of Balstad. On the E. of Vest Fjord lofty peaks of snowy mountains rear their heads far away towards the frontiers of Sweden. I believe there are few views of its kind to be compared to that from the middle of Vest Fjord. On leaving Vest Fjord the steamer winds its way up Rafte Sund, a lovely channel, to Steilo in Ulvöen, a pretty little island almost out on the open ocean. Perhaps one of the most striking features of the Loffodens are the enormous numbers of sea fowl. Gulls and eider-ducks innumerable; so numerous are the latter, and so tame, that it is sometimes necessary for the steamer to go half-speed in the narrow channels to avoid running over the young ones. The famous "Maelström," of which English geography books relate, that whales and other monsters are sucked into it, till "they will roar you, an't were any nightingale," is in a narrow passage between two of the Loffodens. We insert an account of it, taken from *Notes and Queries*, of April 3, 1858.

"The dangerous current and supposed whirlpool of the Mäelström lies at the south end of the Loffoden Isles, between the islets of Moskenæs and Vaeroe. Its real perils are produced by the tremendous current that rushes in and out of the Great West Fjord that lies between the Loffodens and the western coast of Norway. Dangerous currents are thus occasioned between most of the Loffoden Isles, such as the Galström, the Napström, and the Gimström; but the chief current is directed between Moskenæs and Vaeroe, constituting the famous Mäelström. When the wind blows from certain quarters, and particularly from the N.W., and meets the returning tide in the Strait, the whole sea between Moskenæs and Vaeroe is thrown into such agitation that no boat could live in it for a moment. In calm weather it is only three-quarters of an hour before the flood tide that the boatmen venture to cross; for, with the stillest and most glassy water outside, the Mäelström is dangerously agitated, except at the period above mentioned. The 'set' of the tide through the Strait is at first towards the S.E.; it then, after the flood, turns from the S. towards the S.W., and finally, towards the N.W.; so in 12 hours the circle of the current is completed. This is rather a slow proceeding on the part of a whirlpool, but the agitation of the current arises from an immense body of water being forced by the flowing tide into the narrow passage between the isles. In addition to this the depth decreases most suddenly as the stream enters the Straits. Outside, on the west of the Loffodens, the soundings show a depth of 100 to 200 fathoms, while in the Straits, and in the West Fjord, it suddenly shoals from 16 to 30 fathoms, and the whole weight of water from the North Sea is suddenly compressed between the cliffs of Moskenæs and Vaeroe. As to the stories of ships being swallowed up in the vortex, they are simply fables; but any ship that became involved in the current would probably be driven on the sunken rocks and reefs in the Strait if it did not founder from the fury of the waves. The Mäelström is quite out of the track of the Nordland 'Jaegts' with their odoriferous cargo of dried fish, and no other vessels are called upon to take this course. Nor are whales ever sucked down by the greedy whirlpool, though the following circumstances may account for this part of the legend.

"On the Island of Flagstadt, which lies a little to the north of Moskenæs, there is a narrow inlet called Qualviig between the rocks opposite to the farmhouse of Sund. This inlet or passage is at first extremely deep, and then suddenly shoals to about 16 ft. In this narrow cleft a very considerable number of whales have within the memory of man run themselves ashore. We know not what attraction draws these generally wary animals to this narrow creek, but once in the canal it is impossible for the whale to retreat, as he requires a large space to turn his body, and grounding with the falling tide the huge monster is left there to struggle with his fate. Large whales are known to have lived 8 days in this natural trap, and the people say their bellowings and struggles were fearful to behold. About the beginning of the present century an enormous male 'fish' was fast embayed here, and ere the sun was set he was followed by his mate, who shared his imprisonment and death. This happened at the time that Mr. Sverdrup occupied the farm of Sund, and from the good luck that befell him, from 20 whales and more being stranded here during his occupancy, he obtained the surname of the 'King of the Loffodens.'

"EDWARD CHARLTON, M.D."

From Namsös at the mouth of the Namsen to Hammerfest by boat is 83¾ Norsk m. or 584 Eng. From the Hund Station to

Vemundvik, 1¼, upon the coast; and from hence, with the exception of part of one stage, all the rest of the journey to the N. Cape is by water.

Seierstad, 1½. From hence the *Folden Fjord* is crossed to Strand. This little-frequented tract is inhabited by myriads of water-fowl, that breed here undisturbed, and the traveller may chance to have his meditations disturbed by the sudden appearance of a whale close to his boat. —*Everest's Norway*, p. 56.

Strand, 2. Up an arm of the fjord to

Finne, 1¼.

* *Aarför*, 2.

Foldereid, 1. Here the hills are crossed to a branch of the *Bindals Fjord*, down which the stage continues to

* *Teraak*, 2. On leaving the Bindals Fjord towards the end of the stage, the lofty island of Leko is seen on the S.W. Our route now lies up the coast to

* *Steensöen*, 3. The mountains upon the coast now become lofty and precipitous. Torghatten, a curious rock upon the island of Torget, is passed on the left upon this stage. It is upwards of 1000 ft. high, and perforated in the middle. "It is of granite, and its form, as seen from the S., is not unlike the peaked waterproof hats sometimes worn by sailors, whence in fact its name, '*Torget's Hat*.'"—*Forbes's Norway*, p. 44.

* *Salhuus*, 2. The boatmen up this coast are most skilful and excellent, but the squalls from the mountains are sudden and dangerous; and we must again repeat the caution never to allow the sheet to be fixed in sailing, but always to have it kept in hand. The love of finkel is the boatmen's great fault, and in some cases care must be taken to prevent their indulging in too frequent libations.

Forvik, 2½.

* *Sövik*, 2¾. This station is upon the large and highly cultivated island of Tjotöe. In the 11th century it was the residence of a celebrated chieftain named Haarek, a contemporary of St. Olaf. From hence may be seen the extraordinary peaks of mountains called the Seven Sisters; and also the lofty Donna-öe. Von Buch estimates their height at above 4000 ft. At Sövik passengers for Vefsen leave the steamer. Vefsen is one of the best salmon rivers for its size in Norway, by all accounts. The fishing is rented by an English gentleman, who in the summer of 1853 killed a fish of 52 lbs. there.

* *Sannessöen*, 1¼.

* *Kobberdal*, 1¼. Passengers for Ranen land here. The Ranen is a fine river, but the accounts of the salmon-fishing are rather contradictory.

* *Donnaes*, ¾. Upon the mainland to the E. of this is the largest glacier in Norway, with the exception of Justedalsbræ (near Leirdalsören, Route 21). This glacier is between Bejern and Ranen, in the province of Nordland.

In several districts of this province the rivers flow in subterranean passages for some distance, and then reappear; the two largest of these are Jardbluelv, in Saltdal, and the Prugra, in Ranen.

* *Lurvoö*, 2¾. On this stage the coast continues exceedingly mountainous, with wild-fowl in myriads. Some miles to the W. are seen the four peaks of the islands of Threnen, rising erect as towers from the water. Immediately on passing them, the line of

The *Arctic Circle* is crossed, and near that point a curiously formed cliff is seen, called Hestmands-Öen (Horseman's Island); it has the appearance of a huge man on horseback swimming through the water. The coast is here of the wildest description; precipitous mountains piled upon each other in every variety of form, with their hundred snow-capped peaks; "a correct picture of it would appear to be anything but the representation of sober reality."—*Everest's Norway*, p. 63.

* *Selsövik*, 1¾.

* *Sriner*, 2.

* *Stöt*, 2½.

* *Nord Arnæs*, 3½. On this stage the mouth of the *Salten Fjord* is crossed to

* Bodö, 2½. "Nordland's By," the chief and only town in the province of Nordland. The steamers stop here for 6 hours to coal. On the marsh in September and the end of August, ryper and snipe may be found. It is worth while to walk out to the church, about 3 Eng. m. E. of the town. There is a curious monumental slab on the S. wall outside, to a former clergyman there, who died in 1660. The spruce fir is not found farther N. than about the line of the Arctic Circle. Scotch fir takes its place in the forests; this again does not reach much farther N. than latitude 70°, though there may be some stunted specimens farther N. Woodcocks also, and "hjerpe" (the hazel-hen), will not be found N. of the Arctic Circle.

Bodö is a small place, at present containing about 300 inhabitants, three or four of whom are merchants; it is also the residence of the Amtmand, the Judge, and Sheriff.

It was some years since selected by the Norwegian Government as the site of a commercial town, on account of its advantageous situation, and especially of its vicinity to the great fishing banks of Loffoden; but, notwithstanding these advantages, it seems to have remained nearly stationary.

From Bodö to the head of the Salten Fjord is about 6 m., which may be done in from 9 hours to 2 days, depending upon the wind. There is good accommodation at Saltnæs, at the head of the fjord, but dear. The river there is not worth much as a salmon river, and the houses on the banks are dirty. There is little to see on the fjord, except the Saltenström, a whirlpool in a narrow passage of the fjord, like the Mælström in miniature, but, though smaller, more dangerous. The best place to sleep on the fjord, if a contrary wind entails a passage of 2 days, is at Skierstad. The only object in going up the Salten Fjord is to visit an encampment of Lapps, some of whom may generally be seen with their reindeer on the fjeld, within 2 m. of Saltnæs (but Lapps may be seen far better from Tromsöe), or to ascend the Sulitjelma mountains on the frontier of Sweden, the highest peak of which is about 6000 N. ft. above the sea. They are the highest hills N. of Trondhjem, but otherwise there is no object in visiting them. There are magnificent views seaward from the Blaamand Fjeld above Saltnæs.

The scenery around Bodö is of the wildest kind. About 1½ m. S.E. is Biirfjeld, with its picturesque peaks, snowy ravines, and black precipices, while to the S.W. the mountains tower above each other into the far distance. Sandhorn is one of them, and the highest point in this neighbourhood. The view from its summit is of vast extent. The long range of the

Loffoden Islands

is seen 70 or 80 Eng. m. distant, like the jaws of a great shark, so many and so jagged are their points. In the foreground the islands, bays, and lakes are countless. It is in the neighbourhood of the Loffodens that the millions of cod are annually caught during the winter (from the middle of February to that of April), and which form the staple article of trade in the towns upon the W. coast. It has been calculated from official returns that in an average year the cod-fisheries off these islands were carried on by 2916 boats, having 124 tenders, and in all carrying 15,324 men; the produce being upwards of 16 millions of fish, 21,500 barrels of cod's liver oil, and 6000 barrels of cod's roe. (*Laing's Norway*, c. 6.) "The fishery is exclusively carried on in open boats. The fishermen hang up the larger portion of the fish, which is dried and ready for shipment by about midsummer; this is stock-fish. A considerable quantity is, however, sold fresh to traders (citizens) of Tromsöe, Trondhjem, Christiansand, Molde, and Bergen, who enjoy, in common with the privileged merchants of the district, the right of trading during the fishing season; this they salt down in their vessels, and afterwards convey to particular places along the neighbouring coast, where the climate is less humid than in the Loffodens, and also where there is facility for drying it on the flat rocks, 'Klipper.' This is known in commerce as Klip-fish, and differs little from the 'Bacalao' of Newfoundland. The trade of Loffoden was formerly confined to the privileged merchants of Trondhjem and Bergen; but, according to the last trading law (Handel's Lov), passed about 20 years since, any man may sell articles of necessity, but I do not think he could buy more fish than for his own consumption. The restrictions on trade are still considerable; they are remnants of the tyrannical system established by the Hanse towns when they had the absolute control of these fisheries. No one, for example, can set up as shopkeeper, though called merchant, in a town, unless he can pass an examination in book-keeping by double entry, and in a foreign language! Had such a law existed in England, it is doubtful whether the late M. N. Rothschild could have established himself in London. The trade of the whole of the northern coast is almost entirely one of barter; the merchants being constantly under advance to the fishermen, who are thus bound to deliver their catch to their creditors; but they continually try to evade (and are by no means scrupulous as to the means) what appears to them a species of tyranny, although the thraldom is often voluntary. It is a detestable system with a double curse, for the merchants rarely thrive under it. Where it still lingers in the old dependencies of Norway, the Orkneys, and Shetlands, we see its effects in the appeal of these islanders every few years to the benevolence of the English public. Where no money passes there is no inducement to save—very few will hoard perishable articles, such as meal, grits, &c., beyond their consumption for twelve months."—W. There is a beautiful theory as regards the cod-fishery, which may be of enormous advantage to Ireland. The prey of the cod is said to be most abundant upon particular strata, which are supposed to extend from the Loffodens, by the N. coast of Ireland, right across the Atlantic, to Newfoundland. If this be so, it is believed that wherever the depth of water is not too great, cod may at the proper season be caught as abundantly off the coast of Ireland as at the Loffodens or Newfoundland. Fresh herring is the most tempting bait for cod.

* *Kierringö*, 3.

* *Helnæs*, 2½.

* *Lörö*, 2. From hence there are stations to some of the Loffoden Islands, across the *Vest Fjord*, 3 m. dist.

Fikke, 3. Upon this stage the fjord gradually narrows, the Loffodens being close upon the W.; and the scenery is wild and desolate in the extreme.

Baröen, 3. From hence our route winds through channels between the islands and the mainland all the way to Tromsöe, the mountains at times most grand and picturesque in form.

Shortly before the end of this stage the district of *Finmarken* is entered.

• *Sandtorvholm*, 2¼. Upon this stage Trondenæs is passed. Its church is considered to be the handsomest to the N. of Trondhjem, and one of the oldest in Norway; it was the chapel of a monastery formerly situated here, of which it is now the only remains existing.

There is a Normal school established here, supported by the State, for the education of parish schoolmasters.

• *Harvik*, 3.

• *Dyprik*, 2¼.

Sör Russevaag, 1⅞.

• *Gibostad*, 1⅛, on the island of Senjen. This island, according to a certain Danish Count, who frequently comes here, has the reputation of abounding in bears. Between Gibostad and Tromsöe the Malangen Fjord is crossed; the *Mons River* flows into the head of this fjord. The salmon-fishing, it is said, is pretty good in it, but, like most other Norwegian rivers, it is rented by Englishmen. Professor Munch is inclined to place the northern limit of the early colonization by the Northmen at this point for various reasons. Supposing, according to his view, the stream of colonization to have come N. of the Gulf of Bothnia, either round the coast in ships from Archangel, or by forcing a path over the mountains (and there is a pass leading out to this very fjord from Torneå, and Russian Finland), he imagines this to have been the first inviting-looking spot, which might have tempted the early colonists to land, and settle. The names of places along the coast S. of this fjord undoubtedly bear a Scandinavian form, while to the N. of it they are no less remarkably Finnish. For his various reasons for supposing colonization to have taken place by way of the N., see his "Norske Folk's Historie," vol. i. book i.

• TROMSÖE, 3¼. Ludwigsens Hotel; very fair accommodation. This town is of comparatively recent date. It is one of those established on this coast after the Danish octroi system had received its death-blow, and now owes its prosperity to the extensive fisheries along the coast, and the brisk foreign trade which this lucrative branch of industry has created. The town is pleasingly situated on the eastern side of the island, in the centre of the fjord, from which it takes its name. It is the residence of the bishop, Stift Amtmand, and several subordinate authorities, and contains about 1500 inhabitants, being nearly double what the population was 20 years since. The town and district return one member to the Storthing.

There are generally some Russian vessels here from Archangel and the coasts of the White Sea. They bring corn, which they exchange for dried fish. The crews of these vessels are fine, brawny, picturesque-looking fellows. The vice of drunkenness prevails to a fearful extent amongst the lower classes in this place. From Tromsöe there are fine views of the mountainous island of Kvalö on the W.; and from Tromsöe the Lyngs-fjord and its terrific glacier may be visited. The steamer usually stops a day here. The *Ptarmigan shooting* upon the neighbouring mainland and islands is excellent.

They have a curious custom here, and indeed in other parts of Norway, of lighting huge fires and letting off fireworks on the eve of St. Hans day (Midsummer Day). Seen from the hill above the town, they have an exceedingly good effect, though there be a bright sun shining at the time. There is a similar custom of lighting bonfires on Midsummer Day in the West of Cornwall. The view at 10 or 11 o'clock at night from the hill above Tromsöe, if it be fine and clear, is worth walking up to see.

A Lapp encampment is generally to be seen in Tromsdal on the E. side of the fjord. It is more easily reached than the encampment in the valley of Namsen, or on the Salten Fjord. It is a sight worth seeing. The horns of the reindeer grow to an enormous size, reaching as high as a man's shoulder when the deer are lying down. Some of the herd are so tame that they will allow you to step over them, and stand by them, as if they were cows, in the place of which indeed they stand to the Lapp.

On leaving Tromsöe our route continues between the islands and mainland by

* *Finkroken*, 2, pay for 2½. This stage is down the *Ulfs Fjord*, between which and the Lyngen Fjord there is a gigantic chain of mountains.

It is said that the Russians are very desirous to obtain possession of Lyngen Fjord, by fair or foul means, for a harbour on the Northern Ocean, which is never frozen. Only 3 or 4 Norsk miles, say 25 English, intervene at present between the westernmost boundary of Russian Finland and the head of this fjord; and there is no doubt that the Russians are very desirous to make this last stride to the open sea. In 1853 they endeavoured to pick a quarrel with Norway by giving orders that all Norwegian reindeer, which crossed the frontier, were to be shot; at the same time forbidding their own Lapp subjects to enter Norway. There were some able letters on this subject in the *Morning Chronicle* in the autumn of 1854.

Near the mouth of the Lyngen Fjord, and close to the steamer's course, two glaciers are to be seen, coming close down to the water's edge. There is one in Kvænangen Fjord N. E. of Lyngen, which is actually washed by the sea.—*Forbes's Norway*, p. 78.

* *Karlsö*, 2, pay for 2½.

* *Skjervö*, 3, pay for 4¼. About 3 m. S. of this station the *Reisen Elv* enters the fjord. It is a large stream, and little known at present; it was tried once, and did not turn out very well. There is a good deal of water from a glacier in the river. Those who are desirous of visiting

The *Alten River*,

and who do not proceed there by the steamer, should take boat from Skjervö to Alteidet, 3, from there cross the isthmus to Sopnæs (about ¼) on Lang Fjord, and thence again by boat up the Alten Fjord to Talvik, 3 m., and *Alten* (near the mouth of the river), 1 m., in all, 8¼. The *Steamers* to and from Hammerfest call at

Bosekop (where there is a good Inn), in the Alten Fjord, and only 1 m. by land from Alten. A fair is held here in the latter end of November, and in March, which is largely attended by Finns and Lapps from the mountains, as well as by Swedes. The Alten is navigable for about 4 m. from its mouth. A horse-path runs a long way up the valley of this stream, and across the mountains, over a strip of the Russian territory, into Sweden. (See Route 34.)

Altengaard, near the mouth of the river, was formerly the residence of the Amtmand; it is now the head-quarters of a Roman Catholic mission, which has been established about 3[illegible] years, hitherto without making many converts.

Alten is the most extensive and productive valley in the north, and is in every respect, both as to climate and style of scenery, different to the districts which the traveller has been passing through; here vegetation appears to flourish; the fir, the birch, the willow, and mountain ash are abundant; even corn-fields and cultivated meadows are seen; and after the wild and desolate scenery, among which the earlier part of the voyage has been made, this change is a relief both to the mind and the eye.

In several parts of the Alten valley, the traveller will meet with as soft and pleasing scenery as any Alpine country can present; indeed the impression on the first view is that of an oasis, formed by nature as a resting-place in the midst of ruggedness and desolation.

In a lateral valley, on the S. side of the Alten Fjord, lie the Alten Copper Works, belonging to an English company, the establishment of which has contributed greatly to the prosperity of the district. The gentlemen who are resident there are most obliging in giving information as to the best parts of the river, the proper boat to be taken, provisions, &c., as there are no station-houses.

There are some remarkable marine terraces, or ancient sea beaches, near Alten, and indeed on other parts of the coast of Finmark. Those near Alten are remarkable, in that they are not continuous at the same exact level above the sea, but incline in such a way as to show that the coast has not only been raised bodily out of the water, but in an unequal manner, the part towards Hammerfest having emerged less than the part towards Bosekop. The highest is 240 Eng. feet above the sea.—*Forbes's Norway*, pp. 84-90.

As a *salmon stream*, some anglers consider the Alten superior to the Namsen.* It is now quite as well known, and as regularly fished, as Namsen. Mosquitoes swarm here at times. A tribe of Finlanders or Kvæns (*Kvæner* in Norwegian) are settled at Alten; many of the boatmen on the river speak nothing but Kvænish. They are admirable boatmen, but they are not famous for the love of truth and honesty, which generally distinguishes the Norwegian peasants.

The general *shooting* up the valley of the Alten is good (see Route 34), and the numerous falls of the river and its tributaries are highly picturesque.

The *Tana Elv* is a splendid stream, and its tributaries large and numerous. It rises in the mountains S.E. of the Alten, and for a long distance is the boundary between Russia and Norway. It falls into the Tana Fjord about 60 Eng. m. to the E. of the North Cape. The Tana and its tributaries have been explored by 4 or 5 parties of fishermen in the last few years. Undoubtedly there are large fish there, and a great extent of fishing water, it being 20 Norsk m. from Karasjok to Tana mouth. Salmon ascend above Karasjok. A great part of the river, however, consists of broad shallow *lakes*, one may almost call them, where there is no chance of killing a fish, so that the actual extent of water to be fished is considerably reduced. Mosquitoes swarm, and there is no escape from them, except within a tent. There are no houses on the bank, so that all necessaries have to be carried. It would seem from the same party never going there a second time, that the fishing did not compensate for the discomfort to be endured. See Introduction, under head 9. There are two modes of arriving at Tana; one from Alten across the mountains to Karasjok, where boats may be obtained to *descend* the river; the other is by leaving the Hammerfest and Vadsö steamer in the Tana Fjord, and *ascending* the river as far as may be thought fit. By the former route, horses, provisions, and a guide must be taken from Alten: it will

* "I have had a great many salmon opened in my presence—those caught in the Alten Fjord, before they reached the river, were full of young herrings or smelts (the *Salmo Arcticus*, I believe); but I never could discover anything in those caught after they had been 24 hours in the river."—W.

require about 3 days to do the 16 m. between Alten and Karasjok. Some wretched mountain huts exist, where it is possible to sleep on the way. Some little distance up the Alten a horse-track diverges across the mountains to the E. for 3 or 4 m., and then enters the valley of one of the tributaries of the Tana, and keeps along that valley till its junction with the river, about 8 m. The road then continues (with the exception of a small interval) all the way down the valley of the Tana to its junction with the fjord, about 80 Eng. m., and never leaves the Norwegian territory. Care must be taken not to enter the Russian territory without having a passport properly *visé* for Russia, or the consequences may prove unpleasant. From the mouth of the Tana there are water stations to the North Cape, via. from Guldholmen to Hopseidet, 5 m.; there cross a small isthmus, and on by water to Sværholt, 5; and Kjelvik, at the North Cape, 3; in all, 13 m.

The direct Route to the North Cape continued from Skjervö.—Large shoals of a fish called Sey (coal-fish) are seen off this part of the coast; much used by the inhabitants for food. From Skjervö a fine glacier is visible on Kaagöe. The atmospheric effects about here in winter are sublime. The sun is lost early in November, when his rays, for a short time, alone illumine the tops of the mountains. They are of the most lovely rose colour, while clouds and vapour render all beneath and around them dark, mysterious, and indistinct.

* *Loppen*, 2½, pay for 3¼. This small island lies open to the whole force of the Atlantic. Whales are frequently seen about here. From hence the *Sörö Sund* is entered to

* HAMMERFEST, 7, pay for 8¾. This is celebrated as being the most northern town in the world, and also for its lively trade, being the resort of English, Russian, Dutch, Swedish, Danish, and German traders, but particularly Russian, who swarm on the coast during the three summer months: although situated in so high a northern latitude, 70° 49′, the temperature, even in winter, is so mild, that the waters along the coast and at the bottom of the deepest fjords never freeze; the inhabitants are consequently enabled to carry on the sea fishing in boats during the whole winter.

The Spitsbergen trade is likewise a most important branch here. Small sloops of 30 or 40 tons are fitted out for it from hence, and carry 6 or 8 hands. They leave here in May, and wait at the edge of the ice till it is sufficiently thawed to enable them to near the land. Reindeer, walrus, white bears, and eider-down are the objects sought for. This trade has given to Hammerfest a more enterprising set of seamen than any other port in Norway. Their boldness and dexterity in destroying the white bear with lances is extreme. These beasts are not much dreaded in summer, but when pressed by hunger in the winter they become very daring in their attacks. A story is told of two Russians who were playing at draughts by the window of their hut, when a great white paw, pushed through the pane, seized one of them by the neck, and attempted to drag him out. He escaped with the loss of a pawful of his hair.

Numbers of Lapps may be seen here and upon the neighbouring coast. Like their neighbours the Kvæns, they are sadly addicted to drunkenness at times. With this exception the total absence of anxiety of mind among them, their few and simple wants, and the high state of health and spirits engendered by their hardy habits, make them creatures rather deserving of envy than pity. The Lapp will go for 30 Eng. m. through swamp and over rock, take his draught of milk, lie down in his wet clothes, and awake the next morning as fresh as when he began his journey.

Hammerfest is on the island of Kvalöe. The island was once well wooded, but there are now hardly any trees left, having been cut down for firewood, and no young ones having taken their place. Much drift wood is brought by the Gulf Stream here. "Think of Arctic fishers burning upon their hearths the palms of Hayti, the mahogany of Honduras, and the precious woods of the Amazon and Orinoco."—*Bayard Taylor's Northern Travel*, p. 264.

Seyland may be visited from Hammerfest. The summit of the mountain is 3408 ft., and commands very extensive and grand views. The most northern glacier in Norway is upon it.

The Russian Government takes great pains to foster its trade with the northern provinces of Norway, which are mainly supplied with corn from that country. *Mr. Laing*, in his book on Norway, c. 6 (which deserves attentive perusal), fully and ably exposes the supposed views and objects of Russia as regards the N. of Norway.

The *Aurora Borealis.*—Mr. Everest, in his book on Norway, p. 129, thus describes it as seen by bright moonlight in this neighbourhood in the middle of September:—"Across the sky, to the north, stretched a white arch of light with a span as broad as a rainbow, and rather flatter. A large streak, shaped like a comet, lay within the arch, and this was continually changing both its figure and position. Sun, moon, or stars never yet gave so lovely, so hallowed a light." But it is much finer in the middle of November, when it assumes a great variety of forms; at times appearing like a rain of fire—a great fan displaying all the colours of the rainbow—or a hurried indistinct motion of shapes of light which might be compared to a mysterious dance of spirits.

The *Steamer* usually remains here two days prior to her return S. This sometimes gives sufficient time to visit the North Cape and return, so as to catch the boat before her return S. The best chance of doing this is to take the lightest boat and 4 men. It is not a good plan (except for economy) for a party to join in taking the same boat. Where there are two or more boats, a little emulation is created between the crews, and there is a better chance of a quick passage, as the Norsemen are not given to hurry themselves. It is better, however, to go by the Hammerfest and Vadsö steamer as far as Gjæsvœr, and landing there proceed by boat to the North Cape. This boat leaves Hammerfest every other Thursday. After visiting it you can either wait for the same steamer on her return, or hire boats at each station, and return to Hammerfest, a distance of 11 m. from Kjelvik, 5½ from Havösund.

Ladies should not attempt the journey by boats to the North Cape, as they are not only liable to be exposed to considerable hardships, but may be unable to quit the boat for 20 or 24 hours.

Hammerfest to the North Cape.

Dist. 13 Norsk m., or 91 Eng. A stock of provisions, with some brandy for the men, a cask of water, and plenty of wraps to keep out rain and sea, are essential. A glass or two of brandy to the men upon occasions facilitates the passage: a bargain should be made with them before starting, particularly if they are hired for the whole distance. The *scenery* beyond Hammerfest does not repay the expense and fatigue of the voyage. The grand mountains dwindle into insignificance, and all becomes dreary, barren, and of a uniform dull brown. The stations are—

* *Havösund*, 5½. From hence the most direct way to the Cape (should the wind serve) is to make for the bottom of the *Tue Fjord*, upon the island of Mageröe. Thence walk over to the *Riis Fjord*, and there take boat again, and cross the *West Fjord*, landing at *Hornvigen*, a small bight on the North Cape itself. The regular station route from Havösund is to

Kjelvik, 4½, pay for 5½. This station is upon the island of *Mageröe*, and a guide can be obtained for those who like to walk to the Cape, about 20 Eng. m. dist.; or a boat can be taken round the island to Hornvigen, from whence

The *North Cape*

may be ascended. The way up is steep — the highest point 935 feet above the sea. There is no particular wildness of scenery—around upon the island is nothing but a bare moor, and the sea is not more stormy or violent than upon other parts of the coast. No trees grow upon this island of Mageröe, but the sea throws ashore an abundance of drift wood, which supplies the inhabitants with fuel. For food their chief dependence is upon fish and wild-fowl, which abound. The Gyr Falcon (so much prized for falconry) and plenty of eagles may be seen here.

The song in the older Edda, called Valas Spaadom, gives the eagle his proper place in the scenery of the country. After foretelling the destruction of the earth, the prophetess sees it come up again "glorious green. The waterfalls precipitate, but the eagle flies over it, seeking for fish." This is a study from nature, as it still remains.

There are few finer accounts of the North Cape, and of the Midnight Sun, than Mr. Carlyle's. He describes "Teufelsdröckh" emerging (we know not whence) in the solitude of the North Cape, on that June midnight, standing there, on the world promontory, looking over the infinite Brine.

"Silence, as of death," writes he; "for midnight, even in the Arctic latitudes, has its character; nothing but the granite cliffs, ruddy-tinged, the peaceable gurgle of that slow-heaving Polar Ocean, over which in the utmost North the great sun hangs low, and lazy, as if he too were slumbering. Yet is his cloud couch wrought of crimson, and cloth of gold: yet does his light stream over the mirror of waters, like a tremulous fire-pillar, shooting downwards to the abyss, and hide itself under my feet. In such moments solitude also is invaluable; for who would speak, or be looked upon, when behind him lies all Europe and Africa fast asleep, except the watchmen; and before him the silent Immensity, and palace of the Eternal, whereof our sun is but a porch lamp?"—*Sartor Resartus*, p. 109.

The following is the description of the North Cape, also at midnight, by Mr. Bayard Taylor:—"It was now 11 o'clock, and Sværholt glowed in fiery bronze lustre, as we rounded it. The eddies of returning birds gleaming golden in the nocturnal sun, like drifts of beech leaves in the October air. Far to the N. the sun lay in a bed of saffron light, over the clear horizon of the Arctic Ocean. A few bars of dazzling orange cloud floated above him, and still higher in the sky, where the saffron melted through delicate rose colour into blue, hung like wreaths of vapour, touched with pearly, opaline flushes of pink and golden gray. The sea was a web of pale slate colour, shot through with threads of orange and saffron, from the dance of a myriad shifting and twinkling ripples. The air was filled with the soft, mysterious glow, and even the very azure of the southern sky seemed to shine through a net of golden gauze. The headlands of this deeply indented coast—the capes of the Laxe and Porsanger Fjords, and of Mageröe, lay around us, in different degrees of distance, but all with foreheads touched with supernatural glory. Far to the N.E. was Nordkyn, the most northern point of the mainland of Europe, gleaming rosily and faint in the full beams of the sun, and just as our watches denoted midnight, the N. appeared to the westward—a long line of purple bluff presenting a vertical front of 900 ft. in height to the Polar Ocean. Midway between these two magnificent headlands stood the midnight sun, shining on us with subdued fires, and with the gorgeous colouring of an hour, for which we have no name, since it is neither sunrise, nor sunset, but the blended loveliness of both—but shining at the same moment, in the heat and splendour of noonday, on the Pacific Isles." — *Northern Travel*, pp. 267, 268.

Those who expect to find nothing better than Lapps and their huts in this wild district of Finmarken, will be surprised to hear that a party of English and American gentlemen, who missed the steamer from Hammerfest, and were detained till she made her next voyage, passed their time most agreeably amongst the kind and hospitable families. At a dinner party at one of the houses, they sat down 24 in number, which was followed by a ball, kept up till 4 in the morning.

From Hammerfest another steamer leaves for Vadsö soon after the arrival of the steamer from the S., touching at Havösund, Kjelvik for the North Cape, Repvaag, Vardohuus, and other places, arriving at Vadsö on the third day from Hammerfest. She returns in time to catch the steamer going southwards of the succeeding week. *Vardohuus* is a little fort, built by King Christian IV. of Denmark, more than 200 years ago, as a protection for her fisheries, and to guard against Russian encroachments in the Varanger Fjord. *Vadsö* is a wretched little place of about 800 inhabitants, with a summer of 6 weeks and a winter of 10 months. Potatoes can sometimes be grown there. From Vadsö, fishermen wishing to try the Neiden, or the Pasvig, must cross the Varanger Fjord to its southern shore in boats. East of Pasvig, in about longitude 48° 30′ E. (from Ferüe), is the Russian frontier, and near here the sea in winter is frozen: and the Gulf Stream, which has brought warmth from the tropics to soften the rigour of the Norwegian climate throughout the whole length of the country, at length loses its force, and its track is lost in the Polar Ocean.

ROUTE 25.

CHRISTIANIA BY STEAMBOAT ROUND THE COAST TO TRONDHJEM, HAMMERFEST, AND VADSÖ IN EAST FINMARK.

The whole of this Route, comprising near 2000 miles of coast, can now be performed by means of comfortable steamboats, visiting almost every town in the country.

Printed lists of the times of departure and arrival of the *Steamers* at all their places of call upon this Route may be obtained at the steam-boat office on the quay at Christiania, on board the steamers, and at the hotels. Particular care should be taken to ascertain at the steam-boat office whether any and what alterations will be made, which may disarrange plans formed for meeting the steamers at any particular times and places.

The whole voyage from Christiania, along the coast up to the North Cape, may now be accomplished in 14 days. The steamers call at all the towns and settlements upon the coast; and at the towns usually stay long enough to see all the objects of interest they contain.

These steamers belong to Government, have strong crews, and are commanded by officers in the Royal Norwegian Navy, gentlemen who would do honour to any service. The captain and first officer on board all the Norwegian steamers speak English.

The fares of these vessels are very reasonable; see p. 6. A place in the Chief Cabin from Christiania to Hammerfest costs but 35 sps., or 7*l.* 17*s.* 0*d.*, and in the Fore Cabin 22 sps., or 4*l.* 19*s.* Food and wines are cheap and good; they are paid for extra, and may be calculated at about 6 marks, or 5*s.* 6*d.* per diem. This includes 4 meals and a pint of good French wine. The beds are clean and comfortable. Fees expected by the stewards and stewardess, small, and at discretion: and it is usual to give something to the crew.

The scenery upon the land routes across the mountains between Christiania and Bergen, and Christiania and Trondhjem, is so wondrously fine, that the voyage all round the coast by this route is not recommended, except to those persons who from ill-health or disinclination may wish to avoid the fatigue and little discomforts in the way of roughing it, which must be put up with in crossing the country.

The great advantage of these steamers to the tourist is, that they enable him cheaply and rapidly to move from place to place upon the W. coast, landing where he pleases for fishing, shooting, or exploring the most interesting scenery; for description of which see Route 24. The "Nor" leaves Christiania for Bergen every other Thursday at 7 A.M., reaching Bergen on the following Thursday afternoon. If time is an object, this boat is the best to choose, as the steamers for Trondhjem leave Bergen on Fridays. (*See below.*)

For ladies and invalids this coast route offers the greatest advantages, as it enables them to visit some of the grandest scenery in Norway, without the fatigue of travelling much by land, or being but rarely, if at all, exposed to sea-sickness, as the steamers after leaving the town of Stavanger run almost the whole way between a belt of rocks and islands, and the main land. This belt acts as a vast breakwater, within which the sea is quite smooth, let it be ever so rough outside. All the advantages of a sea-voyage are therefore obtained with few of its discomforts.

The society on board is of the upper classes of the Norwegians, and their kindly feeling towards each other, as well as to foreigners (and especially English and Americans), is very great, and adds much to the pleasure of the voyage.

In coming S., passengers can, instead of going up to Christiania, meet the steamer for Kiel at the mouth of the Christiania Fjord. (See Route 20.)

The sunset effects upon the W. coast are sublime. The scenery of the wildest description, and at times most grand and picturesque, but this is the exception and not the rule, till West of Christiansand. The islands and hills upon this iron-bound coast are in some parts quite barren, in others covered with firs and lovely little patches of verdure in the valley. But they are usually too low and rounded in the S. to be picturesque. In the N. they are much grander in height and outline.

Some of the best scenery in Norway lies in the upper parts of the Hardanger Fjord, the Sögne Fjord, and the Stor Fjord, which may be conveniently explored from the towns of Stavanger, Bergen, Aalesund, and Molde. Upon some of the large islands upon the W. coast there are red deer, and occasionally bears are met with.

For particulars as to the fishing and shooting to be had upon the fjords and near the coast, see Route 24. N. of Trondhjem, between the Namsen and Hammerfest, excellent *ptarmigan-shooting* is to be had near all the places at which the steamers call.

Two days N. of Trondhjem the Arctic Circle is crossed, and, about midsummer, the long and solemn twilight of the S. of Scandinavia is replaced by perpetual daylight during all the 24 hours.

One day N. of Trondhjem is the *Namsen*, and a little to S. of Hammerfest the *Alten*. These two are considered the finest *salmon streams* in Norway.

If it be intended to explore any of the scenery of the fjords or inland, then the preliminary information in Route 24, as to requisites for the journey, should be attended to before leaving Christiania. That Route also describes most of the towns upon the coast.

The steamers "Moss" and "Foldin" leave Christiania every *Sunday* and *Thursday* morning at 7 o'clock, for Christiansand and intermediate stations, and continue through the summer every consecutive Thursday.

Since the weekly steam communication has been established with Hull, this, in a commercial point of view, is of great importance, as it enables the man of business to command his time, and to reach any particular locality he may desire, without the necessity of performing a long and tedious land journey.

Any one, however, desirous of reaching Alten or Hammerfest within the shortest period will neither select the coast journey by land or voyage by steamer, but proceed across the Dovre Fjeld, through Gudbrandsdalen to Trondhjem, or through Osterdalen. (See Routes Nos. 20 and 31.) Where time, however, is not so great an object, the coast voyage is very interesting. There is smooth water nearly the whole of the way; the steamer winding her way through the intricate channels formed by the myriads of islands that shelter the coast. The greatest attractions upon this Route for fishing and shooting may be said to commence about Christiansand; the grandest scenery, however, is met with between Bergen and Christiansand, and in the Loffodens.

Steamer leaving Christiania on Thursday, at 7, arrives at

Drobak, at 8½ A.M.

Moss, at 10 A.M.

Horten, at 10½. This town, a few years back, was nothing more than an inconsiderable village; it has now assumed the character of a town, and has become of importance as the chief naval station and marine establishment; a very respectable dockyard has been built, as well as arsenals and depôts for naval stores.

Vallo, 11½ A.M. Here the Copenhagen steamer is met, and the post for the westward taken on board.

Laurvig, 2 P.M.

Frederiksvern, 3 P.M.

In Laurvig there are two respectable hotels. The town is charmingly situated at the head of a small fjord facing the S.E., and is built in the form of a crescent. The church is a picturesque building, and the view of it and the town from the sea is very pretty. The river Lauven falls into the fjord, near to the town on the S.E., and is the best salmon stream in the south of Norway. The fish are large and abundant, and can get a long way up the river. There is a direct route to Kongsberg from this place, 9½ m.; the road keeping along the valley of the Lauven nearly the whole way, presents a variety of picturesque scenery and charming subjects for the pencil. (See Route 23.)

Laurvig carries on a considerable trade with Great Britain, and owns a number of vessels: the last official returns show that 26,029 tons of shipping left the port, and 37,936 tons arrived. The Fritzo Iron Works are situated near Laurvig; it is one of the largest and most perfect establishments of the kind in the country.

In this neighbourhood, a watering-place, called Sandefjord, has, within these few years, sprung up, and is now, in consequence of the medicinal virtues of the waters, much frequented, not only by invalids from the capital, but the neighbouring towns and interiors of the country, as well as from Sweden and Denmark. The baths are open from the 1st of June to the 31st of August. Gouty and rheumatic affections, cutaneous eruptions, scrofula, derangement of the liver, &c., as well as paralysis, have derived great relief, and in some cases entire cures have been effected by the internal use of the waters, together with the external application of an impregnated clay, which abounds in the neighbourhood.

Steamers regularly touch there during the season.

The steamer leaves Langesund on *Friday*, at 4½ P.M.

Kragerõe, at 6 P.M. This small town is celebrated for the goodness of its oysters.

Risöer, 7½ P.M.

Dyngö, 9 P.M.

ARENDAL, 10 P.M. This is a small but pretty town, built on rocks projecting into the channel formed by the belt of islands off this range of coast, and near the mouth of the Nid Elv. Ships lie close to the houses, as the depth of water is ample for the purpose. The quay runs in front of the principal street facing the S.E.; it is broad and well laid out, and, viewed from the sea, the houses built upon it have an imposing appearance. Close to the town, on the banks of a small lake, there are some celebrated iron mines.

The steamer leaves here again on *Mondays* and *Fridays* at 4 A.M.

Grimstad, 5 A.M.

Lillesand, 6 A.M.

CHRISTIANSAND, 8 A.M., is 161 English miles from Christiania. (See Route 24.)

There are two tolerable inns in the town. Christiansand is the capital of the province or diocese of that name, and ranks as the 4th city in Norway. It is the residence of the Stift Amtmand and the Bishop. It was founded in the year 1641, by Christian IV.; its harbour is one of the best in Norway. The cathedral is a fine building of grey stone, and ranks next to those of Trondhjem and Stavanger. The situation of the town upon the Topdals Fjord, and with the rocks rising around it on the land side to a great height, is strikingly picturesque. The Torrisdal Elv enters the fjord close upon the east side of the town. There is a branch of the National Bank here, and a Grammar School, where scholars are prepared for the University. The town is defended by a fortress on the small island of Odderö, at the entrance to the harbour. Christiansand contains about 10,000 inhabitants: it has a considerable trade, the arrivals and departures annually being about 54,345 tons, and 54,548 tons respectively. Great quantities of lobsters are shipped from hence for the London market, 24 lobster smacks being regularly employed in this trade during the season. There is a fine bridge over the river leading to Oddernæs Church, a building of some antiquity, situated about ½ of a mile from the river. In the churchyard are several old tombstones, and a Runic stone, supposed to be as old as the middle of the 11th century, is worthy the attention of the antiquary.

The British Vice-Consul, Mr. J. Mörch, is deservedly noted for his courtesy to British travellers. Three miles up the Torridal River there is a fine fall, "Hel-fos." The road is along the bank of the river, passes through a grand pass, and the salmon-fishing is well spoken of, and is abundant during the season.

Travellers frequently land at Christiansand, and strike into the country at once, either to the Hardanger, Tellemarken, or to Sæterdal. For distances, stations, &c., see Route 24.

The steamers "Hakon Jarl," "Jupiter," and "Nid Elven" leave Christiansand in turns every Monday at noon, touching at Kleven, Farsund, Flekkefjord, and Egersund; and arrive at Stavanger, Tuesdays (from September 7, Wednesdays).

Egersund is one of the numerous ports of refuge on this coast, containing 1700 inhabitants; it carries on a lively trade with our northern ports, and with its lobster trade gives regular employment to several of our lobster smacks.

STAVANGER, although only containing 12,000 inhabitants, is an important town: it derives its importance, however, from the herring-fishery, the annual catch of which averages between 300,000 and 400,000 barrels. It is one of the most ancient towns in Norway, and was a bishopric prior to the foundation of Christiansand. The cathedral, with the exception of that of Trondhjem, is considered to be the most perfect specimen of the architecture of the Middle Ages in Norway. It is well preserved, and very interesting. "It is remarkable that the Gothic of the 13th century in Norway is of the early English character."

The town is built on the N.E. side of a large promontory in Stavanger Fjord, and commands beautiful views over the fjord and the range of mountains in the distance to the E. and N.E., extending up to the Hardanger range. A small island in front of the town renders the harbour one of the most secure on the coast.

There is a considerable trade between the Baltic and this port, as well as with France, the tonnage that enters in and out during the season is considerable; according to the last return, 27,690 tons entered, and 31,408 tons departed.

Excursions from Stavanger are numerous and beautiful. (See Route 24.)

The steamer leaves Stavanger again after a short stay, and touches at *Kobberviy*, *Haugesund*, *Mosterhavn*, *Lervig*, *Teroën*.

For those who wish to explore the Hardanger Fjord, this is the best place to leave the steamer. (See Routes 21 and 23.)

From Bergen they leave every other *Friday* and *Sunday* morning; Aalesund and Molde the following *Saturday* and *Monday*; Christiansund *Sunday* and *Tuesday*, and arrive at Trondhjem same days.

The steamers "Æger," "Prinds Gustav," "Lindesnæs," leave Trondhjem in turn every *Wednesday* at 8 P.M., and reach Hammerfest the following *Wednesday* afternoon. They reach Namsös, at the mouth of the Namsen, on *Thursday* at 1 P.M. From Namsös to Hammerfest the voyage occupies about 6 days. The general features of the coast have been described in Route 24. It has not been thought necessary to give a list of all the petty stations at which the steamer calls. Printed lists (to be obtained also in Christiania) are hung up in all the steamers, which give full information of the days and hours at which the steamer calls at the various stations. She stops 6 hours at Bodö to coal, 24 at Tromsöe, and about 48 at Hammerfest, before commencing her return voyage. From Hammerfest another steamer, in connection with this, proceeds every other Thursday, as stated in Route 24, to Vadsö, in East Finmark, arriving there the following Sunday, and returning to Hammerfest in time to catch the steamer going from Hammerfest in the ensuing week.

The whole voyage, with the exception of the short distance between Grotö and the Loffoden Islands, is among the numerous islands which surround the coast, and which form one of the most extensive and splendid inland navigations in the world; if the weather be fine, which is very likely to be the case during the summer months, the admirer of nature in her sternest form will be amply repaid for the fatigue and expense of the voyage.

Those desirous of proceeding from Trondhjem to the Namsen and Alten Rivers for salmon-fishing will find full particulars in Route 24. *For the Namsen*, passengers can land at Namsös at the mouth of the Namsen, and from thence take a boat to *Spillum*, 4½ m., upon the Namsen Fjord (see Route 24), and only 1¼ m. by land from the Hun Station upon the Namsen.

For the *Alten*, passengers land at **Bosekop*, 1 m. by land from Alten, for which see Route 21.

Prior to the establishment of a steamer, in 1838, the only means of proceeding to the N., after leaving Aargaard, or Foldereide, N. of the Namsen River, was either by hiring a boat with 3 or 4 men for a certain distance, or by the regular post, changing boats at each of the stations *en route*. The names of the stations, and the distances for a boat voyage, are given in Route 24.

This mode of travelling has its charms to the scientific traveller, and especially to the naturalist and geologist, it affords by far the most satisfactory means of investigating the objects he is in pursuit of. The three summer months affording one almost continued day, the ground is quickly traversed, and the traveller has the advantage of stopping and making détours where and how he pleases.

At almost all the water stations N. of Trondhjem comfortable quarters will be found, and the islands and fjords contain numerous fishing huts.

HAMMERFEST, see page 134; also for information as to making the voyage from thence to the *North Cape*.

ROUTE 26.

CHRISTIANIA TO TRONDHJEM BY RAIL TO EIDSVOLD, THENCE BY STEAMER OVER THE MIÖSEN TO LILLEHAMMER, THROUGH GUDBRANDSDAL, AND OVER THE DOVRE-FJELD.

Dist. 49¼ Norsk m., or a little under 350 Eng. The time requisite for this journey is 4 or 5 days. Those who are desirous of going by the steamer from Trondhjem, either southwards or northwards, should ascertain the exact day of its departure at Christiania, so as to regulate their journey accordingly. The post goes twice a week by this road, and Forbud papers can be sent by it.

See preliminary observations, and Route 21. It is possible for travellers to go by road from Christiania to Eidsvold, or Minde on the Miösen. The stations are—Christiania to † *Grorud*, ¾; *Skrimstad*, ¾, pay for 1 m.; †*Klöften*, 1¼; † *Trygstad*, ¾; †*Dahl*, 1¼; *Svendsen*, ⅜; †*Eidsvold* ⅝. From Svendsen, to † *Minde*, 1¾. From Eidsvold to †*Minde*, 1¾; in winter time, when the ice bears on the Vormen, only ½ hr. is required for this stage. These are all fast stations: but the road is so uninteresting, that the railway is always preferred. It may be as well to remark, that a road turns off westwards from Grorud, and joins Route 27 near Sogstad; and that at Klöften, the road to Stockholm through Kongsvinger turns off to the E.: Route 35.

Two passenger trains run daily from Christiania to Eidsvold, and back; one in the morning, and one in the afternoon each way, performing the journey in a little under 3 hours. From June 22 to August 22, there is an additional train up and down, leaving Christiania at 12.30, and Eidsvold at 12.45. During this period the "Skibbadner" leaves Lillehammer in time to arrive at Eidsvold for the 12.45 to Christiania, and returns immediately to Lillehammer with the passengers by the 12.30 from Christiania.

There are now two steamers constantly plying on the Miösen, so that by leaving Christiania by the morning train, travellers can reach Lillehammer at the N. end of the lake the same evening, a distance of 17 Norsk m., or 115 Eng.

The steamer leaves Eidsvold on the arrival of the morning train from Christiania, and after ascending the Vormen to Minde, at the S. end of the Miösen, it proceeds on its voyage to Lillehammer, calling at various places *en route*. The average passage is 6 hours.

FARES.—From Christiania to Eidsvold by rail, 1st class, 6 marks; 2nd class, 4 marks; 3rd class, 2 marks. From Eidsvold to Lillehammer by boat, 1st place, 6 marks 2 skillings; 2nd place, 4 marks 4 skillings.

If the traveller intends to pursue his journey beyond Lillehammer, he had better buy his carriole and all necessaries for the journey in Christiania. The preliminary remarks in Route 21, concerning requisites, &c. for the journey, are applicable here; with this exception, that by selecting his night-quarters carefully, and by sending a Forbud to order horses, and provisions to be ready, the traveller will always obtain eatable food. If he cannot eat the black rye bread of the country, he had better take a box of biscuits from Christiania. On the road it is expedient to have the wheels of the carriole greased every morning, or at least every other morning. Patent boxes, or axles, are not yet introduced.

Near *Eidsvold* there is a mansion formerly belonging to the Anker family, celebrated for being the spot where the members who framed the Constitution of Norway in 1814 met, established and proclaimed the independence of the country. The house has been purchased by public subscription in commemoration of that event.

From *Minde*, Route 29 on the eastern side of Miösen diverges to Lillehammer; and from Kornodegaarden, on that Route, the road through Österdalen up the valley of the Glommen, Route 31, turns off to the E.

From *Svendsen*, ½ m. from Eidsvold on the old Christiania road, Route 28 on the western side of Miösen to Lillehammer turns off. The roads on both sides of the lake are infamous, *experto crede*, and the steamer should always be taken in preference. If obliged to take either, select Route 28 on the western side.

The accommodation at Minde is good, and good grayling fishing may be had towards the end of August, both here and at Eidsvold. The water here is icy cold, so that bathing would be highly imprudent. No salmon can get up here, on account of the falls of the Glommen, of which the Miösen Lake is a feeder. There is a species of fresh-water herring in the Miösen, which is taken in large quantities.

The *Miösen Lake*. This beautiful water extends from Minde to Lillehammer, on the N.W., 63 Eng. m. It has several branches, all on the E. bank; the largest of them is nearly in the centre of the lake, at its widest part, opposite the island of Helgeö. The streams and torrents flowing into it are numerous, but its principal tributary is the Logen, which enters the lake at Lillehammer. Minde is in the Agerhuus district. On the E. bank of the Miösen, 1¼ m. from Minde, the Hedermarken district begins, and continues till near Lillehammer. Two miles from Minde on the W. bank, the Christians' district or province of Thoten, begins, and continues all the way up. The town of Lillehammer is in this district, which extends to the N. of the Dovre Fjeld.

This lake was violently agitated at the time of the great Lisbon earthquake, on 1st Nov. 1755; on which occasion, it is said, that its waters rose 20 ft., and then suddenly retreated. Again in 1860, during the disastrous flood, the water rose to an enormous height. A mark in the railway hotel at Eidsvold shows the level it attained. The scenery towards the end of the lake is more pleasing than picturesque—the hills upon the banks are rather low, and wanting in fine outline; they are covered to the water's edge with woods of alder, birch, mountain ash, &c., and in the lower slopes, and forests of pine and fir above. The farms on both sides are very numerous and valuable. Towards the head of the lake the scenery becomes finer, the hills increase in height, and are more picturesque in form.

The cuisine on board the steamers is moderately good and very reasonable. The wine excellent. Carriages and carrioles are placed upon a barge which is towed by the steamer; there is rarely any chance of there being no room to take a carriage, for if they have more goods and carriages than one barge will carry, they quickly have a second in tow. The steamer calls at ten places for goods and passengers during the voyage. The variety of passengers is amusing, and the habits of many of them most primitive. Tobacco is in great request amongst all classes of the men, and its *consequences* are visible in all directions on the deck. But the honest, open-hearted bearing of the people, added to their constant and sincere desire to oblige strangers, who are visiting the country, make ample amends for all their little eccentricities.

About half way up the lake the site of Stor Hammer is passed; it was formerly a town of considerable extent, and the seat of a bishopric. The Swedes burned and plundered it in 1567. Some considerable and picturesque ruins of the Cathedral still exist, which may be seen from the lake. "They chiefly consist of a wall with four round arches. The Cathedral remained nearly entire till towards the end of the 17th century, when it went to ruin. It was formerly very magnificent, and contained many paintings and ornaments; a large organ, and a miraculous crucifix, that wept blood from a reservoir in the head. There were also three other churches in Stor Hammer, of which no vestiges are left. It is now again a rising little town."—*MS. notes*, W. R. C. N.

Somewhat further up, on the island of Helgeö, are the ruins of a castle, built by Hako IV. It is in contemplation to erect extensive works of defence upon this island, and make it a grand military arsenal of the country.

Opposite this island of Helgeö, on the W. bank of the lake, is the village of Hof, where the steamer calls for passengers. Hof is close to Sogstad, from whence a most curious Obelisk may be visited. See Route 28.

Half way between Stor Hammer and Lillehammer on the E. shore, is the church of Ringsaker, said to be built on the site of one of King Olaf's victories. Inside there is a curious carved altar-piece, painted and gilt.

T.* † Lillehammer. Station-house comfortable, and charges reasonable. Kept by Madame "Ormsrud." There is also a small hotel kept by a man of the name of "Hammer," which is tolerably comfortable, but dear.

Carrioles are sometimes to be bought here. "This town was formerly of considerable extent, and the seat of a bishopric. It had a cathedral and a monastery, both founded about 1160, by Adrian, an Englishman, at that time the Pope's Legate in Norway. He afterwards became a Cardinal, under the name of Nicholas Breakspear, of St. Alban's, and Pope, under the title of Hadrian IV. The place was burned by the Swedes in the 17th century."—*Laing's Norway*, p. 487.

Lillehammer is now a small but rising town, population above 1000. It is situated at the head of the Miösen, on high ground, overlooking the lake, having the river *Logen* on the W., at its confluence with the lake. The trout in the Logen are celebrated, and for some distance up the stream run to a very large size.

There are several sawmills upon a small torrent the Mesna, on the N. of the town. It will be worth while exploring this stream a short distance up. There is a fine fos about 2 Eng. miles from the town, which in the early summer is seen to best advantage. The walks around here are beautiful. From a seat upon the Christiania road, a short distance on the S. of the town, there is a most extensive and lovely view over the lake and surrounding country. It should, if possible, be seen at sunset.

"I cannot take leave of the lovely Miösen Lake, without stating my hearty concurrence with Dr. Clarke and other writers quoted by him, that the banks of this lake, and of its feeding river, the Logen, for the distance of 170 Eng. m. from Tofte, in Gudbrandsdalen, affords a series of the finest landscapes in the world; that it is doubtful whether any other river can show such a constant succession of beautiful scenery. He might have added that the grandeur of the forest-clad mountains which inclose the rich and charming valley of Gudbrandsdal, through which it winds its impetuous course, is quite equal to its beauties, and that the richness and fertility of the banks of the lake are on a par with both."—*Barrow's North of Europe*, p. 371.

In going South from Lillehammer, this Route may be varied by following Route 28, to Krommerbakken, along the W. side of the Miösen. From Krummerbakken, by Route 27, to Grinagermarken, and from there by Route 21 to Christiania. Or along the W. side of the Tyri Fjord to Drammen, Kongsberg, and the magnificent Riukan-fos. See Route 23.

"The most striking features of the road between Lillehammer and Trondhjem are the entrance of Gudbrandsdal between Lillehammer and Moshuus, the pass of Rusten between Laurgaard and Brendhaugen, and the descent of the Driva from Kongsvold to Drivstuen."—*Forbes's Norway*, p. 8.

Gudbrandsdalen. This wondrously beautiful valley commences at Lillehammer, and extends up to the foot of the Dovre Fjeld, about 163 Eng. m. The greater part of it is narrow and winding, with towering mountains on either side, cultivated on the lower slopes, and generally covered with pine forests in the upper parts. Here and there the valley widens for a short distance, but nowhere to a greater extent than 6 or 7 Eng. miles.

On leaving Lillehammer our road continues N., and shortly commands a beautiful and extensive view over the town and lake. A torrent from the E. is crossed soon afterwards, and the road joins the margin of the river Logen, on the left bank. From this spot the beauties of the Gudbrandsdal commence. A succession of rapids and grand cascades are passed, as the road continues to ascend the valley. The colour of the water is of a milky blue, like snow water, but it abounds in fish.

† *Aronsæten i Öier*, 1⅜. About 3 Eng. miles south of Moshuus. The road here is excellent. A diligence runs daily between Lillehammer and Elstad, leaving the former at 6 A.M., and the latter at 1 P.M. Not very first-rate quarters. The shooting as well as fishing about here well spoken of. Near this place the river makes a grand fall, called the *Hunnefos*, beyond which the lake trout cannot get up the river. They come up like salmon to spawn, and some of these monsters have been taken here, weighing up to 30 lbs. Above this fall the fish are smaller, but most abundant in the Logen, and all its tributary lakes and streams, not only trout but various other kinds. The mountains continue to increase in grandeur, as the road proceeds up this glorious valley. Farms thickly studded on both sides. A steep hill occurs on this stage, passing through a pine forest; exquisite views of the river beneath and valley beyond.

† *Holmen i Thrötten*, 1⅜. Station-house some distance off the road, on the right. On the 15th August a large horse fair is held here, which lasts for 3 days. It is well attended. Some of the finest horses in Norway may be seen at it, many of them as much as 16 hands high, and beautifully shaped animals; but for service they are not to be compared with the smaller and more genuine Norwegian breed, which average about 13 or 14.

A little beyond Holmen the *Moxa Elv* dashes across our route, while on the left a by-road crosses the river by a picturesque log-bridge, and leads to a most wild and mountainous country on the N.W. full of small lakes and torrents.

The river forms a narrow lake nearly all this stage. There is no longer any steamer plying on the Losna Vand.

† *Nedre Losnæs i Fodvang*, 1⅛. The *Troms Elv* is crossed upon this stage, up the valley of which stream a horse-track turns off to the E. and joins Route 31, near the Messelt station upon the Glommen.

Near here the road crosses the *Troms Elv*, the bed of which is some 200 ft. below. To the right is seen a picturesque fissure in the mountain. It is called the "Devil's Rock," as the torrent is subterranean for some distance from the spot where it issues from the mountain. The scenery increases in grandeur.

* † *Elstad i Ringebo*, ⅞. The station here is about ¼ mile English off the road to the left. It is good, and more beautifully situated than any other on the road. It is built on the point of a hill, which projects into the valley, and commands extensive and lovely views. There is an excellent new road all the way from Lillehammer to this place.

The station-master is unusually intelligent for his class. The snipe-shooting in the valley below is said to be excellent. By the roadside opposite the turn to the station is the picturesque and antique church of Ringebo.

From hence the valley continues most lovely all this stage, the large stream flowing sluggishly on its course. Two torrents from the E., the *Vaalen Elv* and *Erye Elv*, dashing through picturesque rocky gorges, are crossed about midway on this stage. Near the latter a horse-track turns off on the right to the valley of the Glommen: Route 32.

* † *Listad i Söndre Fron*, 1⅛. Shooting about here is said to be fine.

On this stage the valley widens, and is more highly cultivated, but the upper parts of the mountains still clothed with continuous pine forest. The stream again becomes very rapid, and forms two fine and picturesque cataracts. The land near the river exceedingly rich.

* *Öien i Nordre Fron*, ⅞. Very comfortable quarters. From June 12 the station is removed to † *Nedre Brandvold*, distant from *Listad*, ⅞, and from *Storklevestad*, 1⅛. A torrent, the *Seid Elv*, is crossed near the station, and the road keeps close to the Logen up this rich and splendid valley. Irrigation prevails here extensively, and continues for several stages—the water being led down the mountains in wooden troughs to the different farms.

* † *Storklevestad i Qvam*, 1⅛. Comfortable quarters and reasonable charges; game said to be plentiful about here. Better quarters may be had at Viig, the old station, about 1 Eng. mile south of this. Situation of the station beautiful, on the bank of the stream, and surrounded by mountains. Some of the timbers in this house are shown which formed part of the old house in which St. Olaf was born, and which stood near this spot.

On leaving Storklevestad the valley takes a westerly direction, and winds a good deal, the stream dashing along at a racing pace. Not far from Viig, the church of *Qvam* is passed on the right. Here Colonel Sinclair was buried. The scene of his slaughter and that of his devoted band is passed on the next stage. The *Veglie Elv* is crossed soon afterwards, and about here the road is 863 feet above the sea, according to Forsell's map. About midway upon this stage the valley again turns almost due N. At this bend of the valley the *Hedals Elv*, from the W., joins the Logen. A horse-track leads up the valley of the Hedals Elv to the mountains on the W. A road turns off from Viig to Espedal's Iron Works, distant 4½ m.

From Breden, Moen, and Rommundgaard, the three succeeding stations, there are roads leading through Vaage to Lomb parish.

Thus, from † *Breden* to *Slette*, 1⅛; *Bjölstad i Hedal*, 1; *Söndre Snerle i Vaage*, 1⅞ (pay for 1¼, and for 1⅞ returning); †*Svee*, 1⅛; †*Garmo i Lomb*, 2; † *Andvord*, 1⅛; † *Rödsheim*, 1¼. Hence, pedestrians, or even a horse can go over the Sögne Fjeld to Optun, 5¼ m. in Nordre Bergenhuus Amt; and from Optun there is a track to the head of the Lyster, or of the Aardals Fjord, the two westernmost arms of the Sögne Fjord. From the head of Lyster Fjord boats to Leirdalsören can be taken on Route 21, which see. This route will take pedestrians through some of the wildest parts of Norway: considerable hardship will have to be endured. From † *Breden* or from † *Moen* to † *Nedre Aasören*, 1; *Snerle*, 1⅞, &c. (see above). From † *Rommundgaard* to † Svee, 2 m., and (see above) from Rödsheim, Galdhöpiggen, the highest mountain in Norway, may be ascended. It is 8300 Norsk feet above the sea. A pedestrian may force his way hence over snow-covered fjelds, ascending Glittertind on his way, 7800 feet, to Gjendin Vand, thence to Bygdin Vand, a large mountain lake, 3500 feet above the sea. If not fortunate enough to fall in with a hut, the traveller will have to camp out. There is a hut at the W. end of Bygdin Vand.

From thence along the Tyen Vand to Nystuen on the Fille Fjeld, Route 21. This path should not be attempted without a guide, and it may be no easy matter to get one. It was followed in 1852 by Mr. M., however, without one, but there is considerable risk in the undertaking. From Optun Skagstoltind, 7877 feet, a peak of the Horungerne mountains may be ascended.

For further information, see Route 38.

* † *Breden* and *Bredevangen i*

Sels, 1¼. Dreden is the winter, Bredevangen the summer station. Near here the river forms a small lake, close to the head of which the *Otta Elv* joins the Logen on the W. A little farther up, a torrent from the E., the *Ulen Elv*, forms a picturesque fall, and turns several sawmills. Soon after leaving Solheim, the road passes a very steep hill, called *Kringelen;* the scene of the massacre of Colonel Sinclair, and his Scotch followers. At this spot a small post with an inscription marks the spot where Colonel Sinclair fell. In 1612, during the war between Christian IV. of Denmark and Gustavus Adolphus of Sweden, a body of Scotch troops had been raised for the service of Sweden. The Danes were at that time in possession of Gottenburg; and from Calmar, in the Baltic, to the North Cape, the whole coast was occupied by the subjects of Christian IV. The Scotch, therefore, decided on the bold plan of landing in Norway, and fighting their way across it to Sweden. A portion landed at Trondhjem, and the rest, 900 strong, commanded by Col. George Sinclair, landed in Romsdalen (see Route 30), from whence they marched toward this valley, ravaging the country on their way. At Kringelen an ambush was prepared by about 300 peasants; huge quantities of rocks, stones, and trees were collected on the mountain, and so placed that all could at once be launched upon the road beneath. Everything was done to lull the Scotch into security, and with perfect success. When they arrived beneath the awful avalanche prepared for them, all was sent adrift from above, and the majority of the Scotch were crushed to death, or swept into the river and drowned; the peasants then rushed down upon the wounded and stragglers and despatched them. Of the whole force only two of the Scotch are said to have survived. But accounts differ on this point, one being that 60 prisoners were taken and afterwards slaughtered in cold blood.

Sinclair's lady is said to have accompanied him, and it is added that a youth who meant to join the peasants in the attack was prevented by a young lady, to whom he was to be married the next day. She, on hearing that one of her own sex was with the Scotch, sent her lover to her protection; Mrs. Sinclair, mistaking his object, shot him dead. — *Laing's Norway.* The date of this massacre was the 24th August, 1612.

The rest of the Scotch, with some Dutch, were completely successful in their object. They were commanded by Colonel Mönnichofen, landed N. of Trondhjem, marched upon Stockholm, which they aided in relieving from the Danish forces most opportunely, and enabled the Swedish monarch soon afterwards to conclude advantageous terms of peace.—*Geyer's Histoire de Suède.*

In a house near this place of slaughter it is said that some arms and other trophies taken by the peasants from the Scotch are preserved.

The road now follows the stream, and from the foot of this celebrated hill there is a most picturesque view of it, and the valley and river on the right. Before arriving at the next station the stream is crossed by a new bridge to the right bank.

† *Moen i Sels*, ¾.

† *Rommundgaard i Sels*, ¾. A very excellent station. Here Colonel Sinclair passed the night before the massacre. Shooting around here said to be fine. Reindeer are often to be met with in the *Rundane mountains*, about 3 m. N.E. of this. Also white foxes and wolves. The most W. of this group is 6000 feet above the sea. On the opposite side, a

little higher up, the *Sæter Aae* joins the river. From Laurgaard, the old station, a by-road branches off to the W. by the Vaage Vand, from whence horse-tracks lead across the mountains of the Sögne Fjeld, Route 38, and by the Justedal Glaciers, to the Sögne Fjord (see Route 21). The distance from Laurgaard to Sandtöe is 2 m. Also to the high road on the W. coast between Bergen and Molde, Route 24. Ponies and guides may be obtained at the different stations. The bridge at Laurgaard is 1000 Eng. feet above the sea, and the highest point passed on the next stage is about 1600, descending again, however, considerably to the church at Dovre, which is not more than 1500.

Continuing our route, the road is very hilly on this stage, the scenery grand in the extreme, and increasing in wildness. During this and the next stage the mountains on the W. are those of the *Haalangen Fjeld*. In one part the road is carried over the shoulder of a mountain, called *Rusten*, at a great height above the level of the river, which foams through a narrow rocky gorge to the right.

* † *Brandhaugen i Dovre*, 1. A nice clean station. Reindeer venison is sometimes to be had here. The trout-fishing and shooting about here highly spoken of. The road still continues on the left bank. Numbers of small farms up the sides of the mountains on this stage; the soil light; and vast forests of pine. River close on the left all the rest of the way. The village of Dovre and its pretty church are passed on the left, shortly previous to the next station. The wondrously beautiful Gudbrandsdal is considered as commencing from this village of Dovre, and the fjeld properly begins at

* † *Toftemoen i Dovre*, 1. Road still continues close alongside the river all the way, and gradually ascending. The valley contracts, and the soil becomes more sandy. It is said that the station-master here can trace his pedigree up to Harald Haarfager.

T. * † *Dombaas i Lesje*, 1. Capital quarters. The station stands at some little distance off the road on the left.

Here Route 30 turns off, leading through the magnificent valley of Romsdal to the town of *Molde*, on the N.W.

Our route now quits this valley of the Logen, and turning N.E., the ascent of the

Dovre Fjeld

is commenced, which soon becomes very steep. Splendid views are obtained over the *Lesje Vand*, on the road to Molde. The road passes through a picturesque forest of old Scotch firs before arriving at the next station; and a small lake, the *Fogs Aae*, is crossed, which is the source of one of the large tributaries of the Glommen. The limit of Scotch fir here is about 2870 Eng. feet above the sea: birch ceases about 400 feet higher.

* † *Fokstuen on Dovre*, ⅞, pay for 1. The station is much improved lately; it is 3150 feet above the level of the sea. A short distance from hence the plateau of the Dovre Fjeld is attained, but the road gradually ascends during all this stage. About midway it passes between two desolate-looking lakes, formed by the stream from the Fogs Aae, which runs through them. The lake on the left is the *Volu*, and from thence the stream takes the name of the *Folda*. The scenery wild, and vegetation scanty. A few stunted birch are the only trees to be seen.

* † *Jerkin on Dovre*, 1⅛. An *excellent* station. Everything clean and good, and great attention paid to the comfort of the guests. Charges very reasonable. There are five good

and well-furnished rooms. English gentlemen have stayed here upwards of two months at a time for the sake of the shooting. The station-master is a large farmer—breeds horses extensively, and is quite a genius. The rooms are decorated with his paintings, and his carvings in wood are admirable. Specimens may be purchased, such as spoons, handles for knives, &c., carved in reindeer horn. There also may be seen all the economy of a mountain farm. The dairy at Jerkin is well worth a visit. The landlord keeps 35 cows, and 24 horses. Potatoes grow near the house. In fact, whether for grand scenery, sporting, or comfort, this is one of the most tempting places in all Norway at which to linger, at least for a few days. The postman acts as carrier for anything which may be wanted from Christiania or Trondhjem. Ladies will, perhaps, be favoured with a sight of the family wardrobe, and amused at the number and variety of the dresses hung round the room, furs for winter, &c.

The establishment of Jerkin as a station dates from the early part of the 12th century, together with Fogstuen and Tofte on the S.W., and Kongsvold on the N. They are called *Fjeldstuen* (mountain lodgings), and, as such, are rent and tax free.

This station is seldom without reindeer venison, which is supplied by a man named Per, who lives in the immediate vicinity of the mountain of Sneehœtten. He is said to be a crack shot, and acts as guide and keeper for any sportsman stopping here. He has dogs, but they are useless except for deer or hares. Ptarmigan are plentiful, and a good brace of setters would be invaluable for them. Mr. Laing speaks well of the trout-fishing here; the fish are small, but numerous.

From Jerkin a station-road runs E. for some distance down the valley of the *Folda Elv* (Foldalen), and joins Route 31 in the valley of the Glommen, at *Neby*. The deer-stalking at Foldalen, in the autumn, is well spoken of, and elk, though very scarce, are at times met with there.

Excursion to Sneehætten.—Jerkin is an excellent place from whence to visit this celebrated mountain; horses and guides can be obtained here. A day's provisions, including some brandy, are requisite. The view, from the summit of the mountain, at sunrise and sunset, is sublime. The lover of the picturesque will also be repaid by a visit to Per, the hunter's, dwelling. He and his wife and children reside here throughout the winter, and are the only inhabitants of this wild district within a range of 14 Eng. miles. Sneehœtten is on the N.W. of Jerkin; the ascent is so gradual that much of the effect of its great height, 7714 English feet, is lost. Its peaked summit is only about 3500 feet above the base from whence it springs. It was long considered the highest mountain in Norway, but it appears that *Skagstöls Tind* in the Sögne Fjeld (see Route 38) is 163 feet higher,* and Galdhöpiggen (see Viig, in this Route) is still higher, being 8300 Norsk feet.

"Sneehœtten may be ascended in an easy day from Jerkin; it is 3 or 4 hours' riding to the base of the mountain, and from thence about an hour and a half's walking to the top, most of it over that peculiar kind of snow-ice which is, I believe, found on the highest summits of snow mountains. The ascent is without difficulty. The view is fine; to the N. a very wild prospect of mountains; to the E. an immense table-land of moor. It is well to take horses, as many streams must be crossed. Sneehœtten forms the N.W. extre-

* Forsell's Map, in 9 sheets: published at Stockholm, 1815-1816.

mity of one of those ridges of high snow mountains which rise out of the great table-land of moor, which separates the E. and W. declivities of the Scandinavian mountains. It rises much above the snow line, and contains true glaciers. The mountain itself is very picturesque: at the foot lies a little lake, backed by glaciers, and those again by black precipices, rising above them in the form of an amphitheatre. It is a remarkable instance how much more the height of the snow-line depends upon the accidents of situation and atmosphere than upon latitude, that the table-land about Jerkin, which in summer is entirely free from snow, rises to a height as great or greater than those mountains near Bergen, which, in a much warmer climate, and a degree and a half farther S., contain glaciers reaching down almost to the sea level."—C. T. N.

"On the summit of Snechœtten there is a crater, which is broken down on the N. side, and surrounded on the others by perpendicular masses of black rock, rising out of, and high above, beds of snow that envelope their bases. The interior sides of the crater descended in one vast sheet of snow to the bottom, where an icy lake closed the view at the depth of 1500 feet from the highest ridge. Almost at the top, and close to the snow, which had probably but a few days before covered them, were some very delicate and beautiful flowers, in their highest bloom, of the *Ranunculus glacialis*, growing most profusely; nor were they the only inhabitants; mosses, lichens, and a variety of small herbaceous plants, were in the same neighbourhood; and, lower down, dwarf birch, and a species of osier, form a pretty kind of thicket. The tracks of reindeer appeared on the very topmost snow."—*Sir Thomas Acland. MS. Letter.*

Mr. Laing says: "The most extraordinary feature of this mountain tract is that the surface of the Fell and of Sneehœtten to its summit is covered with, or more properly is composed of, rounded masses of gneiss and granite, from the size of a man's head to that of the hull of a ship. These loose rolled masses are covered with soil in some places; in others they are bare, just as they were left by the torrents which must have rounded them, and deposited them in this region."

On quitting Jerkin, a short but very steep ascent leads to the highest point of the Dovre Fjeld road, 4594 feet above the sea. To the W. the summit of Sneehœtten may be seen in clear weather. The road quickly begins to descend from this grand and desolate region; high poles are fixed on each side of the road to mark the way during snow. Reindeer moss abounds here. Mr. Laing passed this way in February. He says: "A smothering snow-drift came on, and it was scarcely possible to see from pole to pole. I asked the boy who drove the baggage sledge if he was sure we were upon the road. He said they always left that to the horses on this stage when the path could not be discerned; that they would not go wrong if not put out of their pace, but left to take their way themselves. The journeying on this elevated plain, enveloped in a cloud of snow as dense almost as that on which you are driving, makes a sublime impression on the mind. You seem travelling in the sky. What you see and touch of the earth is scarcely more substantial than the snow that is whirling round and above you. It seems all one element, and you alone in the midst of it."

On quitting the plateau of the fjeld the road enters a deep glen, down which the river *Driv* (which rises to the W. of Jerkin) forms a series of cataracts and falls. The way continues by the side of this river, and rapidly descends and increases in grandeur and picturesque effect all the way to Kongsvold. The variety and richness of the moss, lichens, and herbage, and warm colour of the rocks, in passing over the fjeld, form a study for the artist, unique and charming in effect.

* † *Kongsvold on Dovre*, ¾, pay for 1½. Another excellent station. In the event of Jerkin being full, this is the next best place as head-quarters for the fishing and shooting to be had in the region of Sneehætten. It is also a good place from whence to ascend that mountain. This station is 3063 feet above the sea. The road continues close along the right bank of the Driv, nearly all the way now from Kongsvold to Rise. It has been lately made, to avoid the fearful hill of Vaarstige, which formerly existed. It is carried all the way down the valley now by the side of the Driva, being, in many places, quarried out of the face of the rock. It is a striking piece of engineering. Soon after leaving Kongsvold, the river makes two picturesque falls, and a third is passed on the right, about the middle of the stage, where a torrent from the E. joins the river. The scenery is most grand and picturesque; the ravine narrow, with high mountains clothed with birch and fir, and rocks fine in outline, with much colour, chiefly reds and browns. Splendid subjects for the pencil all the way.

* † *Drivstuen i Opdal*, 1⅜. A large farm at this station, and tolerable accommodation. Good trout-fishing in the Driv. Here the Dovre Fjeld is considered as ending; height above the sea, 2220 feet. On leaving this station the road continues rapidly to descend; scenery splendid, and ravine narrow, till near the end of the stage, when it widens, patches of cultivation increase, and the mountains decrease in grandeur. Between Kongsvold and Drivstuen lies the Vaarsti, a very steep hill which is now avoided since the new road was made.

† *Rise i Opdal*, 1⅛, pay for 1¼. Near this station the *Vinstra Elv* is crossed, the ravine gradually widens into a broad valley, and the Driv Elv becomes a fine stream. The hills are said to abound in black game and hares. At the village of Opdal our road quits the river, and runs to the N.E. The elevation of the road near Opdal is 2114 feet, and the peak of the Sneehætten may be seen about S.W.

* † *Ny-Öune i Opdal*, ⅞. A most comfortable station, and excellent quarters for fishing and shooting; the hills about here also are said to be rich in game. The station-master carves well in wood, and specimens of his skill may be purchased. The road continues N.E.; scenery not so fine as hitherto; mountains lower, with much birch and scrub. Here a station-road on the W. branches off, and continues down the stream through Sundalen, towards the town of *Christiansund*, in Route 24. The stations are—*Öune* to *Aalboe*, 1; *Gravöne*, ⅞; *Sliper i Opdal*, 1¼; † *Gjöra i Sundal*, ⅞. From *Gjöra* to *Sliper* pay for 1⅞, but only for ⅞ returning; * † *Storfale i Romfog*, 1⅜; * *Sundalsören*, 1⅜; hence by sea to Christiansund, 4½. The Sundal is highly spoken of as a *salmon stream*.

* † *Nystuen i Opdal*, 1¼. In the early part of this stage the scenery is of the same character as the last; towards the end of the stage the road descends through a thick pine forest to

† *Austbjerg i Remmebo*, 1. New road. Good shooting quarters. In the distance mountains piled above each other, covered with a sea of dark pine and fir. Capercailie and black game are said to be numerous in this neighbourhood.

Between Övne and Bjerkager there is now an excellent new *chaussée*. Before arriving at the next station the traveller will remark a cross carved on the solid rock. It marks the spot whence an unfortunate workman was precipitated to a depth of 700 ft., in 1862. And, on crossing the river, a station-road to the left leads down the valley of the Orkla, and joins the high road between Molde and Trondhjem (Route 24) by the following stages, viz.: Haarstad, 1½; Grudt, 1¼; and † Kalstad, 1. Vide p. 116.

† *Bierkager i Remnebo*, 1. New good road.

* † *Garlid i Soyndal*, 1½. This station is some distance off the road, up the side of the mountain on the left. Fair accommodation here. Charges reasonable. An interesting and most industrious family. They carve well, and make excellent carrioles, with springs, at 18 dollars, which is exceedingly cheap. The knives and other articles of steel and iron, though roughly made by the peasants, are considered much superior to those manufactured in the towns, both as to temper and durability. Near this station a *new road* to the S.E. has been made, which leads into the valley of the Glommen, near the *Neby* station, Route 31, on the way to Christiania.

From Garlid the road keeps along very high ground all the way, through mountain pastures and park-like scenery. The *Villa Elv* is crossed just before the next station.

† *Præsthuus i Remnebo*, ¾. The road from Garlid is good, but a heavy stage going south. Road still runs along high ground, through rich pastures for some distance, and numbers of small farms in all directions. Scenery continues park-like, till a rapid descent leads down the mountain, through a wild, picturesque valley, to

Soknæs i Stören, 1. Poor quarters, but the *salmon-fishing* in the *Gula* (or Gaul) *Elv*, near here, and higher up about Rogstad, is excellent. Soon after leaving Soknæs, the road enters the valley of the Gula, which it crosses, and quickly joins the road from Christiania, through the valley of the Glommen, Route 31. The new railway between Trondhjem and Stören is now open. Keeping N. the road continues along the bank of the Gula, which winds its rapid course through a dark ravine; the mountains on either side and in the distance clothed with pine and fir to their summits. Scenery becomes less wild towards the end of the stage.

Vollan i Horrig, ¾. Road continues along the eastern bank of the Gula, more or less all the way, and is level. Valley highly cultivated, and the hop extensively grown. Soon after leaving Vollan, the stream expands into a small lake, and midway between that and Leer the *Lundesogna Elv* is crossed.

Leer i Flaa, 1½. Road follows the winding of the Gula again all this stage, mountains becoming more rounded and decreasing in boldness towards Meelhuus, but still covered with forests along the higher points. Numbers of farms on both sides the valley. Road hilly and bad.

* *Meelhuus*, ¾. From hence the church forms a most picturesque object, looking up the valley. It is beautifully placed on the crown of a small hill, with the fir-clad mountains towering above each other in the background, and the valley winding away into the far distance on the right.

At Meelhuus our road quits the Gula, and passes over rounded hills and broken, picturesque ground, highly cultivated in places. Lovely views on the S.E., over part of the *Trondhjem Fjord*.

* *Esp i Leinstrand*, ¾. Road continues over well-cultivated and undulating high land. Towards the end

of the stage the road from Christiansund, Route 24, joins ours on the left. There is now an excellent new road to Trondhjem. Before reaching that city, the most lovely scenery is passed. In the foreground are the remains of some old fortifications—beneath, the city and its ample roadstead spread out like a map, and beyond, the fjord, of immense extent, bounded by mountains in the distance. And to the left, on the bank of the fjord, is seen a small hill called Swerroberg, where the renowned King Swerro is said to have lived in the latter end of the 12th century.

T. † TRONDHJEM (or Drontheim), 1½.—*Inns:* Hôtel d'Angleterre, Hôtel Belle Vue: both pretty good and comfortable. People very civil. Hôtel du Nord. And there are several comfortable boarding-houses, which are less expensive than the hotels. The usual charges per diem at the hotels and boarding-houses range from 1 dollar to 1½, exclusive of wine, which is good and cheap, particularly French wines. The two first-named hotels are in the best part of the town, near the cathedral and post-office, and a considerable distance from the jetty, where passengers are landed from the steamers when there is much sea. In fine weather, the boatmen, if ordered, will pull across the roadstead and land their passengers close to the Hôtels d'Angleterre and Belle Vue, but this can only be done at high water.

The *Post Office* is on the S. side of the town, opposite the Frue Kirke, and on the way to the cathedral. Notes may generally be changed for small money at the post-office. See commencement of this Route as to sending Forbud papers by the post upon this road.

The *British Vice-Consul* here is Mr. Knudtzen. His counting-house is on the E. side of the town near the river. He acts as agent for some of the London bankers, and will cash circular notes and bills drawn on letters of credit. Forget not to replenish the stock of *small* money, and that it is often difficult to obtain sufficient, except from the bank, which is only open for about an hour early in the morning. Nothing can exceed the kindness and hospitality of Mr. Knudtzen and his family to British and American travellers. They all speak English perfectly, and the value of their information and advice to travellers is as great as the readiness with which it is afforded to those who seek it. Mr. Knudtzen is the fortunate possessor of several charming works by Thorwaldsen. They have twice been saved from destruction when Mr. Knudtzen's town-house was burned. Two alti-relievi are very lovely. The subjects, Hector's interview with Paris and Helen; and Cupid and young Bacchus.

At Trondhjem the travellers' carriage and harness should be carefully inspected, and damages repaired. Trust not to others; it requires personal attention, and Norsk workmen are slow and procrastinating. The *Shops* are few and poorly stocked. Views and prints of Norwegian costumes may be purchased at reasonable prices; also trinkets of native manufacture; furs and eider-down are very cheap, particularly ermine. The two latter are amongst the best presents which are to be purchased here for friends at home. Mr. Lundgreen's, however, is an excellent shop, where all kinds of groceries, provisions, portable soup, preserved meats, wine and brandy, &c., may be bought. Mr. Hartman's also is a good ironmonger's shop, where shot and Prussian powder are to be had.

Rifle-shooting is a favourite amusement amongst the gentlemen here. E. Hoaas, near the Frue Kirke, can repair them, but he keeps none ready-made.

Capes, hat-covers, &c., of goat-skin are made in Trondhjem, and are excellent, as well as very durable; but the smell from them is disagreeable when damp.

The city of Trondhjem was founded A.D. 997, by King Olaf Trygvason, upon the site of the old Scandinavian city *Nidaros*. The adventures of this king are the most romantic of all the sovereigns of Norway. Born a prince, his mother only saved his life from the usurper of his rights by quitting the country; they were taken by pirates, separated, and sold as slaves; at an early age he was discovered and redeemed by a relative, became a distinguished sea king, or leader of piratical expeditions, married an Irish princess, embraced Christianity, and ultimately fought his way to the throne of Norway in 991. He then became a most zealous missionary, propagating the faith by his sword; death or Christianity was the only alternative he allowed his subjects. In 998 he destroyed the celebrated Trondhjem Temple of Thor and Odin, with the idols of those gods which existed there, and were held in the highest veneration. This temple was a short distance from the walls of the city, and upon its site the church of Hlades was built.

Trondhjem was the royal residence and seat of government, and remained the capital of Norway down to the time of its union with Denmark, when Christiania was made the capital. Its population, by the census of 1855, was about 16,000.

The city is built round a bay, on the S. side of the fjord, at the mouth of the river *Nid*. It has repeatedly suffered from fire, most of the houses formerly being of wood. The last was in April, 1841, when 350 dwellings were destroyed. Since that all the houses rebuilt are, according to law, of brick or stone. The streets are regular and spacious, with large square water cisterns at their intersections. The architecture of the houses is of the plainest description, without any ornament, but they have a great air of cleanliness and comfort.

The *National Bank*.—"This bank was founded 1816, and has its head office in Drontheim, with branches in the principal towns. It is under the direction of 5 stockholders, with a council of 15 representatives of the other proprietors. Its capital was originally raised by a forced loan or tax upon all landed property, and the landowners became shareholders according to their respective payments. In a short time these shares became a valuable stock, and are at a considerable premium. It is a bank for landed property, and discounts bills, &c., only as a secondary branch of business. Its principal business is in advancing, in its own notes, upon first securities over land, any sum not exceeding two-thirds of the value of the property, according to a general valuation of the whole country taken in 1812. The borrower pays interest at 4 per cent. half-yearly on the sum to his debit; and yearly 5 per cent. of the principal, which is thus all repaid in 20 years. In the event of non-payment of the interest or instalment, the bank proceeds by a summary sale of the property by public auction to realise its security."—*Laing's Norway*, p. 283.

The *Cathedral* is the great object of interest here. "Between the years 1016 and 1030 St. Olaf built a church on the spot where now St. Clement's Church stands. He was buried a little to the south of his own church, where the high altar now is. Between the years 1036 and 1047 Magnus the Good raised a small wooden chapel over St. Olaf's grave; and soon after Harald Hardraade built a stone church, dedicated to our Lady, to the westward of this. This group of 3 churches stood in this state in the troubled period that ensued. In 1160 Archbishop Eystein commenced the great transept west of "our Lady's" chapel, and probably completed it about 1163. He or his successor rebuilt St. Clement's Church as it now stands, probably about this time. During the next 60 or 70 years the whole of the eastern part of the cathedral was rebuilt, the tomb-house or shrine being joined on to the apse of the Lady Church. In 1248 Archbishop Sigurd commenced the nave; it is not certain whether it was ever completed. In 1328 the church was damaged by fire: it must have been after this accident that the internal range of columns in the circular part was rebuilt in the style of our earlier Edwards."—*Ferguson's Illustrated Handbook of Architecture*, page 931.

According to Mr. Laing, the W. end, now in ruins, was founded in 1248, and at the end of the 13th century the whole structure must have stood in all its splendour. The extreme length has been 346 feet, its breadth 84; but the W. end, which contained the grand entrance, had a chapel at each corner, making the breadth of that front 140 feet. The whole of this W. end was highly decorated, particularly the entrance, which had 3 doors, over which were 20 delicately cut niches, in which statues were placed, and, judging by the mutilated remains, they were of considerable merit. Many of the existing ornaments of this W. end will amply repay the trouble of seeking them.

The shrine of St Olaf was decorated with the greatest magnificence, and long a favourite place of pilgrimage, not only for the Scandinavians, but for pilgrims from all parts of Europe; and in such veneration was he held, that even at Constantinople churches were erected to his memory. —*Malte-Brun*, vol. viii. p. 518. The body of the saint was found incorrupt in 1098, and also in 1541, when the Lutherans plundered the shrine of its gold and jewels to an immense amount. The ship which carried the greater part of this plunder foundered at sea on its way to Denmark, and the rest was seized by robbers on land. The Lutherans, however, appear to have treated the body of the saint with respect. In 1568 it was removed from the shrine and buried in the cathedral. St. Olaf was slain 31st August, 1030. See p. 120.

Tradition and history alike recount how often this holy pile has suffered from fire; and in various parts of the edifice finely carved stones have been built into the massive walls, betokening but little regard to architectural beauty or uniformity in repairing the ravages of the devouring element. The transept and E. end are the only parts roofed in, and now used for divine service.

"The upper parts of these," Mr. Laing observes, "have probably been rebuilt at various and comparatively recent periods. By these I mean all above the first arches, or those springing from the ground. I conceive that all this higher part has originally been only of wood, and that where the woodwork has been consumed by fire at different periods, the stones of the aisles and arches within the shell now remaining of the W. end, have been employed to build up the present walls of the transept and other parts which were originally of wood. Thus," he adds, "we may account for the paltry taste and execution of all the upper part of the structure, and for the insertion of cut stone mouldings of arches where an arch could never have been intended; but the stones thus built in have evidently been brought from other places, while all that is below, and could not possibly have been injured by any conflagration, is original, and, from its antiquity, style, and execution, very interesting. The round arch with the zigzag ornaments, which we call Saxon, is employed in all this old part, and also in St. Clement's chapel. The present entrance in the north transept is a fine specimen of both; but this simple massive style is mixed with light pointed arches, and adorned with grotesque heads, flowers, and all the variety of ornaments which are usually considered peculiar to a much later period of Gothic architecture; but here the two styles are evidently coeval. It shakes the theory of the Saxon and Norman, the round and pointed arch having been used exclusively in particular and different centuries, and affording ground to determine the comparative antiquity of Gothic edifices. The Norman arch, in its most florid style, is connected with the Saxon in its most simple and massive form, in a building where the known date of the portion containing this admixture is more ancient than the ascertained date of those English edifices from which the theory is derived."

Upon the left, on entering at the N. door, a large and beautiful round arch, highly decorated with the zigzag and other ornaments, was discovered in 1847, and carefully laid open. The general effect of the interior of the cathedral is ruined by the high pews below, as well as those inclosed in the galleries. The choir is octagonal, surmounted by a dome of modern construction. The high altar is surrounded by light pillars and open arches extending to the roof. The whole of the choir is most elaborately and beautifully decorated, and will repay a careful and minute inspection. Over the altar is placed a fine cast of Thorwaldsen's noble statue of the Saviour. On either side of it are casts of statues of the 12 Apostles, which are very inferior as works of art, and ruinous to the general effect of the choir.

"The mixture of round and pointed arches is very remarkable. The upper rows of arches are all round; but in the lower rows only the outer ones, while the inner ones on each side next the choir are fine full-pointed arches. The same peculiarity may be seen in Christchurch Cathedral in Dublin."—*MS. Notes*, W. E. C. N.

Considerable sums have been expended within these few years in repairing this fine cathedral. The Norwegians take much pride and interest in its preservation; but it is evident that none of the authorities here possess either skill or taste for Gothic architecture, for it has been fearfully "churchwardened;" the richest and most elaborate tracery being carefully choked up with coats of a lead-coloured wash.

Trondhjem Cathedral is (according to an article of the Constitution of 1814) to remain the place of coronation for the Norwegian sovereigns. The Bishop of Trondhjem performs the ceremony. Here Bernadotte was accordingly crowned king of Norway.

There are two works published on this cathedral. The best is by Gerard Schöning, in 1762, and minutely describes it as it was in the days of its glory, besides giving several engravings of the most interesting parts. The other is by Assessor Schwach. Both these works have long been out of print, but may be seen at the public library in the Museum. There are also a description by Grimkele, a notice in the "*Norge fremstillet i Tegninger*," and a fine work by Mr. Schrimer, of Christiania, on the cathedrals of Norway.

The *Arsenal.*—On the S. side of the cathedral are some remains of the Royal Palace, which, with the adjoining grounds, are now occupied as a military and naval arsenal. The throne of the old Norwegian kings is preserved here. The naval portion of the arsenal, with its dockyard, are beautifully kept. They are on the left bank of the river Nid; and here are laid up in ordinary a considerable number of gun-boats, each in its own shed, with all that belongs to it, numbered and ready for instant service.

The *Museum* is small and badly kept. It comprises a library; some of the books are said to be very rare; the theological portion are said to be the best; the manuscripts are principally letters of the kings of Norway. —*Everest's Norway*, p. 201. There are likewise collections of Northern antiquities, old armour, minerals, shells, &c., but the best is the collection of Norwegian ornithology.

There is a *theatre* here. The city contains no manufactories of importance. Its trade is chiefly confined to its exports of dried and salted fish, timber, tar, and some copper from the mines at Röraas; and to importing wines, groceries, and other articles of foreign produce, for supplying its own as well as the wants of the neighbouring districts. All the products of the country are exceedingly moderate in price. The French and other wines are also cheap and very good. Of late years Trondhjem has taken a great lead in ship-building, and has become celebrated for building very fast-sailing vessels; but they are exceedingly wet. There is a great air of comfort and well-being amongst the people, and all classes are celebrated for their good looks.

The roadstead is not very safe, being unprotected to the N. and W.. The river Nid, which surrounds great part of the town, will not admit vessels drawing above 10 or 12 feet water. This river is said to be rarely frozen; the cold here, from its proximity to the sea, never being very intense.

Near the Custom-House (according to the opinion of antiquaries) is the spot where the ancient *Ore-thing*, or assemblage of the people, for this part of Norway was held. Here above 20 kings of Norway have been proposed, accepted by the Thing, and proclaimed. It is sacred ground for a king; and Bernadotte testified his respect for it and for the historical recollections of his subjects in 1835. He stopped his carriage, got out, and walked across the spot with his hat off.—*Laing's Norway*, p. 387.

On the E. the city is commanded by a chain of hills, and on one of them there is an old fortress of some extent, which overlooks the town, but is utterly inefficient for its protection.

The *Environs.*—Opposite the city, in the centre of the fjord, stands the small island rock of *Munkholm*. Canute the Great, A.D. 1028, founded a monastery of Benedictines here, the first of that order established in Norway. A low round tower is all that remains of it, and this is within the walls of the fortress. It was in a small gloomy chamber in this tower that the Staatsminister of Christian V. of Denmark, Graf von Greiffenfeld, was immured from 1680 to 1698. He was originally Peter Schumacher.—*Wagner's Handbook*, p. 60. This dungeon is no longer shown, but it is said that he had worn a deep channel in the pavement in walking up and down, and indented the stone table where he had rested his hand in passing it. This fortress has ceased to be used for State prisoners. Great expense has been incurred by the Government in strengthening its defences; but it appears extremely doubtful, in the event of a war, whether it would be sufficiently strong to withstand an attack, or whether, owing to the distance, the guns from its batteries could be of much avail in protecting the shipping or town. It is still the dark solitary rock which Victor Hugo has described in his "Hans of Iceland," looking more like a prison-house than a fortress. Leave to visit Munkholm must be obtained of the commandant in Trondhjem. The Norwegian regalia are kept in the fortress.

Down the fjord, about 3½ m. N.W. of Trondhjem, a small river enters the fjord near the *Uddue* station, in the parish of Rimen. The *salmon-fishing* there is good.

Three miles S. of the city the Nid forms two beautiful falls, known as *Lierfossen*. The perpendicular height of the upper fall is 99 Eng. feet, and its breadth, according to Dr. Clarke, 413 feet. The lower fall is about 1000 yards distant; its height 82 feet, and breadth 122 feet. The upper fall is the most picturesque. The *salmon-fishing* near the lower fall is said to be excellent. Close to the falls are several furnaces for smelting copper, sawing-mills, &c. Leave must be obtained of the proprietor of these works for fishing in the Nid.

From these falls a beautiful excursion may be made up the valley of the Nid to the *Selbo Lake*, across it from Teigen to Qvællo, and thence by land to Stordal, on the Trondhjem Fjord, and back to the city by land or water. The total distance is about 12 m.

Excursion from Trondhjem to Selbo and Tydalen.

From Trondhjem to *Haugan*, 1⅜; *Vigen*, 1⅜, pay for 2⅛, returning for 2; *Fuglum*, 1; thence either across Sælbo Sö to *Havernæs*, ⅛, or round the bottom of the lake to *Scaaas*, ⅛, and to *Havernæs*, 1⅛; *Rolsæt*, 1; *Udhuus*, 1⅛; *Græslid*, 1⅛; *Aunet*, ⅜; *Kirkvold*, ⅜, from which place a bridle-road leads to *Stuedal i Tydal*, 2 m.

Another route is from Trondhjem to *Rönningen*, 1¼; *Teigen*, 1¼; *Havernæsset*, 2⅛ on Sælbo Sö, and thence as above.

Trondhjem to Jæmteland.

Trondhjem to *Levanger*, 7¼ (vide Route 24); *Næs*, 1¼; *Garnæs*, 1. Heavy road, but beautiful scenery. *Sulstuen*, 1⅛, pay for 3; † *Sandvigen*, 1⅜; *Mælen*, in Sweden, 1⅛. Total, 14⅛.

Charming excursions may also be made by boat up the Trondhjem Fjord, and also down it to the sea-coast, where the wild-fowl shooting is capital. In the large island of *Hitteren*, which lies upon the coast about 7 m. N.W. of Trondhjem, the deer-stalking is highly spoken of, as well as the wild-fowl and other shooting. Permission must be obtained to shoot there. "Red-deer shooting is rather expensive work. In the first place leave must be obtained of the proprietor, who not only expects the quarry, but a payment of 3 dollars for every deer that may be killed, and 1 dollar for the guide; and after all it is but tame work compared with reindeer hunting. In the north-western part of the island a fair sprinkling of black game and capercaillie may be found."—*Barnard's Sport in Norway*, p. 34.

The two modes of going to Hitteren are by water down the fjord, in boats from the water stations, or by the steamers which regularly call there; or by the road, which is 10 m. By water it is much farther.

Travellers going northwards, and intending to land on the coast for fishing or shooting, or for exploring the country inland, should take with them from Trondhjem such store of dried provisions, wine, &c., as they may require. A few wax candles in the latter end of August or the beginning of September will be found a great luxury. Of course, if not intending to leave the steamer, these stores will not be wanted.

If going S. the road can be agreeably varied by returning by the valley of the Glommen (Route 31); or going by land, Route 24, or water, Route 25, to Bergen, and from thence to Christiania. Much time, expense, and fatigue are saved by taking the steamer to Bergen, instead of going by land, but the scenery upon Route 24, between Molde and the Sögne Fjord, is the most grand and picturesque in Norway, and all who can afford the time should go that way. It is only practicable for carrioles. *Provisions* and small money should not be forgotten, whichever route may be taken.

Steamer to Hamburg every Friday till December, touching at Christiansund, Molde, and Aalesund on Saturdays; Bergen, Wednesdays; Christiansand, Fridays; and reaching Hamburg the following Sunday. A small steamer also plies from Trondhjem to Steenkjœr, and Levanger in the Trondhjem Fjord all the year round, where Route 24 is joined. Inquire at Trondhjem. See Routes 24 and 25 for stations called at on the way to the Namsen and Alten.

Steamer to Hammerfest every Wednesday at 8 P.M.

ROUTE 27.

CHRISTIANIA TO TRONDHJEM OVER RINGERIGET TO LILLEHAMMER.

Distance 51½ Norsk m., or 360 Eng.

For those who are not going to Bergen this is by far the best route to take in going to Trondhjem, the scenery being much finer than upon either of the more direct roads. See also preliminary observations to Route 26.

From Christiania to † *Thingelstad*, as in Route 21, distance 18¾ Norsk m., or about 58 English. By this road Sundvolden is passed, whence the beautiful view, mentioned in Route 21, over Ringeriget is to be seen on ascending Krogkleven, and also the lovely scenery of Randa Fjord is visited.

At Thingelstad our route separates from that to Bergen, and, after a steep and long ascent across the hills to the N.E., crosses the head of the *Eina Lake*, near

† *Teterud i vestre Thoten*, 1⅞, pay for 2⅛. Soon after leaving this station the descent towards the Miösen Lake is commenced. From Teterud one can go to *Lundhagen i Holbo*, 1¼; † *Kræmmerbakken*, 1¼.

† *Bärsvolden i vestre Thoten*, 1⅞. Good road to this place. Good road to

† *Kræmmerbakken*, 1⅛, where Route 28 is joined.

From hence to Trondhjem as in Route 28; dist. 38½ N. m., or 267 Eng.

ROUTE 28.

CHRISTIANIA TO TRONDHJEM OVER HURDALEN ON THE WESTERN SIDE OF THE MIÖSEN LAKE.

Dist. 48⅜ Norsk m., or about 339 Eng. See preliminary observations, Routes 26 and 29. Since the establishment of the *steamer* on the Miösen Lake, this land route has been comparatively little traversed during the summer months, it being more expensive, and the road hilly and infamously bad.

Its chief attractions are the lovely views it commands over the Miösen, and the pastoral scenery through which it passes; together with the trout and other fishing in the Miösen and its tributaries.

From Christiania by road to *Svendsen*, 5⅝, as in Route 26, where the stations are given; but it is better to go by rail to *Dahl*, 4⅞, and post thence to *Svendsen*, ⅞.

† *Eidsœter i Hurdal*, 1¼, pay for 1⅜. Here the road turns off to the left, passing Hurdal's Glass Work to

† *Garsjö i Hurdal*, 1½, pay for 1⅞.

* † *Grönnen i östre Thoten*, 1⅞, pay for 2, but returning for 1⅞. The first ¾ m. to Grönnen is heavy. The *Stor Elv* is crossed shortly before arriving at

† *Kræmmerbakken*, 1. Here Route 27 from Christiania joins our road. From here to † *Snörrig*, ¼, and to † *Fjeldhoug*, 1½, at both of which places the steamers on the Miösen stop. Near here is *Sognad*, formerly the station, where there is one of the most remarkable remains of antiquity which Norway can boast of. It is an obelisk of fine sand-

stone, and four ells in height, which stands upon *Alfstad Gaard*, where, according to tradition, a king named Alf dwelt. Upon three sides are carved Runic characters, and the figures of four horses, upon one of which is a rider. Over these horses there is a fox, above that again a flying eagle. Wormius read the Runic inscription thus :—

Jurun raisti Stain dini eftir Evin Venis hanna etha aug Gurdu af Hrigariki vien Urula Eivla.

Thus translated—Jurun erected this stone in memory of his friend Evind, who was married to Guri of Ringerige. Evind's friend was Urula.

On the other side—Midl i Vitaholm aug karde sun sini Svartander i Vitaholm. Igli reisti stein dena eftir Thoral aug munti stein eftir dusi.

Thus translated—Midl in Vitaholm mourns his son Svartander in Vitaholm. Egild erected this stone to Thoral, and this stone is in memory of them.

The *Hund Elv* is crossed before reaching

T. † *Gjövig i Vardal*, 1⅝. From hence a station-road leads into that between Christiania and Bergen, Route 21, at the head of the Rands Fjord ; dist. about 3 m.

• From Gjövig the road keeps close along the Miösen all the rest of the way to Lillehammer. The *Stok Elv* is crossed close to

• † *Stokke i Vardal*, 1. From hence along the valley of the Stok to the W. another road leads into Route 21, at *Eidsvold*; dist. about 1⅞ m.

The *Vismund Elv* is crossed on the way from Sveen to

† *Grytestuen i Vardal*, 1⅝. The road passes the head of the lake upon this stage, when the town of Lillehammer is seen across the stream. The road continues up the valley of the *Logen Elv* for some distance. The *Fare Elv*, which flows from the long range of the *Skjalbro Fjeld* on the N.W. into the Logen, is then passed ; and that river is soon after crossed by a long bridge. Then, turning S. down the river, about half a mile distant, is

T. • † LILLEHAMMER, 1⅜, or *Vingnæs*, 1⅝. From hence to Trondhjem is the same as in Route 26, in which see also observations as to the fishing to be had here, and scenery in the neighbourhood, &c. From *Vingnæs* to † *Toft*, 1⅞ ; † *Forseth*, ⅞. From † *Toft* one can also drive to † *Aronsveen i Öier*, 1⅛ (R. 26) ; and to † *Sönstevold i Gausdal*, ⅞. From † *Forseth to Helleberg*, 1½ ; *Sönstegaardsrödningen*, 1½. From † *Forseth* to † *Sönstevold*, ⅞ ; *Holmen i Öier*, 1⅛.

ROUTE 29.

CHRISTIANIA TO TRONDHJEM OVER HEDEMARKEN ON THE EASTERN SIDE OF THE MIÖSEN LAKE.

Distance 49⅝ Norsk m., or 350 Eng. See preliminary observations, and description of the Miösen Lake, fishing there, &c., in Route 26, also Route 28, as to the road on the W. side of the Miösen, which equally apply to this Route up to Lillehammer. Both these roads on the banks of the lake are infamously bad ; so much so, that it is always best to take the *Steamer*.

If compelled to follow either, the road on the western side of Miösen, Route 28, is better than this on the eastern bank.

From Christiania by rail to *Eidsvold*, 6 m., thence by steamer or road to *Minde*, 1⅛, at the foot of the Miösen Lake.

At Minde the *Vormen Elv* is crossed by a ferry to the E. bank. The Hedemarken district is entered just previous to

† *Morstu i Stange*, 1⅛, but pay

for 1½. The road from Minde to Morstu is hilly and heavy. About 14 Eng. m. E. of this place a vein of quartz, containing gold, was worked many years since, but finally abandoned, with considerable loss.—*Everest's Norway*, p. 31.

* † *Korsödegaarden i Stange*, 1⅛, pay for 1½. An excellent station, and good night quarters. Here a road to the right turns off to the valley of the Glommen, Route 31. Ours continues parallel with the lake to

† *Sörholte i Stange*, ⅞. Hence one can post to † *Hörsand i Romedal*, 1½; *Gillundstrand*, ½, where the steamer on the Miösen touches. In winter time one can sledge across Agersvigen to T. † *Hamar*, 1⅜. Or from *Sörholte* to *Togstad*, 1⅛, and thence to *Hamar*, ½, by boat. Midway on this stage to the left a road leads to a ferry across the *Baadsenden*, an arm of the Miösen, on the other side of which there is a road leading into this Route, near Smestad. The *Svart Elv* is crossed, and soon after a road to the S.E. turns off for the Glommen, and joins Route 31, at Gaustad, 1 m. Our route follows that road for a short distance.

† *Louisenberg i Vang*, 1⅜. This station is ⅜ m. from Hamar. A heavy stage to

† *Bjerke i Furnæs*, ⅞. The *Bremund Elv* is crossed during this stage.

† *Fangberget i Ringsaker*, 1. The *Moe Elv* is crossed shortly before arriving at

† *Smestad i Ringsaker*, 1½.

† *Frengstuen i Ringsaker*. About midway on this stage a stream from the *Mesme Vand* is crossed, and soon afterwards the Christians' District is entered. The road on this stage is even, and lies along the bank of the lake to

T. * † LILLEHAMMER, 1⅜. From hence to Trondhjem. See Route 20.

ROUTE 30.

CHRISTIANIA TO MOLDE, AALESUND, AND CHRISTIANSUND, OVER THE MIÖSEN LAKE, AND THROUGH GUDBRANDSDALEN AND ROMSDALEN.

Dist. 45⅞ m. by land, and 11 by water, together 56⅞, or 390 Eng. From Christiania to Dombaas, as in Route 26. Dist., Christiania to Dombaas, 31¾ m., of which 9 are by water on the Miösen.

The scenery from Dombaas to Molde is amongst the grandest and most picturesque of any in Norway, particularly in Romsdalen, and the upper part of the Romsdal Fjord. The mountains are fine in outline, and the whole route affords subjects of the best description for the landscape-painter. The tributary streams, falling into the Rauma, are very numerous; their falls and cascades are highly picturesque. In this land of waterfalls those in Romsdalen rank among the first for number and beauty, although none of them are of any great height. The *salmon-fishing* in the Rauma is good; and the shooting is also well spoken of. Reindeer and bears are found in the mountains, and red deer in the islands off the coast; hares, winged game, and ducks are abundant. Not being the most direct way to Trondhjem, this Route has been sadly neglected by tourists; but all who can spare the time will be amply repaid in exploring its great beauties. Most of the farmers in Romsdalen are substantial men, and the traveller will find no difficulty in comfortably locating himself there, wherever he may desire. The stations, with few exceptions, are good.

From Molde the grand Alpine scenery upon the Stor Fjord can be visited, and tourists can then proceed by land to Trondhjem or Bergen, or by the *Steamer*, which regularly calls there on its way between those cities.

From Dombaas the road keeps along

the bank of the Logen Elv to the *Lesje Varks Vand.* "This lake is 7 Eng. miles long, and 2050 feet above the level of the sea, and is the source of two rivers, the Laagen flowing to the south, and the Rauma to the north. This is a most remarkable instance, and worthy of note; for not only is it a rare thing for two *large* rivers to flow in contrary directions from one and the same source, but the Laagen, by falling into the Miösen at Lillehammer, from the other end of which, at Minde, the Vormen ultimately flows into the Glommen, the whole southern part of the country between Frederickstadt and Veblungsnaes is rendered insular." (*Sport in Norway*, p. 40.) The road keeps along the north side of the lake, which abounds in trout during the rest of this and the next stage.

* † *Holager i Lesje*, 1.

* † *Holseth* (or Holset), 1⅛. Here a horse-track to the left leads to the head of the Vaage Vand, and also to the Justedal Glaciers and Sögne Fjeld on the S.W. See Routes 21 and 38, the latter of which turns off here. Romsdalen begins at this station, and its total length does not exceed 7⅞ m., or about 56 Eng.

* † *Lesje Jernværk*, ¾. Here there is an old iron mine. From hence the road passes three small lakes.

* † *Mölmen*, 1½. A short distance from hence a horse-track turns off on the S., and joins that from Holseth. On this stage the scenery becomes more wild and picturesque. There is a picturesque waterfall to be seen here.

The *Stor Fjord.* Before coming to the next station another horse-path on the left runs to the Stor Fjord, on the road to Aalesund. The scenery of the snow-clad range of the *Lang Fjeld* mountains upon the Stor Fjord is but little known at present. It is of the grandest description. The outline of the mountain is more picturesque than in most other parts of Norway, and full of variety. The Stor Fjord, and its numerous tributary streams, possess equal attractions for the sportsman and the angler, as well as the artist.

† *Nystuen*, 1. Between this and Ormen there is a beautiful waterfall, about 150 yards off the road, which should not be missed. The range of the *Bröste Fjeld* now begins on the left, and from hence the road rapidly descends; the scenery increasing in grandeur and picturesque outline, and the Rauma still foaming along its rocky bed, close on the left all the way.

* † *Ormen i Grytten*, 1, pay for 1½, returning for 1½. Excellent quarters for salmon-fishing. The river makes a picturesque fall here, beyond which the salmon cannot pass.

* † *Fladmark i Grytten*, 1. Small station. On this stage the river flows tranquilly.

† *Horjem i Grytten*, 1. Poor station. Between this and Veblungsnaes lives Landmark, who will take in travellers. He speaks English. Capital fishing, and good opportunities for reindeer hunting. The scenery becomes particularly grand; the road winds between two enormous mountains, *Romsdals-horn*, 2183 feet high, on the N., and *Trolltinderne* (Witch Peaks) on the S.

T.* † *Veblungsnaeset*, 1½. A capital place for head-quarters while fishing, shooting, and sketching up this splendid stream and valley, which end here. Three bears were killed in one day by a farmer near this in June, 1847. The Rauma falls into the *Sis Fjord*, a branch of Romsdal Fjord, close to this station. Near here is likewise the farm where Col. Sinclair landed with his regiment, previous to their slaughter in Gudbrandsdalen. See Solheim, Route 26. Between this and Molde a steamer runs three times a week, and corresponds with the steamers between Christiansand and Trondhjem.

The *Route to Aalesund* turns off here. It proceeds by water down the fjord, where it joins the high road between Aalesund and Molde. Dist. from hence (Veblungsnæset) to Aalesund, 8⅞ m. The stages are, *Vestnæs*, by water, 2⅜; †*Ellingsgaard*, by land, 1; * *Söholt*, by land, 1¼, a good station; *Sorte*, part water, 1¼; *Röseth*, 1⅛; T. *Aalesund*, part water, 1⅛. For description of this town, see Route 24.

Route to Molde continued.—From hence to Molde there are two ways—down the fjord (the scenery upon which is sublime), by boat, 3⅜. This is likewise the nearest way. From 7 to 10 hours are requisite, according to the wind and weather. The other road is partly by land, as follows:—The Isse Fjord is crossed to

Torvig i Vold, ⅞. From hence by land along the E. bank of the *Rodven Fjord*, a small branch of the *Lang Fjord* to

† *Alfarnæs i Veö*, 1¼. Here the head of the fjord is crossed to Söllesnæs: or a boat can be taken direct to Molde, 1⅜.

Söllesnæs i Veö, ⅞. Hence by land to

Dvœrnæs i Bolsö, ⅞. Here the *Fanne Fjord*, a branch of the Molde, is crossed, and the high road between Molde and Christiansund (Route 24) is entered at Strande; or a boat can be taken direct from Dvœrnæs to Molde, 1.

Strande, ¼. From hence the way is by land to Molde.

The *Road to Christiansund* turns off at Dvœrnæs. Distance, 5⅛ m. The stages are—across the Fanne Fjord to *Lonsæt*, ¼; thence by road to *Eide*, 1; *Furseth*, ⅞; *Gimnæs*, 1⅞; by water to *Pladsæt*, ⅜; *Bolgen*, by land, ¾. By water to CHRISTIANSUND, ¼. From Gimnæs one can take boat direct to Christiansund, 1⅜. For the description of this town, see Routes 24 and 25.

Route to Molde continued.—Road close along the *Molde Fjord* all the way, commanding splendid views of the distant mountains of the Lang Fjeld.

T. * MOLDE, ⅞. Population about 1200. This town is built upon a promontory on the N. side of the Molde Fjord, near its junction with the sea. It consists of one long straggling street along the banks of the fjord. There are several handsome villas in the neighbourhood, and the environs are with justice considered among the most picturesque and beautiful in Norway.

"Molde commands a view of the snowy Alps that line the whole of its S. side, and are the N.W. boundary of the Dovre Fjeld. I do not remember such a long-extended range of peaks and pinnacles and shattered ridges, except, perhaps, in the Loffodens. And here one rank peeps out from behind another until they are lost in the distance, and, as they mix with the white clouds, we fancy them like hanging cities or castles in the air. Among them Romsdals-horn appears conspicuous." — *Everest's Norway*, p. 208.

The little trade which exists at Molde is chiefly confined to fish.

The *Steamers* call here regularly every week in passing up and down the coast. It is a convenient place from whence to make an excursion to the magnificent scenery upon the upper parts of the Stor Fjord, and forming part of Lang Fjeld.

For stations and distances between Molde and the towns N. and S. of it on the coast, see Routes 24 and 25.

The fjords about here abound in wild-fowl, including the eider-duck, which is found all along this coast. The habits of this bird are interesting. The nest is made on the ground, composed of marine plants, and lined with down of exquisite fineness, which the female plucks from her own body. The eggs are usually 4, of a pale olive-green. They allow their nests to be robbed of the eggs and down three times; after that, if further molested, the birds desert the place. So avaricious of progeny is this duck, that, when plundered of her own, she will sometimes steal the eggs and young of others. When the female has stripped herself of all her down, the male comes in aid—his is white. In the Storthing of 1847, a law was passed for the protection of game, wild-fowl, &c., and since then the islands along this coast frequented by these ducks have become a valuable property. Each nest during the breeding season produces about ⅛lb. of down, but which, when picked and cleaned, is reduced to ½. So firm and elastic is this beautiful down, that the same quantity which can be compressed between the two hands will serve to stuff a quilt or coverlet, and while its weight is scarcely perceptible, it has more warmth than the finest blanket. For a full account of the eider-duck, and of the manner of preparing the down, vid. "Sport in Norway."

ROUTE 31.

CHRISTIANIA TO TRONDHJEM OVER ÖSTERDALEN, UP THE VALLEY OF THE GLOMMEN, AND THROUGH RÖRAAS.

Dist. 48½ Norsk m., or 336 Eng. But by using the new road from Neby instead of going by Röraas, it is only 46½. See preliminary observations to Routes 26 and 32. The scenery upon this route is not so interesting as that over the Dovre Fjeld, and is therefore seldom traversed by those who are unacquainted with the latter route. But the valley of the Glommen, with its vast pine forests, and picturesque falls and cataracts, is very fine; and the trout and other fish in the river and its numerous tributaries are highly spoken of. The fall near Frederikstad prevents any salmon getting higher up the Glommen. There is no salmon-fishing to be had upon this route until after passing Röraas and arriving at the Gula River; the best is about Rogstad, near where this route joins that over the Dovre Fjeld.

Some of the finest description, as well as the largest quantity, of pine timber exported from Norway, and that chiefly cut up into deals, is produced on the banks of the Glommen and its tributaries. In the spring the logs are floated down to the saw-mills at the falls of the Glommen near Frederikstad. The deer-shooting to be had in the autumn upon this route is said to be excellent; the best is about Foldal, towards the Dovre Fjeld, and the other northern parts of the bailiwick of Österdalen. Elk are at times met with there, though very rarely, and then chiefly towards the borders of Sweden. Bears and wolves are frequently killed in the wild district on the E. side of *Stor Sö*. Ptarmigan and hares are abundant in parts of Österdalen. The country is very wild, and thinly inhabited. The E. side of the whole of the upper part of the Glommen, and from thence to the Klar and Dal Rivers in Sweden, comprises one of the finest sporting districts in both countries. See also Route 62, as to the country between the Klar and W. Dal.

The shortest and best route is to proceed direct to Hamar by steamer on the Miösen from Eidsvold, vide Route 26. From Hamar there is a new railway to Grundset, dist. 3⅞ m. But as only one train leaves daily, the traveller may be unable to avail himself of it, in which case he will proceed to † *Korsödegaarden i Stange* as in R. 29, and thence branch off to the right to † *Koloen i Romedal*, ⅞; and † *Hörsand i Romedal*, 1⅛. The next station is *Bergstuen i Löiten*, ⅞; which is a station on the new railway; and † *Grundsæt i Elverum*, 1⅛, the terminus.

From Christiania to Grundsæt by rail and steamer, is 15¾. The journey may be agreeably varied in going from Trondhjem to Christiania, by keeping down the valley of the Glommen through Kongsvinger. There is a road on each side of the river. The stations on the east bank from Grundsæt are—to † *Bækkevold*, ⅛; † *Elsæt*, 2¼; rest ½ hour at *Hommb.* † *Melby*, 1⅜; † *Austad*, ⅞; † *Kirkenær i Grue*, 1¼; *Brandvold*, 1⅛; thence crossing Gjölstad Sund to T. † *Kongsvinger*, 1⅜. Travellers intending to explore the Trysil district, will proceed from Bækkevold thus to † *Mo i Elverum*, 1⅛, pay for 2; to † *Axelhuus i Trysil*, 2½, pay for 3⅜; to † *Sörby i Trysil*, 2⅛, pay for 3¼. The stations on the W. bank are —Grundsæt to *Berger i Elverum*, 1¼; *Braskerud*, 1⅜; *Oengen*, 1⅛; *Lösaasen*, ⅞; *Holmerydningen*, ⅞; *Næs*, 1⅛; *Nordre Rolstad*, 1¼; † *Kongsvinger*, ⅞. Thence to Christiania, see Route 32. But to continue. From Grundsæt the grand part of the Glommen valley commences—the road keeps along the foot of a steep range of mountains on the W., until it enters the fine valley of the *Austa*, which stream is crossed near

† *Nygaard i Aamot*, 1¾. Upon this stage the *Rren Elv*, from the Stor Sö, enters the Glommen on the E.

† *Arnestad i Aamot*, 1. This station lies 1 English mile off the road; horses may generally be had at Lapstuen, between which and next station pay only for 2 m.

[If going *viâ* Stor Söen, probably arrangements might be made at last station to take the same horse to Disæt. *Route by Stor Söen*, * † *Disæt*, 2 m., pay for 3, a heavy road. * † *Lösæt*, 1, but the same horse will go to Skjörbund, the southern end of the lake, whence the steamer starts daily for Akre. Capital trout and grayling fishing at Lösæt, which is an excellent station to put up at. "In 1861 two Englishmen bagged 120 lbs. of trout and grayling at this place, in one day's fishing."—*Sport in Norway*. A track over the mountains leads to the Klar Elv. Shooting well spoken of.]

The Haft Elv is crossed before reaching

† *Ophustunen i Elvedalen*, 2⅛. This station is on the E. bank of the river. Travellers who are obliged to sleep here generally leave their carrioles at a small hut, where the horses are changed, and are then ferried over to the station. It is a particularly bad station. Four torrents are crossed on this stage, and the *Imsæ* Elv near.

* † *Söndre Mevelt i Elvedalen*, 1⅞. A horse-track leads hence through the mountains to the W., and enters Gudbrandsdal near Losnæs, Route 26. Between Möklebye and the next station, upon the E. bank of the Stor Sö, there resides a hunter, whose services the sportsman would do well to secure, as deer, and sometimes elk and bear, are to be met with on that side of the lake. It is, indeed, one of the finest sporting districts in Norway.

* † *Vestgaard i Elvedalen*, 1. Here our route crosses the Glommen to the left bank, and leaving that river, a very long and hilly stage across the mountains is commenced, great part of which is along the left bank of the Stor Sö. There are two arms of the Glommen to be crossed; one ferry is an operation of some difficulty, when the river is full. The Glommen is left here, and not seen again till Neby. It is a capital station. Where the road crosses the river at Vestgaard, a horse-road leads up the left bank to Stein, at the entrance of Steindalen, from whence a road joins our route higher up at Neby. By this way 40 Eng. m. of the Glommen may be explored, which are not seen upon the direct route.

Akre i Rendalen, 2⅞, but pay for 4. This stage is also very hilly—road all the way up the valley of the *Rena Elv*.

Bergset i Örre Rendalen, 1⅞, pay for 2¼. Indifferent accommodation. The road hence lies through a dense pine forest for 20 Eng. miles, in which hardly a human being is met with. The solitude is very striking. In some parts large tracts have been destroyed by fire; the charred stems of which present a most remarkable appearance. A fine mountain, called "Bellingen," is seen at intervals on the left. Ryper, plentiful about Engen. Here a horse-path leads W. to the Glömmen, where it separates, and to the N. leads to the Dovre Fjeld; to the S. it cuts another track to Gudbrandsdalen, which it enters near Oien. The ascent is very long and steep, up the valley of the Rena, which is twice crossed on the way to

Engen i Tyldal, 3, but pay for 4¼. On the last stage the traveller must rest ½ hour half way, at Midtskoven. The ascent still continues on this stage—the Rena is again crossed, the fine mountains of the *Trons Fjeld*, 5761 feet, are passed close on the W., and the valley of the Glommen is again entered, and the river crossed at

* *Neby i Tönset*, 1½, but pay for 2. From Engen to Neby a very heavy road, requiring at least 2½ hours, going south. Here a station-road runs S. down the right bank of the Glommen to Foldalen, and so to Jerkin, on the Dovre Fjeld, 8¼ m. The stations are—to *Gjelten*, 2; †*Nordre Holm i Foldalen*, 2¼, pay for 3; † *Kroghaugen*, 1; † *Dalen i Örre Foldalen*, 1¼; † *Jerkin*, 1½. Route 32 also turns off here.

A new Station-Road to Trondhjem has recently been made, which, commencing a short distance on the S.W. of Neby, runs up the valley of the *Tunden Elv*, crosses the mountains, and descends by the valley of the *Orkla Elv*, until it enters Route 26, near the Garlid Station. The stations are *Lundsæter i Tönset*, 1¼, pay for 1½; † *Stöen i Qvikne*, 2, pay for 2¾; *Frengstad i Qvikne*, 1¼, pay for 1½; *Nærerdal*, 1¼, returning pay for 1½ (hence in winter one can go to † *Bjerkager i Rennebo*, 1½); † *Garlid i Sognedal*, 2¼, pay for 3. This route, which is now the post-road, is 4¼ m. shorter than by Röraas. (Vide R. 26.)

In going from Trondhjem to Christiania, those desirous of seeing as much as possible of the Glommen may keep that river in sight nearly all the way, by going from Neby to Stein, and thence taking the horse-road which leads down the valley and joins our route again at Vestgaard. See Route 32 for stations on the above road.

From Neby to Röraas our route continues through grand mountain scenery up the valley of the Glommen. The costume of the peasants becomes picturesque. In the Glommen, as well as the Tornea and other rivers, the fish are speared by torchlight, as in Scotland. "Few objects are more exciting to the lover of field-sports, or more interesting to the admirer of the picturesque, than the rugged banks of a mountain torrent lit up by gleaming torches, whilst the foaming stream glitters and sparkles as it bursts amid the rocks here and there at intervals, every object standing out prominently in a blaze of light, whilst at other points of the stream everything is shrouded in the blackest darkness, the whole forming a scene to which no painter that ever lived could render justice." — *Milford's Norway*, p. 250.

Tolgen, 1⅞.

Os i Tolgen, 1¼. The road to this place keeps along the Glommen. In winter, when the ice bears, horses are changed at *Lilleöien*.

T. * † RÖRAAS, 1⅜. This town contains about 3000 inhabitants. It owes its existence solely to the extensive copper mines in the neighbourhood, which were discovered in 1645, and have, with few intervals, been worked to a profit ever since.

The annual produce of these mines has occasionally been as high as 4000 skippunds, 600 or 700 tons; at present it rarely exceeds 250 tons.

The mines are well worthy of a visit, and although sunk to a depth of from 200 to 300 fathoms, the workings are nearly all carried on in the direction of the lode, or bed of ore, which seldom inclines above 15° from the horizontal, so that you can, in most cases, walk to the bottom; in fact, unlike the generality of mines, horses and carts are employed to bring the ore to the surface, or at least to the short perpendicular shafts, by which it is conveyed up.

There are no manufactories, nor is agriculture carried on to any extent in the neighbourhood. The inhabitants are supported solely by the traffic created by the mines.

This town is situated about 3000 feet above the level of the sea; it is consequently one of the coldest districts in Norway, the mercury, during the winter, being frequently frozen.

In the neighbourhood of Röraas, the traveller will most probably have an opportunity of seeing some of the Laplanders with their deer. There is much to interest and amuse in their peculiar habits and mode of life. From Röraas there is an excellent new road into Sweden—thus to † *Ernstgruben*, 1½; † *Skotgaarden*, 1¼; *Östre-Malmoyen i Sverige*, 1 Norsk, and 1 Swedish mile.

From Röraas to the *Oresund Lake* on the N.E. the Glommen becomes a mountain torrent, forming numerous waterfalls, which, though not large, are many of them highly picturesque. Some way from Röraas the Glommen is crossed for the last time, and the ascent continues as the road winds away to the N. from the valley of the Glommen. The summit level of the mountains is attained near

† *Bergan i Röraas*, 1½. A picturesque little station, but the people very poor, and the house dirty. It is about 4000 feet above the sea. The only trees near are birch. This is a very thinly populated district, and a very peculiar dialect is spoken. The small lake passed on the W., before arriving at this station, is the source of the *Gula Elv*, and along the picturesque valley of this stream the road now descends, winding along it for the greater part of the way to Trondhjem. Numerous tributaries of this fine river are passed.

† *Næsvold i Aalen*, ¾.

† *Hov*, ¾, pay for 1 returning.

Grödt i Holtaalen, 1½.

Langlete i Holtaalen, 1.

Kirkvold i Singsaas, 1¾. The Gula is crossed to the left bank after leaving Kirkvold.

Bogen i Singsaas, 1.

* *Rogstad i Stören*, 1. About here the *salmon-fishing* is well spoken of. On leaving this station the Gula Elv is crossed, and the Dovre Fjeld road is joined soon after.

Vollan i Horrig (or Vollan), 1¼. From hence to Trondhjem is the same as Route 26: dist. 4.

ROUTE 32.

CHRISTIANIA TO TRONDHJEM THROUGH KONGSVINGER, AND UP THE VALLEY OF THE GLOMMEN.

Distance 54 Norsk m., or 378 Eng. This route is not to be recommended to those who are unacquainted with the far grander beauties of the Dovre Fjeld road, Route 26. The Glommen is the finest river in Norway. By this route, about 300 Eng. m. of this splendid stream may be explored, the road keeping close by it, more or less, the whole distance. The falls and cataracts of the Glommen, and its many beautiful tributaries, are numerous, and the scenery increases in grandeur towards the N. There is ample occupation for the sportsman, the angler, and the artist. Nowhere can the pine forests of Norway be seen to greater perfection than upon this route.

There is now a new railway constructed from Kongsvinger to Lille-Ström on the Eidsvold line, so that the traveller can go the whole distance from Christiania to Kongsvinger by rail, dist. 8 3/10 m. Two trains run daily up and down, taking about 4½ hours. Fares, 1st class, 1 sp. 4 m.; 2nd class, 1 sp. d. 1 m.; dogs, 1 m. each; carrioles and carts, 1¼ sp. d.

Should, however, the traveller prefer going the whole way *en carriole*, which cannot be recommended as the road is but little travelled, and the stations inferior, he will proceed from Christiania to

† *Grorud i Aker*, ¾ m.

† *Skrimstad i Skedsmo*, ¾, pay for 1.

† *Klöften i Ullensager*, 1⅛. Here the road branches off to the right.

† *Lund i Ullensager*, ¾.

† *Opaker i Næs*, 1⅛. Upon this stage the *Ous Elv* is crossed near its junction with the Glommen.

† *Korsmo i Odalen*, 1⅞, from which place one can be set over to Skarnœs, a station on the railway. From Korsmo one can post to Nordre Odalen; thus

From † *Korsmo* to † *Ekornhol*, 1⅛; † *Östrand*, 1⅞, resting for ½ hr. on the road. When the ice bears on Storsöen it is only ⅞ m. From † *Korsmo* also one can post direct to † *Östrand*, 2⅛, or in winter over the ice, 1⅛.

† *Sundby*, ¾. From hence one can be set over to Sander railway station. From Sundby to † *Östrand*, 2.

T. † *Kongsvinger*, 1⅛. Here there is a bridge over the Glommen. The traveller can now proceed to Grundsæt, 9¾, where R. 31 is joined either on the eastern or western bank of the Glommen, vid. p. 166.

From Grundsæt to Vestgaard is the same as in Route 31; dist. 7⅛. On crossing the river at Vestgaard our route separates, and by a by-road keeps along the left bank of the Glommen to

Hanestad, 4. Near here, on crossing a small torrent, a by-road leads N.E. and joins Route 31 at Bergsæt, 1⅛ m.

Stein, or *Gjelten i Lille Elvedal*, 4. Trout-fishing excellent about here, and the deer and general shooting well spoken of. From hence a station-road leads up Stoindalen to that most excellent station, Jerkin, on the Dovre Fjeld (see Route 26). Dist. 6⅛. The stations are—*Grimsbo i nedre Foldal*, 2⅛, pay for 3; † *Kroghaugen*, 1; † *Dalen i Övre Foldalen*, 1⅛; † *Jerkin*, 1⅛.

Crossing the Glommen here, and keeping up the right bank, the *Tronfjeld*, 5761 feet high, is seen on the R. Shortly before arriving at the next station, the *new road to Trondhjem*, up the valley of the *Tonden Elv*, is passed on the left, see Route 31; and which route our road joins again at

Neby, 2. From hence to Trondhjem as in Route 31.

ROUTE 33.

TRONDHJEM TO STOCKHOLM, THROUGH VÆRDAL AND SUNDSVALL.

Dist. 90 Norsk m., or 610 Eng. This route is quite practicable for ladies. Passports must be *visé* by a Swedish Minister or Consul before entering the country. If they be not, then a Swedish passport must be taken at Stockholm, for which about 3¼ rix dollars are paid, but the bearer is entitled to the passport under which he entered Sweden. It is also most advisable to obtain a good supply of Swedish *small* money, and if in paper it will be more readily taken than silver. Many of the stations are good, but a small stock of provisions should always be taken.

This road, which connects Trondhjem and the capital of Sweden, has been completed for some years; formerly it was impossible to get across to Sweden except on horseback, now there is a capital road, and very tolerable accommodation is to be met with the whole way. The distance from Trondhjem to Sundsvall, the nearest point of the Gulf of Bothnia, is about 350 English miles, of which at least 60 run along the shore of the Trondhjem Fjord, nearly due north as far as Vœrdal, from whence the road strikes directly across Sweden, pursuing with but little variation a south-easterly course until it reaches the Gulf of Bothnia at Sundsvall. The road formerly was steep and laborious, except where it made a considerable détour towards Vœrdal; but of late years it has been greatly improved, and is now as good as any in Norway.

From Trondhjem to *Levanger*, as in Route 24; dist. 7½ m.

The country is much better here than in the immediate neighbourhood of Trondhjem, the soil superior, and the barren headlands of primary rock running into the fjord not so numerous, steep, or rugged. Cultivation extends back into the country as far as the eye can reach, and is not confined to the hollows and skirts of high ground, but spreads over hill and dale. One of the most curious facts is the successful cultivation of the hop plant in this district. "I found a small hop garden even on this farm (near Levanger), and the crop apparently was excellent. It is singular that a plant, which is so delicate and precarious in the south of England, and requires the most expensive culture, should flourish here in lat. 64° with very little attention paid to it."—*Laing's Norway*, p. 84.

On entering Vœrdal the road turns suddenly to the S.E., making quite an acute angle with its former direction, and here opens one of the most beautiful valleys in all Norway, through which the road runs as far as Indal. "I do not know in Scotland so beautiful a valley as this of Vœrdal—the crops of grain so rich and yellow—the houses so substantial and thickly set—farm after farm without interruption, each fully inclosed and subdivided with paling—the grass fields of so lively a green, as free from weeds and rubbish, and as neatly shorn, as a lawn before a gentleman's windows, every knoll, and all the background covered with trees, and a noble clear river running briskly through it. There is a reach or two of Nithsdale which on a small scale resembles this valley, but the soft, living green of the natural grass does not belong to, or is not long retained by, our sown grass-fields. I find that all these beautiful little farms with the substantial houses, and that air of plenty and completeness about them which struck me so much on my way up this valley, are the Udal estates and residences of the peasant proprietors, or bonder. This class of bonder are the most interesting people in Norway. There are none similar to them in the feudal countries of Europe."—*Laing*, p. 92.

* *Næs*, 1½. From hence a road leads across the *Vara River* to the village of Stiklestad, ½ m. distant, which is celebrated as being the spot where St. Olaf was slain. The church there is also very old and interesting, see Route 24. The salmon-fishing near here is indifferent. The river has clay banks, which after rain cause the water to come down a muddy-white colour. There is some good trout-fishing in some of the tributaries.

From Nœs the road keeps up the S. side of the valley, near the Værn River, great part of the way, and crosses a fine tributary to it shortly before arriving at the next station. It is a heavy stage. The beautiful Guddingsbakker are passed before arriving at

Garnæs, 1. Here a station-road runs to the N.W., and joins the coast road, Route 24, between the Röske and Steenkjær Station, about 4 m. distant.

During this stage the road twice crosses the river, and by a very steep ascent winds up to the head of the valley at

Suulstuen, 1¼, pay for 3. From hence the ascent continues through grand mountain scenery to Kongstuen, where the summit level of the mountains is attained, and horses are baited before finishing the stage. A short distance beyond this the *Swedish Frontier* is crossed; the descent on the E. side of the mountain commences, and the next station is reached at

† *Sandvigen*, 1⅞.

Mælen, 1¼. This is in Sweden. For some distance beyond this place there is little of interest in the scenery. The general shooting is good. Ptarmigan are said to be particularly abundant. The scenery, with but little exception, from the Swedish frontier to Stockholm, is of a less grand character than upon the Norwegian side.

For the rest of the Stations in Sweden, and *Steamers* from the towns upon the coast, see Route 64, "Handbook for Sweden."

ROUTE 34.

ALTEN TO TORNEA AND HAPARANDA (AT THE HEAD OF THE GULF OF BOTHNIA), ACROSS THE MOUNTAINS.

Dist. 63⅞ Norsk and Swed. m., or 430 Eng. In winter, when the snow is in a good state for sledging, this journey is usually performed in 6 or 7 days. In *summer* it takes longer.

From Torneå and Haparanda the route can be continued along the E. side of the Gulf of Bothnia to St. Petersburg, or along the W. side to Stockholm, Route 65.

Torneå and Haparanda lie nearly due S. of Alten. There is no road until the valley of the Torneå River is entered; previously to that it is a mere horse-track across the mountains, but the stations are arranged as in the S. provinces, the whole way from Alten to Torneå.

A supply of provisions must be taken upon this route; and, if possible, some Swedish money should be obtained at Alten. Care should be taken to have a Russian *visé* to the passport, before entering the territory of the Emperor. For Sweden it is not so essential, the rule there being, that if a traveller enters the country without a Swedish *visé* on his passport, he must take a new one, for which about 3½ rix dollars (4*s.* Eng.) must be paid; but the bearer is entitled to have returned to him the passport under which he entered Sweden.

In Winter

this route is much frequented, particularly during the fair at Alten, in the latter end of November. It can then easily be traversed in sledges. At that season the journey, as far as Muonioniska, is performed in a pulk, drawn by one reindeer. From Muonioniska to Torneå with horses and sleighs.

The charge for a reindeer from Alten to Kautokeino is 4 orts, or 96 skillings, and from Kautokeino to Niska the same sum. Each traveller generally hires 3 reindeer; 1 for himself, 1 for his luggage, and 1 to relieve the other 2. He must also hire 1 for his guide, to whom 4 orts are also to be paid.

It is essential to be provided with the warmest clothing. The best plan is to adopt the dress of the Laplander, which consists of a good warm cap, and, over the ordinary clothes, a pæsk or coat of reindeer skin. This is a large loose garment reaching from the neck to below the knees, and belted round the waist by a leathern girdle; the lower parts of the dress are called bællinger, which are leggings, and reach from the ankle high up the thigh; they are somewhat in the form of spatterdashers, but with this difference, that they are whole, not having buttons at the sides, but being fastened at the top by a running string that tightens them, and covered at the bottom by the skalkomager, or shoe of reindeer skin, which is confined by a long narrow band, going several times round the ankle, keeping the whole tight together, and preventing the possibility of any snow getting in. These shoes are well stuffed with soft dry grass (*Carex sylvatica*) called senne; and over a pair of good worsted gloves are worn reindeer mittens, also stuffed with dried grass. No other kind of dress can supply the place of this, which is admirably adapted from its material and make to enable the wearer to sustain the severity of the climate. The reindeer skins are worn with the hair outwards, and from the peculiar closeness and thickness of their texture, it is impossible for the cold to penetrate them. Every article of clothing which is tight, and liable to occasion numbness by pressing against the skin and impeding the circulation of the blood, should be avoided. The sleeves of the pæsk are in general so large, that the arms are easily drawn out and replaced in them without the garment being taken off.

The *pulk*, or sledge, in which the traveller is conveyed, in form somewhat resembles a canoe with the stern cut off. It is 5 feet in length, about 16 inches broad, and 8 deep, the back board being about twice that height. The head of the pulk comes to a sharp point, the stern is flat, in order that it may be leant against conveniently, and the bottom is convex; it has an oval half-deck in front, covered with seal skin, to prevent the snow being driven in. To this pulk only one deer can be attached. The harness consists of a collar of reindeer skin; to the lower point of this collar a single trace of strong leather is attached, which passes between the legs of the deer, and is fastened by a small transverse piece of wood to an iron ring at the front of the pulk. Round the body of the deer is a broad belly-band of coloured cloth, through which the trace passes. Round the neck is a broad loose band or collar of cloth, to which is suspended a bell, the sound of which enables the different members of a party to keep together. The head-stall is merely a strip of seal skin fastened round the head of the deer, and tied in a knot under its left ear; to this knot the rein or bridle is fastened, which is likewise only a strip of seal skin.

As soon as the traveller is seated the deer sets off at full speed. The rein is held in the right hand, being sometimes fastened round the wrist by a slip knot, but more usually it is wound once or twice round the hand to keep it firm. From the knot being tied under the left ear, the side on which the rein would consequently hang is the left; but it is necessary that it should always be on the right, to enable the driver more readily to strike the animal on the flank when he wishes to increase its speed, as also to swing it suddenly round on the left side to cause the deer to stop. There is some knack required to keep the rein on the right side, as it is continually getting over to the other. The difficulty of preserving the pulk upright is at first very great, and it is only by exactly balancing his body that the traveller can keep it in an upright position.

An inexperienced person will inevitably be rolled over, not merely once or twice, but several times; but on account of the lowness of the vehicle no bad consequences are likely to ensue. If the pulk were constructed upon any other principle, it would scarcely answer the purpose; the nature of the country, and the snow through which it has frequently to plough its way, require that the bottom of the pulk should be like that of a canoe; were it broader, the inequalities of the ground it passes over, the depth of the snow, and the steepness of the ascents, would render it impossible for the animal to drag it.

In Summer

this route is also interesting. The scenery for a considerable distance on the Norwegian side is very grand. The naturalist will find abundant occupation in the botany, geology, and mineralogy of the varied districts traversed. Bears are by no means rare on the Norwegian side; and in the upper parts of the mountains wild reindeer are sometimes met with, but from the number of tame deer, which now feed on this fjeld in the summer, and which drive the wild ones, not so frequently as formerly. Ducks and plover are plentiful about the end of August, but not later than September, when they are frozen out, and migrate southwards and westwards. But few *ryper* (woodgrouse) are to be found, as the route for the most part is at a greater elevation than the scrub grows, which these birds frequent. Neither will the traveller have much time to diverge right or left from the track in pursuit of them, as it is necessary to get from one *Fjeldstuen* to the next before night closes in. Trout are plentiful in the small lakes and streams; and *salmon* in the Muonio and Torneå rivers; in the upper parts of which these fish are chiefly speared by torchlight. It is said that salmon in these rivers, and indeed in all those which flow into the Gulf of Bothnia, will not rise at a fly. It is doubtful what is the cause of this. It has been stated, that they are a different species of salmon, but the more probable explanation seems to be, that the Gulf of Bothnia and the Baltic contain so much fresh water, that the salmon never reach the sea, and consequently are never in such good condition, or so hungry for a fly, as those on the W. coast of Norway. Their flesh, when cooked, is certainly much whiter. The journey is fatiguing; but gentlemen need not fear taking it, as it was accomplished a few years since by an elegant Parisienne in returning to France with her husband from a tour they had made to Spitzbergen!

After the first 2 or 3 m., throughout the entire distance from Alten to Kautokeino, there is not a single inhabited house, but here and there some Lapland tents may be met with, as all the mountain Laplanders are Nomades; there are, however, chalets or huts, erected at the public expense for the accommodation of travellers; and though the interior merely contains a rough bench, and a square hearth, with an aperture in the roof for the egress of the smoke, the traveller, after the fatigues of the day's journey, hails them with gratitude.

The first stage from Alten to Kautokeino is 16 Norsk m., or 112 Eng., and can only be traversed on foot or horseback. For horses an agreement must be made before starting. The luggage taken should be as little as possible, and will be most readily carried in saddle-bags. The river is navigable for about 4 m. from its mouth; and from Alten, for some distance towards Kautokeino, there are two horse-tracks, one of which keeps up the grand valley of the

Alten, and follows the winding of the river until it joins our route, which is the more *direct* and usual one, and keeps to the W. of the Alten. It was this latter track which Von Buch followed, whose description of it is most interesting; and according to which, during about the first 20 hours from Alten, the way is very steep and mountainous, the fir and other trees become gradually stunted, and the birch at length is alone seen at about 893 feet above the sea. The ascent then becomes less rapid, a large tract of dreary levels is passed, and at their termination the last glimpse of the sea near Alten is obtained. The ascent then continues again, until a vast table-land, abounding in reindeer moss, is attained; the highest part of which is *Nuppi Varu*, 2655 feet above the sea. This hill commands a most extensive view. To the N., the snowy chain of the *Lyngen* is seen, while beneath and around extends a dreary waste, with numerous small lakes. To the S. it is level, and of immense extent. Here Laplanders, with their herds of reindeer, may usually be met with in summer. About 2 m. before the end of this stage a descent is commenced, and the deep and rapid *Siaberdasjock*, which is the principal source of the Alten River, is crossed, shortly before arriving at Kautokeino.

Perhaps a less fatiguing and more interesting way is to ascend the Alten River in boats, for about 4 m. from its mouth, having previously arranged to have horses in waiting at the hut, where the track diverges from the river; thence, to cross the mountains to another point of the Alten River, where boats from Kautokeino should have been ordered beforehand to meet the travellers. This can be done by writing from Alten some days before starting. Information of the days when the mountain post goes would be furnished at Bosekop. This plan was followed by a party in the summer of 1854. We have been favoured with some notes of the route, which we shall insert.

"Aug. 26. We left Alten in the evening in two boats, and were poled up the river to a small house on the W. bank, about 4 m. from the mouth, accompanied so far by some friends to see us off. We were joined here by a Norwegian gentleman, who was returning to Kautokeino. This house, in which we slept, is about 20 feet long by 14 wide. It is divided into two rooms. In the outer one, about 14 feet by 8, 11 adult men, 1 woman, 1 child, and a baby, slept. The next morning we started about 7; our luggage, consisting of two oblong baskets, covered with tarpaulin, a cooking apparatus, and 2 waterproof carpet bags, was slung upon 2 horses. There was a third for riding. The baskets contained our provisions, which consisted of a ham, some bacon, some bread and biscuits packed in tins, coffee, sugar, portable soup, and a tin or two of preserved meat, which we fortunately had with us. Our course lay about west, away from the river, up a valley through birch and fir trees, against which the horses bumped our baggage considerably. Part of the forest had been lately burnt: the trees were still standing, but dead and bare, the picture of desolation. It is stated that when a fir forest is burnt, birch trees spring up in its place, and *vice versâ*. About 3 hours brought us up on to the bare fjeld, from whence we obtained a fine view backwards of the hills on each side of the river, and of some mountains to the N.E. We fancied they were the mountains of Seiland, at the mouth of the Alten Fjord. A little farther on we had a view of the mountains near Kvænangen Fjord, on the W. When the fjeld is attained, it is an undulating plateau, with very gentle ascents and descents for a great extent. Nothing around but reindeer moss (*Cenomyce rangiferina*), a little reedy grass, and bare stones. No birds, or living creatures of any kind. The extreme silence and stillness is, perhaps, the most striking feature. This was only broken by passing a Lapp encampment with a few deer about it. About 8 we reached *Ladne-jaure*, where we again came upon the river, descending to it over an abrupt cliff, which only Norwegian horses would attempt to descend. This is reckoned to be 6 fjeld miles from the hut, where we had slept the night before. We were fortunate enough to find a *gamme* of boughs here to sleep in, constructed by our Norwegian friend, which was some shelter from the pouring rain. We had ordered two boats from Kautokeino to meet us here.

"Aug. 28. The next morning we started about 9. The river here widens out into still shallow lakes, with little stream through them, so that with rowing and sailing we proceeded at about the rate of 1 Norsk mile an hour. There were plenty of ducks about, of which we were fortunate enough to shoot some for dinner, to which, boiled with portable soup, they were a very great addition. We regretted much we had no spinning tackle with us. There must be trout of very great size in these entirely unfished waters, and at times the boats were not going too fast to admit of trying for them in our course. There were occasionally some fishing eagles on the banks, one of which my companion with some difficulty shot. I had seen, the week before, in the Alten River, an eagle make an attempt to carry off a salmon, which was too large for him. I heard a great flapping of wings on the water in the stream at the bottom of the pool, and on looking down, saw a great fight between the fish and the bird. The bird could not lift the fish out of the water, but could bring him to the surface. At length the fish dragged the eagle under water, and all was quiet. Presently they reappeared, and the same contest took place on the surface once more. This was repeated three times, and at last the eagle was dragged down, and I saw no more of them. My boatman informed me, that instances had occurred of salmon being taken in their nets, with the body of an eagle attached to them, both dead of course: the eagle having been unable to withdraw its claws. There is a somewhat similar case to this in the Museum in Truro in Cornwall. A cormorant was picked up by some fishermen with a large conger eel round its neck, having evidently strangled it. The specimens are preserved together. But to continue.—We had dinner at Masi, an old Lapp church, but unused for 100 years. There is no roof, and a birch tree was growing in the middle of it. All the baulks of timber, of which it is built, must have been brought up singly over the snow by reindeer from Alten. About 5 P.M. we reached a fine fall of about 50 feet in height, over which a great volume of water was falling. The boats had to be dragged over land here, and as this operation took some time, we passed the night on an island in the middle of the river: our Lapp boatmen lighting an enormous fire, and making a shelter by turning the boat upside down. The next day we reached Kautokeino in about 4 or 5 hours: the banks of the river getting lower and lower, as we ascended, till near Kautokeino they were but little above the river. The distance from Alten to Kautokeino by this route we roughly calculated to be about 19 miles. With a strong north wind it might very easily be done in 3 days. The expenses for 2 were—3 horses from Alten to Ladnejaure about 16 sp. d. The bargain should be made before starting. From

Ladne-jaure to Kautokeino, 2 boats with 4 men, 18 sp. d. The most favourable time for this trip is in the middle of August, before the days shorten sensibly. The melting of the snow in June, and early in July, converts every stream into a torrent, and every spring into a morass. The mosquitoes in July and the *beginning* of August are so troublesome as to deprive the trip of all pleasure. In September the days shorten so considerably, and the nights become so cold, that camping out becomes unpleasant."

Kautokeino, 16 m. over the fjeld all the way, or 19 m. by Ladne-jaure and Masi. There is a small colony of Kvœns settled here; their ancestors came from Finland. Kautokeino is situated in a shallow valley, or basin, opening towards the north-east. The country around is perfectly bare of trees. In winter the cold is intense. On the southern bank of the river the ground remains frozen the whole year round. Grain and other supplies have to be brought up all the way from Alten. The population in winter consists of about 800 Lapps, but in summer of not more than 80. Still, for some years past, the stationary population has been on the increase, and the church is now kept open all the year round. It was built in 1660, and stands on a slight eminence. In summer, the inhabitants of this village gain their principal subsistence by fishing in the numerous lakes about these mountains, and in collecting fodder for their cattle in winter. Here also many Lapland families keep their stores of winter clothing, &c., as at that period they descend from the higher ranges and congregate about this place. Kautokeino is 834 feet above the sea. A track leads from hence to the N.E., at Karasjok, 8 m., where it joins that from Alten to the *Tana River*, mentioned in Route 24.

The Lapps are generally quiet, well-disposed people, but in 1852 Kautokeino was the scene of some religious disturbances, which resulted in the murder by the Lapps of a Norwegian merchant, and the Lensman resident there. Subsequent inquiries have shown that a private grudge existed in the minds of the ringleaders against these two men. But at all events they made use of the religious frenzy then existing to denounce them, and to get together a sufficiently strong party to come down and murder these men, with circumstances of great cruelty. The two ringleaders, Aslak Jakobsen Hetta and another, were beheaded at Bossekop in October, 1854, and the rest of the party condemned to various terms of penal servitude, or *slaverie* as it is termed; measures which have had a very wholesome effect in quieting the excitement prevalent among them. There is a good explanation of the probable motives which led to this murder, in an article in the first number of the "Theologisk Tidskrift," published in Christiania.

There are no horses to be had in Kautokeino, and they must be ordered beforehand from Karesuando, in Sweden, distant about 10 m. They should be ordered by writing from Bossekop, and time must be allowed for them to come.

From Kautokeino the country is comparatively level, the mountains seen being detached, and rarely exceed about 500 ft. from the surrounding plain. The ascent, however, again commences from Kautokeino, but is very gradual until it reaches the small lake of *Jedeckejaure*, 1378 feet above the sea.

"Aug. 29.—We started in the afternoon from Kautokeino, and went 2 miles up the river again to a wretched Lapp house, where we slept. The next day we started about 8, and crossed the Russian frontier about mid-day. This strip of territory runs out between Sweden and Norway, to within 25 miles of the Lyngen Fjord, on the W. coast of Norway, the country continuing much the same: a level undulating plateau, but with more dwarf birch and juniper undergrowth. We saw more ryper to-day, but no great quantity. About 8 P.M., we found a house to sleep in in the Russian territory. It was exceedingly dirty, but the only house anywhere near: this was about 5 miles from our quarters of the night before, and 7 from Kautokeino.

"The distance hence to *Karesuando* in Sweden, which we reached the next day, is about 3 m. Forests of fir and birch closed in on our track again on this last day, being first seen at an elevation of 1327 feet above the sea: but there was little else of interest.

"*Karesuando*, 10 m. from Kautokeino. Our expenses for three horses from Kautokeino hither were 21 sp. d. Karesuando is on the southern side of the Muonio, which is a fine river, dividing Swedish Lappmark from Russian Finland. The river at Karesuando is more than 200 yards wide, although it must be more than 250 Eng. m. from the sea. There is a nice church here, and an appearance of prosperity very striking after the desolation of the fjeld. Barley ripens here.

"The next day we took a boat with 8 men, and got as far as Muonioniska. The boats are of the same construction as the Alten boats, but larger; 35 feet long, 4 wide, and 3 or 4 narrow planks deep. Two men row, and one steers with a large paddle. The stream is very rapid, and the cataracts numerous, but the boatmen are very expert. Dense forests clothe the Russian bank; there are greater attempts at agriculture on the Swedish side. Half way between Karesuando and Muonioniska, Palajoensuu, where the winter road joins the river, is passed."

Muonioniska, 10 from Karesuando by water, or 16 from Kautokeino by the winter road. "The station is on the Russian side, but we were most kindly taken in on the Swedish side, it being judged imprudent to enter so large a village as Niska, where Russian officials reside, during the time of the war. After the dirt and discomfort of crossing the fjeld, a Russian bath is a great luxury. They are generally to be had in any town or village of the Finmark, Lappmark, or Finland. There is a small building devoted to the purpose. A pile of hot stones are heaped up, in one corner, on which water is thrown. The patient is seated on a shelf high up near the roof, and gently flagellates himself with a bundle of birch twigs, while the steam ascends all round him. 125° Fahr. was as much as I could bear comfortably, though the natives, with whom this is a weekly custom in winter, take it much hotter. They go from this heat, and plunge in cold water, or roll in the snow for a short time. After which they return to the bath, and are soaped and washed by an old woman, who is in attendance. M. Leouzon le Duc, in the notes to his translation of the Kalewala, 25th Runa, states :—'Que les paysannes Finlandaises accouchent toujours dans le bain.' Whatever may be the case in Finland, this is not the practice in Norway. There is also a good account of the descent of the Muonio rapids in his notes to the Kalewala."

From Muonioniska.

In summer the usual and most delightful mode of making all the rest of the journey to Torneå is by water. The boats used are sharp at each end, and as buoyant as nutshells. They are only calculated to contain two passengers besides the boatmen; two rowers sit in the bows, and in the stern of the boat is the steersman with a heavy paddle with which he guides the boat. The river is broad, of an imposing appearance, and broken by innumerable cataracts; nevertheless, it is not so difficult or dangerous as some travellers have represented it to be, the rapidity of the descent being lessened materially by its great length. Sometimes the inclination of the water is scarcely to be perceived; at others, the waves rush boiling and foaming against the rocks, appearing to carry the devoted boat to destruction, which, however, no sooner nears the apparent danger than it is whirled off and passes by in safety. It is at these critical moments that the dexterity of the helmsman is called into requisition; the most experienced and boldest boatman is always selected for that office, and it is surprising to observe with what calmness and steadiness he guides the boat through the greatest dangers.

The banks of the river, which are somewhat flat, are covered with vegetation, and thickly wooded with the birch, pine, fir, and a variety of willow. There is little of interest, however, all the way down from Niska to Torneå. Hardly a word of anything but Finlandic is understood before reaching Matarengi.

Mr. Bayard Taylor's "Northern Travel" suggests a vocabulary of Finlandic words, which were sufficient to carry him through the country. They are pronounced as spelt. The spelling of many words is wrong.

1	*Yxi.*
2	*Kari.*
3	*Golme.*
4	*Nelja.*
5	*Visi.*
6	*Gusi.*
7	*Sehtima.*
8	*Kahdexan.*
9	*Yhdexan.*
10	*Gymmenda.*
½	*Boeli.*
Horses	*Hevorste.*
A bed	*Sungy.*
To go	*Minne.*
To eat	*Sua.*
Good	*Huwa.*
Large	*Esas.*
Boat	*Venne.*
House	*Tupa.*
Where	*Missa.*
Are you ready?	*Ongus sia walmis?*
Look sharp	*Happosta.*
How much	*Goinga bailon.*
Good night	*Huwaste.*
Drive on	*Ayo perli.*
A mile	*Peligorma*
Bread	*Leiba.*
Meat	*Lika.*
Milk	*Maito.*
Butter	*Voyda.*
Fire	*Valkja.*
Not	*Ala.*
Over	*Boiki.*
To sleep	*Nukko.*
Bad	*Pâhâ.*
Small	*Pieco.*
Come here	*Tuoli denne.*
Bring here	*Towa denne.*

On leaving Muonioniska small farms appear, and fields of barley, which is the only grain that can ripen about here. Half a mile from Muonioniska are the rapids of Eyanpaika, or *Muonio-koski*, the steepest and most dreaded on the river. These rapids continue for nearly an English mile, rushing between naked rocks, which stand like encampments on each side; a few solitary trees overhang the banks, and excepting these nothing is to be seen but the clear blue sky above, and the foaming waters which appear to be whirling you to destruction. Not a sound is heard but the roaring of the waters, as they foam and dash against numberless obstructions. It is a grand and most exciting spectacle.

"The most dangerous part of the whole consists of two nearly perpendicular falls, one about 100 yards distant from the other. The higher one is of a horseshoe shape, with a sheer fall of about 6 feet, stretching apparently right across the river. There is, however, on the eastern side a creep, through which the water rushes, instead of falling perpendicularly, and it is through this that the boat shoots at railway speed. The roar increases as you approach this, the stream boils more and more, the rowers quicken their stroke, and the boat is whirled into the tumbling bay between the two falls. It is necessary to cross this; for the passage down the lower fall is on the western side, the descent of which is very similar to that of the higher one, except that the boat floats out into some back water immediately below, while the men quietly commence baling. Perhaps the most dangerous part of all is between the two falls, for the stream has to be crossed with the boat, at times, broadside to the waves. This space is full of rocks also, and there is barely time to get the boat's head straight, before it is whirled into the second fall. Till quite of late years this rapid was esteemed quite impassable, and boats were dragged overland, but a certain Karl Regina, looking from the bank one day, thought he saw that a clear course was possible, and made the experiment alone, letting the boat down stern foremost by rowing against the stream, and so retaining steerage way. He was quite successful, and since that time he is the recognised pilot, and receives a regular fee for taking boats down."

"From Muoniovara" (about 2 English miles from Muonioniska on the Swedish side), writes Mr. Bayard Taylor, "we reached Parkajoki in seven hours, being obliged to go at foot's pace all the way. From thence to Kildangi it took us six hours, for the snow was very deep, which place is about 24 English miles from Kolare."

The stations are as follow :—

Kolare, 10.

Kexisvara, 3. The house on the Swedish bank of the river, if it be the station, is very dirty and uncomfortable. Soon after quitting this station the *Torneå River* comes rushing in by a grand fall upon the W. through a narrow opening of the rocks. The body of water is very great, and swift as an arrow. Iron ores abound about here, and in the upper parts of the Torneå, actually form whole mountains. These ores are very rich, but do not produce good iron unless smelted with others of a different quality.

Kengis Bruk, at the junction of the Torneå and Muonio, will be found a better place to put up at. It is about one hour's drive south of Kexisvara. There is no regular station, but the manager of the ironworks will take in travellers.

Kardis, 3¼.

Pello, 2½. The country now becomes very rich, and the Armenian-like costume of the peasants is picturesque. The rest of the stations are—

Tortola, 2.

Juskengis, 1.

Mariosara, 1¼.

* *Matarengi*, 1. Capital quarters. There is a good summer road all the way down on the Swedish side from hence to Haparanda. In winter the road is chiefly on the frozen river, diverging occasionally to the Russian or Swedish side to cut off a bend. Even Muonio-koski itself is frozen over in winter. Matarengi is nearly on the Arctic Circle. East of it is the mountain of Avasaxa, which many travellers have ascended to see the midnight sun. Celsius, Maupertius, and the French Academicians, came here in 1736 to make astronomical observations. In the last century it seems to have been the "but de voyage" of many distinguished personages, who have left inscriptions in the village of Jukas-jervi, to signify

that the world ended about here. Regnard and his companions left the following inscription :—

"Gallia nos genuit, vidit nos Africa, Gangem
Hausimus, Europamque oculis lustravimus omnem
Casibus et variis acti terrâque marique
Sistimus hic tandem, nobis ubi defuit orbis."

De Fercourt, Corberon, Regnard à Jukasjervi. 18th August, 1681.

Another long inscription contains the following sentence :—"Multum fui et terris jactatus et cataractis, multum quoque et *culicibus* passus."

S. Stewart, civis orbis, 3 *Julii,* 1787. ("Walking Stewart.")

Finland is not much changed in the matter of "*culices*," whether they be mosquitoes or fleas.

Another inscription is—

"Justice bids me record thy hospitable fame
And testify it by my name."

W. Langhorn, United States of America, Juli 23, 1787.

Niemio, 1¼.

Pakkila, 1¼. There is a fine old red-brick church, with a handsome belfry.

Korpikula, 1⅝. A large new inn here.

Kukkola, 1⅜.

Vojakola, 1⅜.

HAPARANDA and TORNEA, 1. A short distance north of this, a white obelisk is passed with the words "Russian Frontier" written on it. There are good quarters here. For description of those towns and roads to Stockholm, see Route 65. In 1854 the Stockholm steamers started from a small fjord, about a Swedish mile (6 Eng.) west of Haparanda. We had some little trouble in finding this fjord.

The *Expenses* of the trip of course depend on the number of horses and boats used. Ours, for 2 persons, amounted to about 83 sp. dollars, or £19. The items were—

	sp. d.
Alten to Ladne-jaure, 3 horses	20
Ladne-jaure to Kautokeino, 2 boats	13
Kautokeino to Karesuando, 3 horses	21
Karesuando to Muonioniska, 1 boat, 3 men	5
Muonioniska to Matarengi, 1 boat, 3 men	15
Matarengi to Haparanda, by road..................	5
Sundries	4
	83

The time consumed was 12 days, including one whole day's rest at Kautokeino, and another at Muonioniska.

ROUTE 35.

CHRISTIANIA TO STOCKHOLM, THROUGH KONGSVINGER, CARLSTAD, AND BY THE NORTH OF THE MALAR LAKE.

Dist. 59⅜ Norsk and Swed. m., or 404 Eng. This is the most direct route between the two capitals.

Before leaving Christiania a good supply of Swedish *small* money should, if possible, be obtained. The peasants in Sweden still prefer paper money to coin. A little stock of provisions should be taken, as for some distance the stations are not good.

After the majestic beauty and grandeur of the scenery in the N. and W. of Norway, this route is comparatively tame and uninteresting to the lover of mountain landscape. Yet some of the scenery is picturesque. See also preliminary information to Route 67, which is joined upon the Swedish frontier.

From Christiania by rail. Vid. R. 32 for road route.

T. *†KONGSVINGER, 8⅛. This small town was formerly of some importance, being considered as one of the keys of Norway. During the last war between Norway and Sweden the fortifications were repaired, and several additions made to them, but since the union with Sweden they have been abandoned, and in the year 1823 the garrison was entirely removed. The citadel is upon a commanding eminence above the town, which is built upon a high point of land, round which the Glommen makes a sudden bend from S. to W., forming a lake, and thus rendering this old frontier fortress a strong position. This lake, in high floods, communicates with another, which sends a considerable body of water by the *Wrongs Elv*, into the Wenern Lake; and this probably has been, and still would be, the course of the whole body of the Glommen, but for the sudden deflection at a right angle to its previous course, which it takes at Kongsvinger. —*Laing's Sweden*, p. 26.

On crossing the Glommen at Kongsvinger our route keeps S.E. along the bank of the Wrongs Elv, which runs towards the Wenern, sometimes spreading into a long winding lake, partly hidden by trees and picturesque rocks. The whole country, when seen from the heights, appears a moving sea of woods. The timber felled in these forests may be sent into Sweden by the Wrongs Elv and Wenern Lake, on the E.; and on the W. by the Glommen, into the North Sea.

† *Branna*, 1¼. From hence a by-road leads through the hills to the lower parts of the Glommen.

† *Magnord*, 1½. Midway upon this stage

The *Swedish Frontier* is crossed. The boundary line is here an avenue cut through the forest, with piles of stones within view of each other, and these are carefully kept up along the whole line of this long frontier.

Morast, 1. From hence to Stockholm, as in Route 67, "Handbook for Sweden."

ROUTE 36.

CHRISTIANIA TO STOCKHOLM, BY FREDERIKSHALD AND THE SOUTH OF THE WENERN LAKE.

Dist. 71 Norsk and Swed. m., or 463 Eng. This route is considerably longer than the last, but the scenery upon it is more picturesque, and it embraces all the towns on the eastern side of the Christiania Fjord, besides the *Falls of the Glommen*, and of the Gotha River, at *Trollhättan*.

As to money, &c., see preliminary information to the last route, and also to Route 69, which this joins at the Swedish frontier.

The traveller can avail himself of the steamer to Frederikshald, which runs twice a week in April, May, September, and October, and three times in June, July, and August. The average passage is eight to nine hours. There are several ways of reaching Frederikshald by land. The best and usual route is by the new road on the eastern shore of the fjord to

† *Lian i Aker*, 1.

† *Riis i Aas*, 1⅜; from Riis one can post to Dröbak, 1¼.

* Dröbak is built upon the E. bank of the Christiania Fjord, and in the narrowest part of it. The population is about 1500. It has a small export trade in timber and deals. Opposite the town is a little island, upon which the Government have constructed a fortress, intended to protect the capital against a *coup de main* by steamers, or other vessels coming up the fjord. Proceeding from this, the next station is

*† *Sandbye i Vestby*, 1¼. Hence to Dröbak, 1½.

† *Smorbak i Soner*, 1⅛. Towards the end of this stage the road is again close along the E. bank of the Christiania Fjord.

T. * † Moss, ⅞. This town is picturesquely situated on the bank of the fjord. It is the capital of the Amt of

Smaalehnes, and the residence of the Amtmand. It has about 4000 inhabitants. There are several saw-mills in the neighbourhood, and it has a large export trade in timber and deals. The church is a handsome building. There are baths in the town, which are much resorted to in the summer season by the inhabitants of Christiania. When the Swedes under Bernadotte invaded Norway, in 1814, it was at Moss, on the 14th of August in that year, that the convention and armistice were agreed upon, and which immediately preceded the final union of the two crowns.

On the opposite side of the fjord is the small town of *Horten.* Those who desire to proceed to the W. of Norway from Moss can do so by the following stages. Tronvigen, ⅝ m. Thence across the fjord to Horten, 1⅛. Bruseröd, 1⅛, where Route 24 is joined, on the way to Drammen or Kongsberg. Or from Horten the same route can be entered at Fyldpas, 1⅜, on the way S. to Laurvig and Christiansand. Continuing our route from Smorbæk, the next station is

* † *Dillingen i Rygge,* 1⅜. Dillingen lies ⅞ m. E. of Moss, and is not used if the traveller is going to or from Moss, in which case he proceeds to Carlshuus, 1⅞.

T. † *Carlshuus i Raade,* 1. From hence a road to the S. diverges from our route, and leads by † Krabberod, 1⅛, and after crossing the Glommen by a ferry to the town of T. † FREDERIKSTAD, ⅜. The greater part of this road is along the bank of the most W. branch of the Glommen, which is crossed by a ferry near the town. The population is about 3000. Formerly it had a considerable trade, but, since the erection of Sarpsborg, its commerce has greatly diminished. This is a fortified town, and was of considerable strength, but of late years the works have been much neglected. In 1716, Charles XII. of Sweden attempted to carry it by a *coup de main,* but failed; and, moving upon Christiania, was so roughly handled by the brave Norsemen, that he was compelled to retreat, with the loss of 4000 men, and thus ended his invasion of Norway for that year. A *steamer* calls here every morning, about 11 o'clock, on her way from Frederikshald to Christiania. (See Route 20, p. 70.) From Frederikstad our route can be joined at Sarpsborg, 1⅝; or at the station at Öiestad, 1⅜, through which a road leads from hence to Frederikshald. The splendid fall of the Glommen, known as *Sarp-fos,* is about 1⅛ m. up the river from Frederikstad, and about the same distance by the road. For description of the fall, see below, at Sarpsborg.

Direct Route continued.—Shortly after leaving the last station, Carlshuus, a road upon the N. is passed, which leads up the valley of the Glommen to Christiania. The W. branch of that river is subsequently crossed, and the stage ends at

† *Haraldstad,* 1¼, pay for 1⅜; from which place one can post to † *Sarpsborg,* ⅞ m., and join the direct road again at *Öiestad,* 1⅜.

T. † SARPSBORG. This was formerly a town of considerable importance, containing no less than 7 churches. In 1567, it was entirely destroyed by the Swedes, and not rebuilt. The site of the town formed part of the estate of *Borregaard,* which was purchased many years since by Sir J. H. Pelly, Bart., who obtained permission from the Storthing for the rebuilding of the town, which, after a lapse of nearly 3 centuries, is now fast rising into its former consequence. The population at present is about 1000. The town is situated on the right bank of the Glommen, nearly an English mile below the celebrated fall. Timber ships of the largest class come up here.

The *Sarp-fos.* The finest views of this splendid fall are from a short distance below the distillery, and from the opposite bank, at Hafslund. The height of the fall is 72 Norsk feet. This branch of the majestic Glommen is much contracted immediately before it arrives at the fall. On the brink a projecting mass of granite divides the stream, which falls almost vertically and unbroken. The body of water is very great, and there are some large masses of granite about the bottom of and below the fall, through and over which the foaming water rushes for a short distance, and then flows gently onwards to the sea. The numerous sawmills and buildings close to the fall on both sides detract from the picturesque grandeur of this Schaffhausen of the North. The volume of water which thunders down here at all seasons may be judged of by the fact, that in summer, upon the brink of the fall, the stream measures 116 Norsk feet in width, by 26 in depth at the deepest part; and in spring, after the melting of the snow, that depth is sometimes increased by as much as 30 feet.

A great portion of the right bank of the stream at the fall, and for a considerable distance below it, is chiefly composed of a stiff blue clay, and formerly the river flowed by Sarpsborg in a succession of magnificent rapids. At that time a very fine mansion, with its numerous outbuildings, stood near the termination of those rapids.

On the 5th of January, 1702, a fearful catastrophe occurred. The mansion, together with everything in it, sunk into an abyss 100 fathoms deep, and was instantly covered with the foaming waters. The house was doubly walled, but of these, as well as of several high towers, not a trace was left; 14 persons and about 200 head of cattle were engulphed, and perished on this awful occasion. The cause of this event is attributed to the fact of the Glommen having gradually undermined the high bank on which the mansion was situated.—*Everest's Norway*, p. 276. At the present mansion-house of Borregaard, there is a large picture of the rapids of the Glommen and the adjoining country, which was painted the year prior to this accident; it is most interesting, as it enables the alterations which have taken place to be accurately traced.

The noble water power at this fall has long been turned to great account for sawmills. The left bank is in the occupation of a company, whose business is exclusively confined to timber. The right bank is entirely occupied by an extensive establishment, not only of sawmills upon the newest principles, but also a large iron foundry and agricultural implement manufactory; a flour mill, distillery, and a brick yard, besides a large farm, and buildings in proportion for the numerous horses and cattle, which must all be housed in winter. The system pursued here combines all the economy of a Norwegian farm with the most approved modes of English agriculture. The company give employment to about 300 hands, and their establishment is the largest of its kind in Norway. The old and horrid system of paying the men partly in rations of brandy has been abolished, and the most zealous efforts are being made to promote their comfort and permanent well-being, as well as that of their families. The tramway leading from the sawmills to the quay was the first constructed in Norway; a large tunnel (amply sufficient for a single line of railway), used for floating the timber into the yards, from above the falls, was made in a novel manner. A small aperture was blasted in the usual way in the face of the rock. In this a fire was then lighted, and kept burning till the granite around it became thoroughly heated, when the embers were hastily removed, and 4 men with heavy sledge-hammers striking the rock as quickly as possible, it gradually peeled off. The fuel used was the waste outside pieces cut from the logs. Eight men were employed in gangs of 4 each, and the fires were kept up night and day until the work was finished, which was accomplished in two years. The distance cut per month was 2 fathoms 6 inches.

From Sarpsborg the Glommen is crossed by a suspension bridge just above the fall, and the road continues through a poor country to

† *Oiestad*, 1¼. From hence, on the E., a road leads to Christiania, and on the W. to Frederikstad, 1⅜ distant.

Near the end of this stage a road upon the E. turns off from this route, and leads to T. FREDERIKSHALD, 1⅝ m. This town is built in the angle formed by the picturesque *Idde Fjord* at its junction with *Swinesund*. It has an excellent harbour, in which the largest vessels can be moored. The old name of this town was Halden, to which Frederick III., in 1665, added his own name, in commemoration of its gallant defence against the Swedes. There are several handsome edifices in the town, which is neat and well built, and carries on a considerable trade in timber. In 1759 nearly the whole of the place, as it then existed, was destroyed by fire. The population is now upwards of 4000.

The fortress of *Frederiksteen* is built upon a perpendicular rock, 400 feet high, on the S.E. of the town. The view from it is very beautiful. This place is celebrated not only for the numerous sieges it has stood, but as the place where Charles XII. of Sweden was killed. Having failed in carrying Frederikshald when he marched upon Christiania, in 1716, he devoted nearly two years to raising another army for the conquest of Norway. General Armfelt, with a division of 7000 men, in Sept. 1718, marched through the mountains to attack Trondhjem, but abandoned the attempt, and in their retreat nearly his whole force perished in a snow-storm, which literally overwhelmed them. Charles himself moved upon Frederikshald, and directed the operations of the siege. He was killed in the trenches on the 11th Dec., and, when found, his hand was firmly clenched upon the hilt of his sword, which was half drawn from its scabbard. The cause of his death was a shot in the temple, which passed through his hat. This hat lies upon his tomb in the Riddarholm Church in Stockholm, and a careful examination of it proves, by the size of the ball, and the horizontal direction it took through the thick felt, that he was slain by a pistol-shot upon the same level as that upon which he stood, and not by a gun-shot from the fortress, which was considerably above him.

Frederiksteen was formerly of great strength. On 3 sides it is inaccessible. On the 4th, close under the walls of the outer works, a few stones, rudely fastened together, are said to mark the spot where Charles XII. fell, but no inscription commemorates that event.

Excursion from Frederikshald.—"About 3 Eng. m. E. of the town there is a considerable lake, the *Fem Söe*, the stream from which flows into the fjord close to Frederikshald. The body of water is not considerable, except in May and June, and after heavy rains; but at all seasons the *waterfalls* upon this stream are the most picturesque in the S. of Norway. It is from the sawmills and manufactories established at these falls that Frederikshald owes its commercial importance. There is a pretty walk or drive along the bank of the river from the town to the falls. A few hundred yards above them from the mansion, Wein, there is an extensive and charming view over the Fem Söe, and to the S.W. over the beautiful valley (Tistedalen), and the wooded banks of the Idde Fjord. Crossing the bridge over the falls, there is a pleasant drive back to Frederikshald by Frederiksteen."—J. P.

From Christiania to Frederikshald viâ *Grönnesund*, 11 *m.*

† Christiania to † *Lille Steensrud*, 1⅝; † *Bovim i Haaböl*, 2¼; *Hesleborg i Spydberg*, ⅜. Ferry over Grönnesund. † *Houg i Eidsberg*, 1½; † *Fladestad i Rakkestad*, 1⅝; † *Eng i Rakkestad*, 1⅞; † *Kjölödegard i Berg*, 1; † *Frederikshald*, 1½.

Or by *Rödenæs and Aremak*, 15½ m. From Christiania to † *Bovim*, 3⅞ (see above); † *Bilet i Askim*, 1⅝, bridge over Glommen; † *Vister i Eidsberg*, 1⅞; † *Kaldan i Rodenæs*, 1½; *Krogtad i Ödemark*, ⅞; *Ytterböl i Aremark*, ⅜; *Pangö i Aremark*, 1¼; *Skodsberg i Aremark*, ⅞; † *Ugjestebye i Berg*, 1⅝; † *Kjölödegaard*, ⅞; † *Frederikshald*, 1½.

Or by *Fet and Höland*. † Christiania to † *Finstad*, 1½; † *Nedre Hauge i Fet*, 1⅛; † *Aanerud i Fet*, 1; *Larsbraaten i Höland*, 1¾; † *Hellegaard i Höland*, 1⅛; † *Kaldan i Rödenæs*, 2¼. See above.

A *Steamer* during the summer months leaves Frederikshald every morning, about 7, on her way to Christiania, where she arrives about 4 P.M. Carriages are taken on board, and the fares are exceedingly moderate. (See Route 20, p. 70.) The whole length of the Swinesund is highly picturesque. One of the finest views of Frederiksteen is from the water, about ½ an Eng. m. to the W.

From Frederikshald a road leads back to our route at the Westgaard Station, ⅞.

Continuing the direct Road from Öiestad, the next station is likewise

† *Westgaard*, ⅞. Upon this stage *Swinesund* is crossed by a ferry. There is good accommodation to be had on the Norwegian side. It forms the boundary between Norway and Sweden.

† *Högdal*, 1⅞, pay for 1½. This is the first station upon the *Swedish frontier*. From hence the road to the *Falls of Trollhättan* and Stockholm is as in Route 77 to Uddevalla, and from thence as in Route 69, "Handbook for Sweden."

ROUTE 37.

CHRISTIANIA TO HELSINGBORG, THROUGH GOTTENBURG.

Dist. 52⅜ Norsk and Swed. m., or 358 Eng.

Nearly all the station-houses in Sweden upon this route are wretched places, and there is no scenery, or anything of sufficient interest to compensate for the fatigue, discomfort, and cost of this long journey by land. From Christiania to the Swedish frontier is the same as in Route 36; and from thence, as in Route 77, to Helsingborg. By taking the steamer from Christiania to Frederikstad, near which are the *Falls of the Glommen*, and going by land from thence to the *Falls of Trollhättan* and on to Gottenburg, some of the finest scenery in this part of Norway and Sweden will be seen, and the least interesting and most fatiguing avoided. For *steamers* from Christiania and from Gottenburg, see those towns.

By the direct road from Christiania to Gottenburg it is 30 Norsk and Swed. m., or 204 Eng.

ROUTE 38.

LEIRDALSÖREN (IN ROUTE 21) TO ROMSDALEN (IN ROUTE 30), OVER THE SOGNE FJELD AND HAALANGEN FJELD.

Dist. 17½ Norsk m., or 122 Eng. Four days must be allowed for this journey, the second and fourth of which are long and fatiguing. This allows for reaching Optun Station the 1st night; Hoff the 2nd; Blaker the 3rd; and Holseth the 4th.

"The scenery upon this route is most grand, and it includes *Skagstöls Tind*, which is 7877 feet,* being 163 higher than Sneehættan (see Route 26), which was long supposed to be the highest. It is now ascertained, that *Guldhöpiggen* (see an excursion from *Viig* in Route 26), is higher than Skagstöls Tind, being 8300 Norsk feet. Excepting the first 35 E. m. by water, the journey must be performed either on horseback or on foot, but the fatigue will be amply repaid, and the undertaking is not so arduous as to deter any one in good health and of average pedestrian powers.

A small supply of food should be taken, but no luggage except what can be stowed away in a knapsack or pair of saddle-bags.

The stations from *Leirdalsören* are—

Solvorn i Hafslo, 2½ by water.
Döven i Lyster, 1¼ by water.
Skjölden i Lyster, ¾ by water.

From *Leirdalsören* to Skjölden, at the head of the Lyster Fjord (which is the extreme N.E. branch of the Sögne Fjord), the scenery is grand and sombre. About 1¼ m. before reaching Skjölden on the E. is the *Feigum Fos*, a fine waterfall, said to be 200 feet. Some distance higher up in the mountains the same stream makes another fall of 700 feet.

The *Sögne Fjeld.*

Skjölden, 4¾ m., by water the whole way. From this station to the N.E., across the Sögne Fjeld to *Blaker* in Lomb, upon the Vaage Vand, is 8¼ Norsk m., or 60 Eng. There are two ways from Skjölden, mere horse-tracks, and for many miles steep and of the roughest description; they are both about the same distance. The western passes along the W. bank of the small lake at the head of the Lyster Fjord, and thence up the valley of the Eide Elv, nearly due N.E. But the grandest scenery is upon

The *Eastern Track*, which crosses the river at the head of the Lyster Fjord, and passes by the E. bank of the lake to the village of

Fortun, ¼ m., and thus far the road is tolerably good. Close here a tributary stream is crossed, which flows from the E. into the Eide Elv, and quitting Fortunsdal, the track follows the right bank of this stream by a very steep and rocky ascent up a wild and romantic valley to

Optun, ¼ m. This is a large mountain farm, not a sæter. I passed the night here; the accommodations are rough and indifferent, but the people civil and obliging. Here a pony and guide can be obtained to cross the mountains, but some hours' notice is requisite, and on that account it is better to pass the night at this place, so that they may be ordered in good time and ready for the journey early next morning. The stage is a long one of 35 E. m., and the same pony and guide are taken the whole way to Kvandesvold. The charge for a pony is about 8 sp. d., and the owner, who acts as guide, will expect 1 or 1½ ort for himself. There is no occasion to take a pony for the guide, as the Norwegian mountaineers are excellent pedestrians. These ponies require no guidance, and, when left to themselves, pick their way amongst the rocks and stones with perfect safety to the rider, thus enabling him with ease and comfort to enjoy the scenery. There is nothing to prevent a *good* pedestrian from accomplishing the whole distance on foot. I think it would be impossible for a traveller to cross the Sögne Fjeld, for the first time, without a guide; and certainly it would be highly imprudent to at-

* Forsell's Map, in 8 sheets, published at Stockholm, 1815-1826.

tempt it. These mountains are never crossed in winter. The price paid for ponies is fixed, as in other parts of the country, but the charges for them are higher, from the length and difficulty of the stage.

On leaving Optun the path continues very rough and rocky as it ascends the valley, and gradually winds towards the N.E. In about an E. m. it emerges on the mountains, and the ascent then continues gradual and winding until the summit of the pass is attained. This most grand valley, through its length, divides the range of the Hurnugerne (or Hor-Ungerne) mountains on the S. from those of the Sögne Fjeld upon the N., and about midway up the pass from Optun, the gigantic *Skagstöls Tind* is passed, on the S. The peaks of this mountain, which form part of the Hor-Ungerne range, are most fantastic, like those to the S. of Molde. They are best seen from the summit of the pass, from whence, looking back to the S. and W., the scenery is of the grandest Alpine character. "The peasants have a tradition that these Hor-Ungerne mountains were the offspring of an incestuous marriage, and therefore changed to stone. The name in the Norsk tongue indicates the misconduct of the mother." —*Everest's Norway*, p. 243.

From this point the track continues for many E. miles over a table-land, by numerous lakes and tarns, and amongst rocks and snow. I passed a lake on these mountains on the 1st July still covered with ice. This table-land forms the summit level of the Sögne Fjeld, and about 3 m. from Optun, still continuing to the N.E., the descent commences, while upon the N. may be seen the *Lomb Fjeld*, 6830 feet. In about ½ m. from the commencement of this descent

Sæteren Bævertkun is reached, 3½ m. from Optun, or 25 E., and the only habitation during the whole distance. At these two sæters, or mountain dairies, it is essential to halt for the refreshment of the pony and guide. About an hour will be sufficient. Some milk, and a seat by the fire, are all the accommodations these sæters can offer. From hence to the next station at Kvandesvold is 1½ m. The track soon enters the valley of the *Baver Elv*, and becomes less rugged. In about ½ N. m. a fine waterfall is passed a short distance off, on the N.W. I was 13 hours on the way from Optun to Kvandesvold, but this included the delay of an hour at Sæteren Bævarthun.

Kvandesvold, 5 m. from Optun. At this station another pony and guide can be obtained; but to prevent the delay attendant on procuring them, it is advisable, if possible, to take on those from Optun. It will cause no diminution in speed, for these mountaineers and their ponies seem never to tire, and particularly if the former be allowed to ride a short distance occasionally.

From Kvandesvold the track continues rugged in places, but is, on the whole, tolerably good, and winds down the valley of the Baver Elv to

Hoff, 1 m. This station is at a large farm, and I found the people very obliging and kind. The accommodations are superior to those at Optun.

The path from hence continues down the valley of the Baver Elv, the scenery of which is picturesque to

Blaker, in Lomb Parish, 1½ m. The station here is good. *Blaker to Laurgaard.* A carriage-road to the E., along the Vaage Vand, leads to Laurgaard, on the high road between Christiania and Trondhjem (Route 26), by these stations, Blaker to Gardmo, 1½; Sandbo, 1½, by water; Laurgaard, 2.

From *Blaker to Romsdalen.* Those who desire to make this journey by carriole should go to Sandbo, as above, from whence there is a tolerable by-road through Haagenstadt, Slandalen, and Hatreinsbræn, close to the Holseth station in Route 30.

The *Haalangen Fjeld.*

This *Mountain Route* from Blaker to Romsdalen, after the first mile, can only be traversed on foot or on horseback. It is inferior in scenery to that over the Sögne Fjeld. The views from the mountains are, however, extremely grand, yet, if the additional fatigue were an object, would scarcely repay those who have crossed the Sögne Fjeld. Wild reindeer are found upon these mountains.

To avoid stopping on the road, it will be best, if possible, to hire a pony and guide at Blaker to go the whole way to Holseth, 4 m.

A carriage-road from Blaker leads up the valley on the W. to

Skeager, 1 m., which is a dirty and bad station. From hence a horse-track commences, which soon crosses the *Otto Elv*, near its junction with the Vaage Vand. A smaller stream is also crossed soon afterwards, and the ascent of the Haalangen mountains then begins. It is very steep and rocky the whole way up. In about two hours' time the elevated table-land of the field is reached, across which the direction of the path is marked by piles of stones. It is rugged in the extreme the whole way, but a pony goes quite safely over it. After crossing the Otto Elv, the track leads nearly due N. for about half way over the mountains, until it enters Loordalen. Here the track separates, one branch going N., and entering Romsdalen near the Mölmen station. The other leads down Loordalen, and, in about an hour afterwards, *To Sæteren* is reached. These are the first habitations on the way from Skeager, and a halt at them is requisite for the pony and guide.

On leaving To Sæteren the track soon enters a pine forest, through which it continues, and is very rugged nearly all the way to

† *Holseth*, 3 m. This station is on the high road to Molde, see Route 30. Including stoppages, I was 14 hours in going this 3 miles from Skeager to Holseth.—S.C.

ROUTE 39.

CHRISTIANIA TO HAMBURG, IN WINTER.

The usual winter route is from Christiania to Helsingborg by Gottenburg (see Route 37). Thence across the Sound to Elsinore, and by diligence to Copenhagen. From Copenhagen by rail to Korsör (see Route 1), whence a steamer goes to Kiel. From Kiel to Hamburg by rail in 4 hours (see Route 1). Doubtless when the present unhappy state of affairs is readjusted, the old route will be used. At present it is worse than useless to attempt to give more detailed information.

INDEX.

I.

J.

K.

L.

P.

Q.

R.

S.

T.

Woodfall and Kinder, Printers, Milford Lane, Strand, London, W.C.

www.ingramcontent.com/pod-product-compliance
Lightning Source LLC
Chambersburg PA
CBHW030325270326
41926CB00010B/1500

* 9 7 8 3 7 4 1 1 7 7 7 0 5 *